PUBLIC ADMINISTRATION
ETHICS FOR THE 21st CENTURY

PUBLIC ADMINISTRATION ETHICS FOR THE 21st CENTURY

J. MICHAEL MARTINEZ

PRAEGER
An Imprint of ABC-CLIO, LLC

A B C CLIO

Santa Barbara, California • Denver, Colorado • Oxford, England

Library of Congress Cataloging-in-Publication Data

Martinez, J. Michael (James Michael)
    Public administration ethics for the 21st century / J. Michael Martinez.
      p. cm.
    Includes bibliographical references and index.
    ISBN 978-0-313-35880-7 (hard copy : alk. paper) — ISBN 978-0-313-35882-1
(hard copy pbk: alk paper) — ISBN 978-0-313-35881-4 (ebook)
    1. Public administration—Moral and ethical aspects. 2. Political ethics. I. Title.
    JF1525.E8M375 2009
    172'.2—dc22   2009015780

13 12 11 10 9   1 2 3 4 5

This book is also available on the World Wide Web as an eBook.
Visit www.abc-clio.com for details.

ABC-CLIO, LLC
130 Cremona Drive, P.O. Box 1911
Santa Barbara, California 93116-1911

This book is printed on acid-free paper ∞

Manufactured in the United States of America

CONTENTS

FIGURES

ACKNOWLEDGMENTS

No one writes a long work without assistance. Accordingly, I am deeply indebted to Robert Hutchinson, senior editor at Praeger Publishers/ Praeger Security International, for his advice and assistance through every step of the publication process. Thanks also to Rebecca L. Edwards, senior project manager at Cadmus Communications Corporation; Devon Hay, marketing coordinator at ABC-CLIO; and all of the dedicated and talented professionals who contributed to the production of this book.

In addition, I appreciate the assistance of three colleagues who reviewed my original manuscript proposal and provided testimonials: Dr. William D. Richardson, the Odeen-Swanson Professor of Political Science, chair of the Department of Political Science, and director of the W. O. Farber Center for Civic Leadership at the University of South Dakota; Dr. Anthony DeForest Molina, director of the Master of Science in Administrative Studies Program and an assistant professor of political science at the University of South Dakota; and Dr. Jeffrey L. Brudney, the Albert A. Levin Chair of Urban Studies and Public Service at the Maxine Goodman Levin College of Urban Affairs at Cleveland State University. Thanks also to Dr. Barry Bozeman, the Ander Crenshaw Professor of Public Policy at the University of Georgia, for providing a testimonial.

My good friend Keith W. Smith offered encouragement at key intervals when the going got tough. My students at Kennesaw State University have been a source of inspiration, as always. Colleagues at Dart Container Corporation also have been supportive of my research and writing activities. Finally, I would not have made it through this lengthy ordeal were it not for the love and support of my wife, Paula R. Martinez. With her, I am everything; without her, I am nothing.

INTRODUCTION: THE QUEST FOR ADMINISTRATIVE ETHICS

As a part time political science instructor at several Georgia universities for more than a dozen years, I often have lectured my students on ethics, politics, and the link between these two admittedly interrelated, but maddeningly indistinct, concepts. Invariably, one or more frustrated students seeking a way out of the morass of theories and concepts will ask, "Why can't we just do the right thing?" Is identifying an appropriate standard of behavior and acting consistent with that standard so difficult that we must risk being paralyzed by indecision lest we make a mistake or risk exacerbating an already difficult situation?

The answer is yes, identifying an appropriate standard of behavior is difficult. "Doing the right thing" or "acting ethically" is frequently in the eye of the beholder. Notice what this statement means, and what it does not. It means that identifying and articulating a workable standard that can be applied in all, or substantially all, cases is immensely difficult for reasons that will be discussed throughout this book. In some instances, even discovering an appropriate source or content of ethics can be problematic. It does not mean that all ethics or ethical precepts are situational and relative, although it does not preclude such a conclusion, either. Rather, ethics is a difficult subject to explore because it can be approached from a multitude of perspectives using a variety of ideas, concepts, and intellectual tools.

One minor point on terminology bears mentioning. Although the terms typically are used interchangeably, "morals" and "ethics" have slightly different meanings; the former generally refers to a person's individual beliefs about right and wrong, whereas the latter refers to a standard of personal behavior that applies to all persons within a certain category. This book will touch on morality, but it primarily focuses on ethics, which depends on one's individual perspective on the world and the way in which an individual interacts with the world as a justifiable standard of conduct. Ethical perspective develops based on a variety of factors—character, judgment, experience, and the role one plays in a given situation. Because every individual reacts to these factors in different ways, the number of permutations and combinations involved in ethical decision-making on a case-by-case basis is virtually infinite. As will soon become clear, the number of schools of thought and approaches to ethics can be daunting, especially to the novice who seeks an answer to an ethical conundrum under severe time pressure.

Having said that ethics is context-specific and the number of contexts is innumerable is not an invitation to embrace relativism. The study of ethics is more complicated than it initially appears, but this realization does not mean that all hope is lost, and anything goes. Despite the large number of situations faced by individuals throughout their lives, commonality exists in the way an individual chooses to face certain situations. Two approaches readily spring to mind—deontological and teleological ethics. The former refers to duty or principle, whereas the latter emphasizes outcomes or consequences.[1]

The great eighteenth-century German philosopher Immanuel Kant is often called the intellectual father of deontological ethics, although such a title is not technically true. Kant was not the first philosopher to explore the implications of deontology, nor was he the last; however, he developed the most comprehensive and influential deontological theory, at least in the post-Enlightenment Western intellectual tradition. For that reason, his thought is a natural starting point for understanding the idea of a permanent standard of ethics that applies anytime, anyplace, anywhere in the world across space and time.

Kant was deeply disturbed by the relativism of his age. During the turbulent eighteenth century, many individuals and governments justified their actions by referring to the consequences as a measure of their ethical content. Any action, no matter how repugnant it might be to observers under ordinary circumstances, could be legitimized as morally desirable if it produced a desirable result. For Kant, such situational, or relativistic, ethics invited moral decay. Without immutable, eternal, never-changing standards, a person or a society was trapped on a slippery slope where anything was allowed if it achieved one's goals. Such relativism allowed tyrants to practice all forms of misbehavior, including genocide, in the name of a higher good. Moreover, individuals were isolated from each other because no one could say with certitude that one act was superior to any other act. The modern standard of "whatever gets you through the night is all right" is tantamount to no standard at all, because it allows any sort of egregious behavior as long as a practitioner of that behavior can latch on to any reason, no matter how lame or self-serving, as a justification.[2]

In direct contrast to consequentialists who contended that moral worth was inextricably tied to the consequences of an act, Kant argued that moral laws are universal imperatives and cannot be violated regardless of the consequences. In his well-known articulation of the "categorical imperative," Kant wrote that, "I ought never to act except in such a way that I can also will that my maxim should become a universal moral law." In other words, the proper analysis in reaching an ethical decision is to ask whether I would want to live in a world where others reached exactly the same conclusion that I reached and acted accordingly. This insight is akin to the Golden Rule: Do unto others as you would have them do unto you. If I choose to lie in this situation, I am tacitly allowing others to lie. Do I want to live in a world where everyone lies? If this answer is "no"—and presumably a person does not want everyone around him to lie—then I should refrain from lying.[3]

Kantian moral philosophy has an elegance that is naturally appealing, especially in troubled times when political figures are routinely caught lying, cheating, and engaging in sordid, scandalous acts. At the same time, Kant's view of ethical duties is sterile and antiseptic; it has been ridiculed widely by subsequent thinkers as far too pie-in-the-sky and naïve to be workable in a world where universal maxims are few and far between. A search for absolutes may be quixotic when compromise is the order of the day.

First, consider the practical difficulties. A philosophy predicated on "right is right and wrong is wrong and never the twain shall meet" does not provide practical guidance in situations where universal maxims conflict with each other, and an accommodation is required. Consider two examples of what most people would consider universal imperatives— "human life is precious" and "a person should tell the truth." It is safe to say that a large percentage of respondents in a public opinion survey would subscribe to these maxims. The problem occurs when and if the maxims collide, as they often do. The old adage portrays a scene where a person fleeing a would-be murderer brandishing a large knife tells an onlooker he is trying to hide so he will not be slaughtered. Suppose the onlooker instructs him to take the left fork in the road. Moments later, a knife-wielding marauder appears and asks which way his intended victim fled. Faced with these two maxims, how does the onlooker respond? If he decides he must tell the truth, he is at least indirectly responsible for the resultant murder; therefore, he has violated the maxim that human life is precious. If he deliberately lies and misinforms the marauder about the path of his intended victim, the onlooker has violated the maxim of telling the truth. In either case, the onlooker can try to justify his or her behavior—"I told the marauder the truth, but I did not actually kill anyone" or "I lied, but I did it in the interests of a higher good, namely saving a person's life"—but he or she deliberately compromised a universal maxim. He has sought to strike a balance between the maxims by seeking a compromise. For all of his high-minded rhetoric and the elegance of his theory, Kant's ethical teachings have diminished practical value in a world where individuals sometimes are forced to choose between competing sets of values.[4]

An alternative approach is found in teleological ethics. Instead of focusing on a person's duty, which theoretically does not change regardless of the time, place, or circumstances, a teleological approach emphasizes the consequences. A consequentialist, in contrast to a Kantian, argues that the end result of an action is the appropriate focal point, which means that compromises may be required if a person has his or her eyes focused on the prize.[5]

Utilitarianism is the quintessential example of consequentialism. According to proponents of utilitarianism, life is filled with numerous moral choices, some of which require individuals, and nations for that matter, to compromise their principles in the pursuit of a higher good. The clash of two immutable moral principles that potentially hobbled deontological ethics does not present insurmountable logical barriers for utilitarianism. The famous maxim "the greatest good for the greatest number" associated with the English Utilitarians, a group of nineteenth-century philosophers who heralded teleological ethics as the appropriate moral grounding, suggests that some preferences invariably must give way to other preferences if society is to operate.

A utilitarian recognizes that the world is complex and moral choices have to be made—even in situations where one choice precludes another choice when both are deemed worthy, necessary choices. Policy-makers and elected officials face such tough, difficult choices all the time. One group of constituents desires A, another desires B, and still another desires C, but choices A, B, and C are mutually exclusive. Assuming the policy-maker is not already philosophically predisposed or required by the party or other negotiation to select one alternative from among the others, making a defensible choice is daunting. Where Kantianism does not provide a means for resolving competing claims, assuming each is a universal maxim, utilitarianism offers a possible solution. A decision-maker must engage in a cost-benefit calculation weighing the advantages of each choice against its disadvantages while taking into consideration the number of people affected. A rational policy-maker will choose a course of action that provides the greatest good for the greatest number, although the basis for making this determination can be subjected to interpretation.

Utilitarianism has been a much-touted feature of democratic governments. By setting forth a means by which choices can be made, however controversial the actual calculations prove to be in practice, utilitarianism, as the most prevalent and influential incarnation of a teleological approach to ethics, avoids the pitfalls inherent in a deontological approach. Nonetheless, teleology is not without its problems. Because compromises must be made, one might argue that once the universal standards of the Kantian system have been rejected, ethics is a slippery slope where bargaining and negotiation, dressed up with eloquent rhetoric, allow for all manner of rationalization and mischief.

Even if the mischief is not intentional, the calculations can become hopelessly confused. How does a policy-maker weigh the depths of preferences? A large percentage of the population may be against providing millions of dollars for, say, medical research into AIDS, but their opinions are not deeply held. In contrast, a small percentage of the population may strongly believe that millions of dollars are required for AIDS research, but their preferences are in a distinct minority. Should the policy-maker strictly adhere to the desires of the larger percentage, many of whom are only marginally interested in the issue, at the expense of the smaller group that desperately seeks the funding for important medical research? A strict utilitarian calculation does little to provide an equitable resolution to a significant, and by no means merely hypothetical, policy problem.[6]

This is a book about the dilemmas inherent in ethical decision-making, especially in the field of public administration, regardless of whether a deontological or a teleological approach is favored. The text focuses on administrative ethics; that is, it presupposes that unelected employees working in the nation's administrative agencies face ethical challenges that are contextually distinct from the challenges faced by persons acting outside of an institutional setting and not employed by a public organization.

To set the stage for a full-blown discussion of administrative ethics, however, it is necessary to step back and consider ethics through broader lenses. In Chapter 1, the text explores the various approaches to administrative ethics that have been identified by leading scholars in the field of public administration. Chapter 2 provides a synopsis of modern ethical theory apart from the administrative context. Many books focus on descriptive ethics versus normative ethics; that is, they differentiate between the "is" and the "ought," between how ethics works and how it ought to work. This book explores both perspectives with an understanding that an administrator seeking immediate guidance will be less interested in the niceties of theoretical distinctions and more concerned with a step-by-step approach to problem identification and resolution.

Chapter 3 returns to the administrative realm by discussing an administrator's role inside an organization and the potential problems that develop when an individual's ethical precepts clash with the values of the larger organization. Chapter 4 explores the role of an administrator as an independent moral agent, and Chapter 5 develops a model for resolving ethical issues that arise in an administrative context. Although no book can honestly purport to solve all ethical dilemmas, the goal is to provide a clear statement of the issue as it relates to American public administration and offer tools for resolving ethical problems. The difficulty, as the text repeatedly notes, is that administrative ethics does not have an agreed-upon, uncontested set of propositions or theories that serve as the central tenets of the subject, although some general theories, concepts, and approaches can be suggested. Engineering, medicine, and law, in contrast, represent a more-or-less agreed upon body of knowledge that can be researched and taught with a level of precision and specificity absent from, or at least not readily apparent in, the study of ethics.

Ultimately, the development of a workable model for public administrators to practice administrative ethics is the crucial objective. Along the way, the book will confront the challenge identified by numerous scholars, especially Terry L. Cooper, Paul Appleby, Dwight Waldo, and Herbert Simon, that the public administration literature has a poor grasp of what constitutes the "good" because it lacks a satisfactory theoretical underpinning. The key to improving the literature on administrative ethics is to explore what constitutes the "good" according to several schools of thought and how public administrators can come to know the "good" and behave in ways that advance the "good" within their respective organizations. Once the "good"—or what Cooper has called the "Big Questions" of public administration—has been identified and satisfactorily explicated, a suitable model for administrative ethics can be developed.

This book suggests that the "good" can be interpreted in numerous ways, and no one conception of this admittedly amorphous concept can be found. Leaving it to other works to grapple with the meaning of the "good," this text argues in favor of a process approach to administrative ethics. In other words, the text does not sift through the competing approaches that Cooper identified and pronounce one as preferable to the others because of its superior intellectual content. Instead, the book assumes that various individuals interested in administrative ethics will grapple with the questions and decide on the appropriate content. Assuming that an individual can reasonably justify his or her decision on the appropriate content of ethical standards, any of the approaches that Cooper identified will suffice as long as certain steps in the decision-making process are followed. Accordingly, Chapter 5 will set forth five stages that lead to an ethical decision.

The discriminating reader will read this thesis and conclude that, to some extent, it begs the question. A large part of an ethical decision involves the content, or source, of ethics. To say, simply, "pick one approach and then follow these steps" appears to ignore the difficult decisions inherent in addressing ethical concerns. The point is well taken. Nonetheless, many works have been written about the primacy of each approach. In fact, Chapter 1 summarizes the literature on administrative ethics for each approach, and Chapter 2 summarizes the broader literature on ethics in general. Rather than rehash what has been written previously, this book argues that a reasonable case can be made for any of the approaches or schools of thought. An administrator is well advised to consider each of the theories. After the administrator has chosen an appropriate approach or source of ethics, what comes next? This book addresses that question and provides suggestions for taking action.

An ambitious intellect may attempt to blend together the schools of thought into a unified theory. Would that such an enterprise were possible or, for that matter, even desirable. Each approach argues for a different source or content of ethics. To blend them together is to create an artificial theory that recognizes ethics as originating from multiple sources, some of which conflict with others. The search for a unified theory is a wonderful intellectual exercise, food for thought sufficient to feed a multitude of scholars and philosophers indefinitely. Public administrators do not have the luxury of such intellectual gymnastics. They must have clear, reliable guidance that is relatively easy to grasp. It is to these embattled public servants, and students of the discipline, that this book is aimed.[7]

1

FIVE MAJOR APPROACHES TO ADMINISTRATIVE ETHICS

Ethics is a topic that has captured the imagination of scholars and the public alike since antiquity. Man always has questioned the premises upon which he acts, and so he has sought guidance for treating like cases alike, the quintessential definition of "equity," a key feature of ethics. "Treating like cases alike" means that distinctions are made based on identifiable actions that allow for praise or blame to be assigned based on the nature of an event. Some actions are deemed morally praiseworthy, whereas others are viewed as contrary to the standards of "right conduct." The general goal of identifying ethical precepts is relatively straightforward—to develop standards of "right conduct" that are known and knowable beforehand and apply to more or less everyone—but maddeningly difficult to specify with precision, and even more onerous to practice.[1]

Aside from the general study of ethics, the more specialized field of administrative ethics as a rigorous area of academic inquiry first emerged from the shadows of the broader public administration literature during the 1970s. Scholars and practitioners in the public sector were not oblivious to ethical concerns before that time, nor were they amoral automatons disinterested in questions of right conduct. Rather, administrative ethics as a systematic field of study before the 1970s was amorphous and undeveloped. No more-or-less agreed set of normative assumptions and theoretical propositions existed as part of a generally recognized body of literature, nor did academics and practitioners agree on a well-established set of empirical techniques. A well-read student of administrative ethics might contend that a well-established set of normative assumptions and empirical techniques remains a missing piece to the puzzle that is the field of administrative ethics, and the point would have to be conceded. Nonetheless, the literature on public administration and ethics has grown tremendously since the 1970s, and attempts have been made to develop the necessary analytic tools even if a satisfactory synthesis of the disparate theories and schools of thought has not been forthcoming.

It was little wonder that the field, if it could even be called that, was in disarray before the Watergate era. In earlier decades, public administrators focused on questions of efficiency as though individuals staffing public agencies did not exercise discretion in decision-making. As a consequence, an "ethical" administrator was someone who sought to understand the legislative will or the orders issued by administrators ranked higher in the organizational hierarchy and acted as quickly and efficiently as possible. The idea that unelected public servants had a hand in developing policy and, therefore, inevitably faced potentially intractable questions of right and wrong in exercising discretion was unfathomable.[2]

In retrospect, the emphasis on maximizing timely efficiency was an ironic understanding of societal needs and values. Progressives at the end of the nineteenth century professed their concern for the injustice of machine-controlled politics and sought ways to root out cronyism and corruption from the public sector. On the federal level in the United States, passage of the Pendleton Act in 1883 was an initial step, although by no means the only one, toward the goal of establishing a professional civil service where recognizable standards of merit trumped the proverbial smoke-filled back rooms where public employment and political favors were bandied about as though they were little more than market-driven quid pro quo transactions. By creating an efficient system of public administration where knowledge was more important than political contacts, progressives hoped to equalize the playing field for the talented albeit not well-connected masses. This level playing field, they contended, would lead to a more "scientific," hence more equitable, public administration. The irony, of course, was that efficiency and justice were viewed as interrelated concepts where one would be fully realized only when the other was maximized. In time, the idea that efficiency and justice are blood brothers would be severely criticized as a chimera. For many scholars in the latter half of the twentieth century, justice and efficiency, although perhaps not antithetical, were at best distant cousins who were not always on good speaking terms.[3]

Scholars began to assail the positivism that had influenced the growth and development of American public administration, especially after World War II, and this led to important changes in administrative ethics. As the American Founders had recognized during the eighteenth century, efficiency has its rewards, but it also has its problems. An efficient government can lead to abuses of power when efficiency is transferred from a means to the end of serving the populace. When efficiency is an end in itself, the government makes decisions based on maximum return for minimum investment. If efficiency is to be adopted as a political value, it must be analyzed and tested.[4] Nobel Laureate Herbert Simon famously argued that so many of the well-accepted axioms in public administration were little more than homilies that had remained unexamined throughout the history of the field. The "proverbs of administration" needed to be identified and understood or the field could not advance beyond its static approach to fundamental questions of governance. Similarly, Dwight Waldo questioned whether supposedly value-neutral terms such as "economy" and "efficiency" were not value-laden. The idea that a concept is value neutral is itself a value-laden conclusion. Simon and Waldo used the rapidly developing tools of social science to devastate the muddled thinking of a previous age.[5]

On the few occasions when administrative ethics received academic scrutiny before the 1970s, the analysis generally concerned the need to develop a code of ethics akin to the codes used to police professionals such as lawyers. The quintessential call for an ethical code came from Fritz M. Marx in 1949, although he was not alone in this assessment. Marx argued that public administrators needed to be "conscious agents of a democratic community." Their values could not be based on their own personal predilections; rather, they had to be predicated on a deep understanding and appreciation of a democratic ethos, especially the American version of a republican form of government. Administrative ethics, therefore, must be developed broadly, keeping in mind the values of the regime. This approach, as we shall see later, became one of the major approaches to the study of administrative ethics.[6]

Another influential public discussion about codes of ethics occurred in the famous Friedrich-Finer Debate, which focused on the differences between "internal" and "external" controls on the behavior of public administrators. In his opening salvo, Carl J. Friedrich argued that an individual sense of moral responsibility is a crucial behavioral control. If people do not internalize a sense of ethics, nothing apart from around-the-clock surveillance can force them to behave appropriately. Friedrich wrote that "[r]esponsible conduct of administrative functions is not so much enforced as it is elicited."[7]

The idea that individual responsibility lies at the core of any system of ethics is a crucial component of modern ethical theory, but Friedrich wrote at a time when the politics-administration dichotomy was still widely accepted within the field of public administration. The primacy of personal responsibility implies that administrators are more than automatons carrying out directives issued by leaders placed higher in the hierarchy. It implies that discretion is possible, nay even desirable. Discretion requires public servants at all levels of an organization to shoulder no small measure of responsibility for their role, however insubstantial or unheralded, in the policy-making process.[8]

Herman Finer presented the counterpoint to Friedrich's arguments. "Moral responsibility is likely to operate in direct proportion to the strictness and efficiency of political responsibility, and to fall away into all sorts of perversions when the latter is weakly enforced," he wrote.[9] It sounds promising to rely on individual conceptions of ethics, but the problem is that such conceptions almost always are suitably vague or ambiguous and, thus, meaningless. Absent some form of external control, it is difficult, if not impossible, to hold an administrator accountable for his or her actions. Individuals will either misunderstand democratic values or they will pursue their own interests. Although Finer later acknowledged that public administrators may enhance their accountability by educating themselves to appreciate public opinion and technical and professional standards, the paramount issue in ensuring ethical conduct is to improve external controls to the extent possible. Democratic government operates best when behavioral controls are external and ethical behavior is clearly defined in a codified, rule-based system that is known and knowable beforehand.[10]

This concern with whether a code of ethics is desirable is a crucial question, and not one that is easily resolved. On one hand, a code replicates the specificity of a positivist law, which allows for precision in identifying standards of conduct and holding administrators accountable for knowing violations of the code. On the other hand, a code of ethics cannot address every situation that will arise. Moreover, if the principles of right conduct are not sufficiently understood and internalized, the rules may be nothing more than a series of obstacles that must be negotiated with no appreciation of the underlying ethical values.

Speaking of values, notice also the concern with democratic values. A key feature of administrative ethics is that public servants, by virtue of their positions, wield enormous power to affect the lives of citizens. Consequently, the public nature of their positions necessitates a thorough understanding of the needs and pressures of a political and legal system based, at least in part, on the consent of the governed. The difficulty with linking the consent of the governed to public servants working within administrative agencies is that those servants do not stand before the populace in periodic elections. Direct accountability is absent. If public servants are to serve citizens faithfully and still be held at least somewhat accountable to those who are governed, an appreciation of, and adherence to, what are sometimes called "regime values" or the "democratic ethos" is critical. This point will be more fully developed later in this text.

Suffice is to say that these issues, among others, lurked under the surface of administrative theory and practice, especially for a quarter century after the end of the Second World War. During this period, administrative ethics was not well developed or understood. The field of public administration in those years focused on administering a burgeoning executive branch as the power of government grew in tandem with the complexity of American society.

Enter the 1970s. The lingering effects of the Vietnam War and the public scandals of the Nixon administration in Watergate focused attention on public sector ethics in a manner previously unimaginable. Despite Paul Appleby's well-known warning that the study of ethics should involve a broader inquiry than merely focusing on "crude wrongdoing," administrative ethics was revitalized, if not revolutionized, by the increased attention to public malfeasance. It is little wonder that assaults on the imperial presidency and the bureaucracy, including the 1973 War Powers Resolution and the Federal Election Campaign Act, date from this era. Public administration as a field and administrative ethics as a topic of occasional academic discourse may have started much earlier, but the study of administrative ethics as an ongoing, well-developed body of literature begins with this period.[11]

From a perspective of public administration, the systematic study of administrative ethics was born out of the political strife and fears of corruption. Much of the literature from the early 1970s lamented the "neglect of metaphysical speculation" and the focus on step-by-step practicality. Perhaps if administrative ethics focused more on the values underlying the public sector and the ideals of a democratic polity, instances of public malfeasance would be reduced or eliminated, or so the thinking went among many leading scholars.[12]

Despite all the advances in the public administration literature since the 1970s, administrative ethics remained a relatively amorphous set of theories and concepts without a satisfactory grounding. As this book will discuss in subsequent chapters, administrative ethics lacked a core set of principles and, for that matter, an uncontested view of how an ethical administrator should act. A well-known ethical theorist, Terry L. Cooper, noted in a 2004 *Public Administration Review* article, "Big Questions in Administrative Ethics: A Need for Focused, Collaborative Effort," that the "interesting but highly disparate" literature on administrative ethics lacks "anything like a focused effort by groups of scholars to study specific sets of significant research questions in a sustained and systematic fashion." He attributed the absence of a systematic approach to ethics as a result of the failure to build consensus on "specific theoretical perspectives, sets of related problems, or significant issues."[13]

Cooper is correct that a theoretical grounding must precede the development of any systematic approach to administrative ethics. Moreover, a theoretical grounding varies according to the type of regime involved and its underlying values, so it is important to examine and articulate underlying regime values. The problem is that the values of a regime can be as varied and numerous as the commentators who seek to identify and understand them. Because the regime means different things to different people, its values can be interpreted in innumerable ways. This multiplicity of legitimate ideas about what constitutes the core values of the United States makes the search for regime values a never-ending process.

Building on Cooper's insights, the question addressed in this book is whether a theoretical perspective (or a combination of perspectives) can be developed from the broad regime values in the United States and the disparate literature on administrative ethics and, if so, whether a workable model for practicing administrative ethics can be developed. The answer to the first question is no, whereas the book suggests that a workable model for ethics can be developed even in the absence of a satisfactory theoretical basis.

It may seem unusual to argue that a unifying theme or perspective is not possible, but this insight need not be surprising. Many thinkers have tried to develop an all-encompassing theory of ethics, but all have failed. They failed because the task itself is misguided. The source and content for standards of right conduct vary because individuals have freedom of choice. One person may believe that his or her conduct should be governed by principles expressed in the Christian Bible, whereas another may subscribe to a Kantian deontological view that is not necessarily at odds with Christianity—indeed, it may be a slightly different articulation of similar values—and still another individual may suggest that a pragmatic consequentialism is an appropriate system.

The temptation is to spend one's time arguing among and between schools of thought until the best possible argument can be crafted in support of theory A. No matter how well the argument is crafted, however, others will support and defend theory B or theory C. In the meantime, the harried administrator working in a public organization calls out for assistance in discerning a pragmatic approach to determining what constitutes right conduct. No amount of theoretical groundwork will assist each administrator in determining an incontrovertible source of administrative ethics. In Chapter 5, therefore, this book "cuts to the chase," as they say. It outlines a decision-making process that provides a framework for taking action in the absence of a clear, overriding ethical theory.

Despite the lack of a clear, coherent theoretical foundation for administrative ethics, many clarion calls have been issued for improved public sector ethics, and it is instructive to understand the most prevalent theories. As Terry L. Cooper has suggested, the public administration literature over the last three decades generally has reported on administrative ethics using one of at least five theoretical approaches: (1) ethics as virtue; (2) ethics as regime values, constitutional theory, and founding thought; (3) ethics as citizenship; (4) ethics as social equity; or (5) ethics as the public interest. Cooper does not limit administrative ethics to these, and only these, approaches. He also recognizes that some overlap occurs as theories incorporate parts of each approach. To some extent, however, each of these approaches has developed its own distinct literature as though the schools of thought were mutually exclusive; that is, each approach has been studied and written about as though no overlap occurred with other approaches. Thus, researchers who touted ethics as virtue often have assailed researchers who believe the most fruitful source should be ethics as social equity. In some cases, researchers have discussed overlapping approaches, but they have not done so in a systematic way, as Cooper has noted. Although this book is not designed to champion one school of thought over the others, a summary of the major features of each approach can provide perspective on the difficulties inherent in administrative ethics.[14]

ETHICS AS VIRTUE

Virtue is a concept that harkens back to the ancient Greeks. Today, the concept has no precise meaning, filtered, as it has been, through the prism of the Victorian age. In its basest, and silliest, sense, it can mean the reluctance of a woman to submit to the whims of an ardent suitor, or it can mean the shouldering of a heavy burden while displaying admirable fortitude. For Plato and Aristotle, however, it referred to qualities of excellence necessary to govern oneself and, ultimately, one's regime. Virtue was an excellence that came from the imposition of rigid self-discipline, from the ability of reason to conquer appetite and desire through personal will and self-control, and from the willingness of the individual to strive for goals and thereby grow while working at maximum capacity. A person displayed virtue when he overcame his base instincts and, through habit and ongoing dedication, practiced asceticism. To be virtuous was to display qualities and traits that few possessed, thus becoming a sine qua non for public leadership.[15]

Niccolo Machiavelli, the great Florentine philosopher of the early sixteenth century, assailed the Greek notion of virtue as an immutable feature of self-control, hence, ethics and good government. Reflecting a more skeptical philosophy than was possible during the apex of the Hellenistic age, the Italian obfuscated the distinctions between "virtue" and "vice," insisting that such concepts were artificial constructs that had lost their usefulness, if they had any to begin with, in an age of realpolitik. For Machiavelli, "virtue" was a woman who, if immodestly attired in a cloak of self-righteousness, would be raped by stronger forces unaccustomed to, and disinterested in, the niceties of abstract concepts such as "right," "wrong, "good," and "evil." In its place, Machiavelli argued in favor of "virtu," a far more resilient, indelible concept. "Virtu," although suitably vague, was his idea of an ethical value that could change as time and circumstances changed. "Right conduct," according to this view, occurs when a person or a nation acts in ways that advance one's "values," however they might be defined.[16]

Machiavelli is a disturbing figure for anyone interested in absolute standards. He seems only a half-step removed from the doctrine of "might makes right." If the ends justify the means, if "virtue," in the classical sense, betrays weakness, if appearing to act virtuously is preferable to acting virtuously, ethics becomes situational. Whatever must be done to accomplish a task, however odious the task and however suspect the means of accomplishing the task, ethics becomes a thin veneer of supposed justification for all manner of bad behavior. In Plato's world, Machiavelli was a sophist who preached that his adherents should embrace any activity as long as it got him close to his desired ends.

After Machiavelli passed from the scene, "virtue" seemed an antiquated idea, an old-fashioned and naïve version of ethics. Anyone espousing faith in a higher virtue over and above the size of one's army or the weapons in his arsenal was seen as masking an inner weakness that no amount of abstract ethical theory could erase. Individuals and nations often were content to speak of virtue in the light of day but practice realpolitik in the dark of night. It would be Kant's task almost three centuries later to rehabilitate the deontological perspective.[17]

Why, then, would a school of thought champion administrative ethics as virtue? Surely such an approach in the modern era would be summarily dismissed as out of touch and more than a little jejune. As with many old concepts that reemerge fortified by a richer intellectual tradition than they previously enjoyed, the "ethics as virtue" school is more subtle and nuanced than the conception of virtue that Machiavelli found contemptible.

As noted previously, prior to the 1970s, many theorists focused on developing ethical rules and codified systems of ethics for public sector agencies. In 1981, researcher Mark T. Lilla challenged this analytical emphasis, which he derided as simply training public administrators to memorize lists of rules without fully exploring their meaning or consequences. Absent a normative foundation, Lilla argued, ethical rules are hoops that must be jumped through, but they do not provide guidance for resolving situations where the rules do not seem to apply. In addition, codified rules can be manipulated in different ways to rationalize all sorts of behavior. Lilla concluded his appeal by arguing that a "democratic

ethos" must be cultivated in public organizations as part of character formation. A democratic ethos, of course, is the idea that administrators are
first and foremost public servants; as such, they must understand and act
on the principles found in any regime built on the consent of the populace as a principle of legitimate rule.[18]

"Character formation" initially resembles a politically conservative
call to return to the halcyon days of yesteryear when people of "good
character"—for example, Ivy League-educated, white, Anglo-Saxon, Prot-
estant males—formulated American public policy based on the values
they had acquired through privilege, connections, and schooling in traditional notions of statecraft. Although some apologists of the "ethics as virtue" school may, indeed, yearn for a bygone era, the approach is more
nuanced than it might originally appear. Virtue as character is the idea that
certain more-or-less uncontested core values exist, and actions based on
those values occur when people who understand the values and can act on
the courage of their convictions are in positions of trust and authority. The
values might be broadly identified as a belief in the beneficial aspects of
pluralism, the creative possibilities inherent in diversity and conflict, the
importance of safeguarding liberty and property interests, the need to protect minority rights through "mitigated democracy" created and maintained by institutional controls of government, and the relative sovereignty
of citizens who participate in consensual self-government. Internalizing
and thereafter championing these values requires a public servant to do
more than pledge allegiance to an external oath or set of codified rules. If a
public servant is going to "walk the walk" and not simply "talk the talk," a
life-long commitment to a republican form of government is required
through study, habituation, and practice to face, and ultimately resolve, the
moral crises that invariably spring up in the context of a life and career.[19]

ETHICS AS REGIME VALUES, CONSTITUTIONAL THEORY, AND FOUNDING THOUGHT

Identifying the source of ethics has always presented a major difficulty
in setting forth a normative grounding for administrative ethics. If a public servant is to be held accountable for his or her actions, it is helpful to
understand beforehand what constitutes "right conduct" in the public
sector. Unlike Justice Potter Stewart's much-ridiculed observation that he
could not define obscenity, but "I know it when I see it," ethical standards

must have some form of precision if administrators are to be judged by how well they adhere to ethical standards. Where do these standards originate, and what constitutes the substantive content of such standards? Proponents of constitutional theory suggest the answer by arguing that the system of American government established by the Founders is the appropriate source of ethics.[20]

According to this perspective, the Founders created the American regime; therefore, it is appropriate to look to the Founders for a source of ethical principles because they set into motion the political regime that exists today. Their values—which rested on the bedrock notion of "republican virtue," an ideal whereby citizens elect officials to represent their views and citizens act partially out of self-interest and partially out of a sense of the common good—are the values that persist and are reflected in our governmental institutions as well as our political culture.[21]

Of course, this endeavor is not without its challenges. The United States has changed in innumerable ways, large and small, since the inception of the regime. The Founders did not foresee, and could not have envisioned, the complexities found in the world of the twenty-first century. As strict constructionists from the "original intent" school of jurisprudence have discovered, determining what the Founders did, or should have done, in specific situations based on their writings and ruminations requires no small measure of broad interpretation; therein lies the heart of the conundrum. Looking to long-dead champions of a republican form of government for guidance from general articulations of regime values is a Herculean enterprise. As Publius observed in *Federalist 37*, "All new laws, though penned with the greatest technical skill and passed on the fullest and most mature deliberation, are considered more or less obscure and equivocal, until their meaning be liquidated and ascertained by a series of particular discussions and adjudications."[22]

Despite potential pitfalls in identifying the Founders' views on crucial ethical issues, proponents of "regime values" argue that although it is impossible to determine how earlier thinkers would handle specific situations, the "higher law" background of American government can be identified and communicated to the current crop of administrators.[23] Note what this process involves, and what it does not. According to John Rohr, arguably the best known of the proponents of the "regime values" school of thought, the process involves delving into authoritative pronouncements of what a regime stands for in an effort to understand the crucial ideas that lie beneath the nation's institutions. To use a crude analogy, regime values are the hardware upon which the institutions, or the operating software, depend. To the extent that the United States "stands for" anything, its stands will be reflected in regime values. To understand these values, therefore, administrators need to read and digest a variety of sources that provide a window into the American Founding, but especially opinions of the U.S. Supreme Court.[24]

Because the court must decide hard cases involving specific, concrete litigants, it is the one place in the American system where the high ideals of the Founders meet the real-world, day-to-day concerns of ordinary citizens eking out a life in the country. Because the Justices must vote to reach an opinion that will resolve current disputes and because the decisions of a majority of Justices become the law of the land, U.S. Supreme Court opinions provide an almost ideal perspective on the salient issues in American life at a given period in time but against a backdrop of current societal concerns. Added to the usefulness of the majority opinion as a method of understanding changes in the law, dissenting and concurring opinions shed light on alternate perspectives not fully captured by the majority.[25]

Consider two vastly different landmark segregation cases as an illustration. In 1896, the U.S. Supreme Court upheld legal segregation as constitutionally permissible in *Plessy v. Ferguson* by a 7–1 vote (with one justice not participating). Justice John Marshall Harlan the elder, the lone dissenter, argued that the U.S. Constitution was color-blind, and a citizen's race should not be a determining factor in extending constitutional protection to individual rights.[26] Fifty-eight years later, the high court reversed *Plessy v. Ferguson* in *Brown v. Board of Education of Topeka*, one of the most influential court decisions in history. A unanimous court held that segregation was not constitutionally permissible. Instead, it was a discredited doctrine propagated by a legal system steeped in an earlier, less progressive era.[27]

Plessy and *Brown* offer valuable insights into the regime values of the United States during different times in the nation's history; they are snapshots into national values. In 1896, the United States was still very much a nation controlled by the white power structure at the federal, state, and local levels. Blacks were denied the equal protection of the laws and were systematically denied access to public accommodations throughout much of the country. Although some progressives, white and black, lamented the sorry state of race relations, by and large blacks were relegated to submissive positions in society, and they had little recourse but to accept their inferior places in the economic, political, and social strata. The nation changed during the ensuing six decades. By the 1950s, even as the modern civil rights movement was about to emerge, thinking in many parts of American culture had evolved. Segregation and other discriminatory laws were America's shameful burden. A revolution was in the air. Regime values had shifted, and this shift was reflected in authoritative pronouncements of American courts, especially the highest court in the land.[28]

In *Ethics for Bureaucrats*, John Rohr argued that searching for regime values in published court decisions avoids problems associated with asking public servants to study great works of philosophy to locate ethical guidance. Court decisions provide a context in which issues are framed and explanations provided for why a recognized, authoritative governmental entity decided a case in a certain way. The general principles of the regime are fit to specific legal problems. In contrast, asking administrators to consult philosophical works can raise as many questions as they resolve because such works often are vague, difficult to understand, and open to multiple interpretations. The "real-world" application of principles and rules discerned from legal cases avoids the ambiguities inherent in reading general works of philosophy. "A haphazard perusal of the works of the great philosophers will yield nothing more than a gentleman's veneer," Rohr contended, because it will never provide a context for decision-making the way a court case provides a context.[29]

Despite Rohr's desire to provide administrators with an authoritative source for identifying regime values, "black letter law" is not always readily apparent in court decisions. Sometimes, legal rules are in flux, and different courts reach different conclusions. In addition, the search for regime principles presupposes that law and ethics coincide. In many cases they do, but not in every case. As illustrated in the *Plessy* case, the law may decide to treat persons differently based on characteristics that ethicists would argue are indefensible. In such cases, an authoritative entity does not provide the clear guidance that John Rohr and others seek in their quest to identify regime principles.[30]

Other scholars have contended that the search for regime values is a useful enterprise even if the results do not always convey the precision that Rohr sought. Ronald Moe and Robert Gilmour suggested that grounding administrative ethics in public law requires administrators to meet the needs of society while simultaneously protecting the constitutional rights of citizens.[31] Similarly, David H. Rosenbloom argued that public administrators must understand and protect the public law heritage of the United States.[32] Laurence J. O'Toole, Jr. suggested that a lack of constitutional grounding led scholars to create a hypothetical politics-dichotomy that may have served as a useful tool for analysis during the early years of the field, but it failed to reflect the reality of administrative operations. Although today the dichotomy has been rejected by most students of American public administration, it still provides "statutory framing" for bureaucracy.[33] Another influential public administration theorist, Charles R. Wise, championed regime values as they are articulated by the courts because judicial decisions, especially U.S. Supreme Court opinions, influence the manner in which the bureaucracy operates.[34]

For all proponents of regime values and Founding thought, the key point is to understand and apply the values of the Founders to a world that has changed significantly. As noted previously, this is neither a simple task, nor one free from controversy. Assuming that twenty-first century researchers can set aside presentism, which is the tendency to interpret past events through the values and sensibilities of the modern age, understanding the Founding perspective can be challenging but a worthwhile effort "to the end of trying to actualize the ideal of the Founders to become a republic of virtue."[35]

ETHICS AS CITIZENSHIP

The "ethics-as-citizenship" approach requires public administrators to do what they can to ensure that people within the regime are treated and respected as citizens. The term "citizens" has a precise meaning in this context; it refers both to the status of an individual and to the practice of participating in civic life. Citizenship status is the idea that persons who reside under the authority of a particular government because of geographic boundaries possess a litany of rights and responsibilities such as the right to vote, freedom of speech, press, religion, and assembly, and an obligation to obey the laws of the regime. Participating in civic life is the next step aside from a person's status. This ideal suggests that persons who see themselves as citizens will actively seek to engage in civic affairs by running for political office, serving on juries or in the armed services, as appropriate, and seeking to know and honor the public good.[36]

Ethics as citizenship highlights a fundamental problem in the history of ethics—indeed, the history of human beings as individuals with aspirations toward collectivity. Individuals often are motivated by self-interest to maximize private concerns even if this means they sacrifice the common good. This is exactly the issue that political economists call the "tragedy of the commons," which, as explained in a well-known article by Garrett Hardin, is when individual users of a resource that is not privately owned (a "common pool resource") have an incentive to use as much as they can, even if they exhaust the resource, to satisfy their individual desires. Because they take a short-term view of their actions, individuals potentially destroy the resource. Hardin's article highlights the need to engage individuals and remind them that as citizens, they have a civic duty to act on interests over and above their own self-interest.[37]

Proponents of citizenship ethics emphasize common themes. First, they insist that citizens, once they are empowered, can exercise authoritative judgment over political issues. This democratic ethos typically is expressed as a means of limiting the power and influence of elites. In the meantime, empowerment and action move good citizens to think in terms of the public interest, however it is defined. An emphasis on the public interest is not to suggest that citizens will be compelled to renounce "self-interest, properly understood," in Tocqueville's words.[38] Instead, they will recognize that self-interest can be maximized only when the public good is protected through the organs of government.

Citizens understand the value of education as a tool for improving public affairs. If a democratic government requires eternal vigilance to ensure its continued success, as many commentators and theorists have argued, citizens of a regime must be instructed on appropriate regime values and the processes and procedures required to govern with a democratic ethos. Education includes not simply rote memorization of key facts and data related to the regime, but it provides citizens with the tools to think about political and ethical problems analytically, with an emphasis on appreciating a common heritage and practical problems associated with governance.

An appreciation of a common heritage can lead to the final insight, namely the importance of community. With its emphasis on the primacy of individual rights, a democratic political system and a capitalist economic system can lead to a life where citizenship is not valued. People are satisfied to labor in pursuit of their own interests with little or no regard for the interests of the collectivity. Citizenship ethics seeks to transcend this cramped notion of life in a democratic/capitalist regime by fostering a sense of mutual regard among and between the denizens who live in a polity. When mutual regard exists, the regime stresses that the rights of every individual citizen are equal to the rights of every other citizen. Public administrators can foster this spirit of citizenship by remembering that they work for citizens, and they must engage in their duties in a manner that respects citizenship.[39]

Citizenship ethics recalls the notion of a shining city on a hill, but for many skeptics, this ideal seems impossible to attain and naïve to attempt. According to researchers Linda de Leon and Robert B. Denhardt, among others, skepticism about the ideals of citizenship is hardly surprising. Since reform movements emerged in public administration during the 1990s, especially the New Public Management and Reinventing Government, scholars and practitioners alike have championed the market model, focusing on customers rather than citizens, which invariably leads to "glorification of entrepreneurial management." The market model posits that government should be organized, operated, and evaluated as though it were a private, for-profit business. Despite the appeal of holding government agencies accountable through measures of efficiency and effectiveness, de Leon and Denhardt suggested that government has other values—e.g., constitutional protections and a belief in the primacy of individual participation—that preclude close adherence to a market model. Moreover, focusing on customers undermines the advantages of treating people as citizens. Citizens have duties and obligations in a democratic society that extend far beyond a customer-supplier relationship, which rests on the idea that customers express their needs and desires, and suppliers jockey to meet those needs and desires. Citizens have rights and obligations that are absent from the customer-supplier interaction.[40]

ETHICS AS SOCIAL EQUITY

At its core, the term "social equity" seems to refer to concepts of fairness and justice, but these concepts are so vague and open to interpretation that they seem to have little value apart from serving as a crude Rorschach test for determining a person's liberal or conservative political values. One person's "fairness" or "justice" is another person's "impediment" or "interference with markets." Equity, to some extent, is in the eye of the beholder. Nonetheless, in the context of public administration, social equity refers to the delivery of government services in a fair and impartial manner regardless of the economic resources or personal traits of the recipients. Moreover, goods and services must be provided equally or at least in such a way that the disadvantaged receive a greater degree of benefits.[41]

Supporters of social equity contend that when the Wilsonian paradigm of a politics-administration dichotomy was rejected after the 1930s, the resultant change in thinking allowed administrators to recognize their duties were broader than merely carrying out orders set forth by political appointees placed higher in the bureaucratic hierarchy. Administrators at all levels act on behalf of the public welfare, which means they have a heightened responsibility for ensuring that members of the public are treated fairly and impartially. Because so many people have been denied fairness and impartiality on account of their gender, race, ethnicity, or age in times past, disparities continue to exist in the American regime. To the extent that such disparities can be recognized and rectified by administrators, they are obliged to promote social equity.[42]

Arguably, the most famous articulation of social equity as a concern for the least fortunate in society was found in the landmark 1971 work of John Rawls, *A Theory of Justice*. Rawls was arguing in a broader context than public administration; however, his defense of equity applies in this context. According to Rawls, the reason social equity is controversial is because people know their position in society. Decision-makers in the upper echelon of government are elites. They secured their positions by virtue of superior knowledge, education, or political contacts. Although some elites will champion social equity as a desirable goal, many other elites will see social equity as an illegitimate means of assisting the disadvantaged by redistributing wealth, thereby violating the rights of all citizens.

Rawls contended that elites arguing against "handouts" for the least advantaged are guided by self-interest, as are most human beings. Because many elites cannot fathom themselves as the least advantaged, they are safe in arguing against social equity. Would they propound a laissez-faire position if they were ignorant of their social position? Rawls believed they would not. He constructed a hypothetical "original condition" where decision-makers must decide on how goods and services will be distributed in a society, but the decision-makers are ignorant of their status. Rawls labeled this hypothetical construct the "veil of ignorance."

A rational decision-maker acting under a veil of ignorance would design a society so that the least advantaged would not be made worse off by any policies developed and implemented by government. Because no decision-maker can be assured that he or she is an elite, the decision-maker must consider the possibility that when the veil of ignorance is lifted, and persons in the society move beyond the original position, he or she will be poor and destitute. This insight—that people should design a government and a society without reference to one's own socioeconomic status—is essentially an argument in favor of social equity. Because the disadvantaged exist and require assistance, administrators have a moral, and perhaps a legal, obligation to provide assistance.[43]

Social equity has been criticized for being too lofty and left-leaning in its political sensibilities. The New Public Administration, which reached its apex during the 1970s, was dedicated to promoting social equity through government programs, but the movement fell on hard times in the Reagan era when smaller government was heralded as the solution to problems of malaise and stagflation. Moreover, many academics were troubled by the notion that unelected public administrators would determine what constitutes "social equity" and take action to implement their vision inside their respective agencies. To conservatives of the "live-and-let-live" school of thought, administrators who championed social equity as a political ethic were the worst sort of activists; they were engaged in "social engineering" without directly answering to the electorate, a frightening prospect for social and political conservatives who believe that government is best which governs least.[44]

Beginning in the reform-minded 1960s and 1970s, a movement arose within the field of public administration dedicated to legitimizing the exercise of broad administrative discretion within a political and legal system based on the rule of law. If decisions that affect a large percentage of the population are made by public administrators who are not directly accountable to the population, the concept of a truly democratic nation is potentially threatened. Proponents of the "legitimacy movement," as it came to be called, argued that career public administrators must exercise discretion based on "legitimate" sources of authority such as the U.S. Constitution, statutory law, and well-worn rules and regulations. These theorists use terms such as "statesmanship," "stewardship," and the "public interest" to explain how and why unelected public officials have an obligation to protect the public. The key insight is that public administrators must demonstrate how and why they make principled decisions based on reasons they can articulate and defend—in short, something far removed from arbitrary and capricious grounds. This heightened duty to perform the work of the public stands in stark contrast to the duty imposed on persons laboring outside of government service.[45]

ETHICS AS THE PUBLIC INTEREST

Closely related to equity is the old adage suggesting that government should be devoted to protecting the public interest, whereas business should be left to pursue private interest. Yet, this simplistic definition does not differentiate between divergent conceptions of the public interest. According to one interpretation of the term "public interest," the core objective is to achieve procedural balance so that all rights and interests are protected equally without regard to the status of the individuals involved. In the realm of constitutional law, the concept is embodied in the term "procedural due process." The process, not the end result, is the important insight; the public interest is served if each person is afforded his or her day in court, even if the outcome is not ideal.

A competing view of the public interest might be thought of as a substantive debate over the ends of a democratic government. According to this view, which is referred to in constitutional law as "substantive due process," a government that purports to be founded on the consent of the governed necessarily protects individual rights from abrogation or encroachment by obdurate, potentially tyrannical governments. If citizens enjoy liberty and property rights, for example, government cannot infringe on these rights absent a justifiable cause based on the actions, rather than the status, of the individual. The protection and advancement of these rights is a substantive ethic; that is, a government cannot undermine these rights without eroding fundamental elements that comprise a democratic government.

Whichever view is adopted, the paramount consideration is that the protection of individuals leads to a higher good, the notion of a community. Whether it is seen as an amalgamation of individual interests or a wholly new, somewhat mystic creation, a "community" is greater than the sum of its parts. It is a belief that we are all in this together, that to be an "American" (or Czech or Swede or Russian or whatever) is more than a national myth. It is a value that sets us apart from other nations and other forms of government.[46]

Throughout the history of the United States, the public interest has been a compelling concept, one endlessly debated but never satisfactorily resolved. The public interest is ambiguous. As Barry Bozeman has written, "So long as public interest concepts are hopelessly ambiguous, usage will necessarily be inconsistent, measurement efforts have little likelihood of success, and it will be difficult systematically to consider 'a great number of examples.'"[47]

Bozeman's comment about the inconsistency and imprecision in measurement helps to explain, at least in part, why the market model has been so persuasive compared with the public interest model. The market model suggests that rather than focus on the substantive or procedural rights that give rise to a sense of community, we should focus on the individual as the unit of analysis. What, exactly, is the amorphous, ambiguous public interest, and how would one know it if he or she encountered it? How does one measure the public interest? In contrast, private interest, as reflected in the marketplace, can be measured relatively easily. If an entrepreneur introduces a product into the marketplace to advance his or her interest in increasing personal wealth, the measure of whether this private interest is advanced is whether the product sells. The outcome can be quantified through monetary measures.

This easy quantification resonates with the public in a way the more imprecise, ambiguous concept of the public interest cannot. Asking a taxpayer to forgo income or pay a higher income tax rate so that wealth can be redistributed to assist the less fortunate through government assistance programs in the name of the public interest or the common good is a hard sell. The taxpayer feels and can quantify the loss of monies, the slight diminution in his or her private interest, but the resultant benefit to the public interest—especially in light of stories about abuses within public assistance programs—remains theoretical and therefore unreal.[48]

CONCLUSION

It is unlikely that any work can adequately sift through the disparate literature on administrative ethics and develop a unified theory that resolves all the nagging questions that abound. Part of the problem is inherent in the nature of ethics as opposed to, for example, law. The latter is a known and knowable system of positivist rules developed to resolve public disputes in an equitable manner and enforced, as necessary, through state sanctions. Law is designed to resolve specific cases in a manner that allocates fault and/or property among and between parties. Because legal proceedings frequently pit one party against another, the process generally is adversarial; one party achieves most or all of its goals at the expense of the other party. In contrast, ethics generally is a set of heuristic principles that guide individuals in decision-making, but the principles are less clearly defined than legal rules. As a result, ethical inquiries often are vague, amorphous, and open to multiple interpretations. When the law is vague and open to competing interpretations, this is seen as a failure to draft an appropriate set of rules because precision is needed to resolve disputes. When ethics is less well-defined and precise than law, the ambiguity can be deemed profundity.[49]

Having recognized the fundamentally amorphous nature of ethics, all hope is not lost. A fruitful effort can and should be made to wade through the literature and make sense of the disparate schools of thought. Each of the five theories of administrative ethics identified by Cooper explores different features of ethical thinking; therefore, they reach different conclusions. That schools of thought focusing on different aspects should reach different conclusions is to be expected. Any intellectual inquiry that uses one conceptual framework versus another will naturally emphasize different aspects than another school of thought employing a separate framework. The task here is to examine the commonalities among each framework and offer insights into mutually agreeable premises. A suitable starting point for this endeavor is to review recent literature on ethics to discern how theories of administrative ethics fit into a larger context.

As mentioned in the Introduction, this book argues on behalf of a process approach to administrative ethics. In lieu of arguing that one of the five approaches to ethics discussed above is favored, this text suggests that as long as one of these approaches is adopted and can be defended through argumentation and persuasion, the crucial component to ethics is in the process of reaching a decision and taking action. It is helpful to know the universe of approaches and theories before making a decision, and it is to the various systems of modern and postmodern ethics that we now turn.

2

————•◦•◦•————

CONTEMPORARY LITERATURE
AFFECTING ADMINISTRATIVE ETHICS

The literature on ethics and the public interest outside of public administration is voluminous and thus far beyond the scope of a single book.
Nonetheless, it is essential to understand the more influential trends that
have helped to shape the development of administrative ethics since writers and thinkers who specialize in the field operate within a framework of
broader ethical concerns and concepts. Accordingly, this chapter will
review contemporary literature on ethical theory as a prelude to exploring
questions of administrative ethics.[1]

THE NATURE OF PHILOSOPHIC INQUIRY

Ethics is the branch of philosophy that is concerned with how and why
people act based on the choices they make. Philosophy, as distinguished
from science, is the idea that human beings can discern the answers to
fundamental questions about how life ought to be lived based on reason
and rational inquiry as opposed to experimentation. In other words,
whereas science seeks answers to fundamental questions through empirical research that supports the development of hypotheses, or educated
guesses, about how the world works, philosophy relies on the ability of
human beings to explore crucial issues through thinking and deductive
reasoning. Because philosophy does not rely on empirical research apart

from general observations about the world, it cannot provide answers to many basic questions about human beings and their world, but it can raise questions that can be empirically tested, and it can enrich human life by identifying questions that are fundamental to the human condition. Philosophy is not antithetical to empirical research; rather, it exists separate from empirical investigations, serving as the foundation for later experimentation.

Philosophy can be thought of as a means of inquiry into the nature of things. In some cases, it is speculative, which generates knowledge for the sake of knowledge regardless of its practical effect. Metaphysics, a branch of philosophy, argues for the pursuit of knowledge regardless of how the results might be used in a concrete, real-world application. This approach is vastly different from philosophical traditions such as logics, ethics, or aesthetics, which seek to provide guidance on practical action and behavior.

Theorists who delve into ethics typically immerse themselves in the concrete applications of philosophical principles. According to many modern theorists, metaphysics does not provide a useful foundation for ethics because it is so abstract and generalized that the knowledge gleaned from metaphysical musings is not readily applicable to the everyday world of a public administrator, for example. For a philosophy of ethics to be useful in making day-to-day decisions, it must be focused on the kinds of problems that human beings face as they travel through their lives, and it must be presented in a manner that allows decision-makers to take action based on the ideas and concepts covered.

For the concerned public administrator who seeks to "do the right thing," a philosophical inquiry can be maddening. Despite the desire of many ethicists to produce a practical system of ethics, the truth is that multiple schools of thought that champion radically different concepts of ethics can leave a harried administrator frustrated at the lack of specificity in ethical theory. This frustration is responsible to some extent for the many attempts to develop codes of ethics in professional fields. Codes of ethics can provide a small measure of specificity, to be sure, but they cannot address every instance where a human being confronts an ethical dilemma. For that reason, if for no other, it is helpful for all administrators, even those "street-level bureaucrats" about which much ink has been spilled, to have at least a passing familiarity with some of the modern theories of ethics that provide a foundation for codes of ethics and positivist bases of right conduct.

Theories of ethics vary, and different schools of thought exist. Much of the difficulty in reconciling schools of thought and competing theories of ethics occurs because theorists, and to some extent practitioners, talk past each other. Some ethicists contend that the important inquiry concerns descriptive ethics (the "is"), whereas others argue for normative ethics (the "ought"), and still others champion analytic ethics (sometimes called "meta-ethics," an offshoot of normative ethics that questions the premises that support moral judgments). Moreover, one group of thinkers posits a system that focuses on the individual as the appropriate unit of analysis, whereas the other group contends that the collectivity is the paramount consideration.

The analysis of the factors that ground ethics also varies widely among and between schools of thought. The twentieth century witnessed the publication of numerous books and articles about ethics. Whether these publications successfully improved upon preceding works on the subject remains open to debate; nothing is new under the sun. Theories must grapple with perennial questions of deontological and teleological approaches to ethics, but the manner in which they proceed and the quality of their arguments determine which works endure and which slip into obscurity.[2]

This chapter will review a few of the most influential and salient theories of ethics in the modern and postmodern era. Although each system has much to recommend it (and much to undermine it, for that matter), each is not "the answer" to resolving ethical dilemmas. If one were to experience a "Eureka" moment and become ecstatic at the prospect of having found the "right answer" to administrative ethics, the epiphany no doubt would have occurred far before this moment in this text. What this brief summary will do is provide a snapshot view of the most engaging theories on ethics in the literature beyond the field of public administration. At the conclusion, the question will remain: As compelling as many of these schools of thought appear, how do they assist in the reconciliation of the competing perspectives identified by Terry L. Cooper in Chapter 1? As discussed in Chapter 5, reconciliation may be impossible, yet decision-makers must not become paralyzed by indecision. A decision-making process, whatever school of thought rules the day, becomes crucial.

THE CONTINUED VITALITY OF UTILITARIANISM

Utilitarianism has been, and remains, one of the most influential philosophical doctrines in the Western intellectual tradition, largely because it strikes even those persons unaccustomed to philosophical discourse as intuitively justified. Democratic theorists and elected officials have taken refuge in the notion that public policy must be developed with an appreciation of how many citizens (and voters) will be affected by a particular policy. Although utilitarianism has not suffered from a shortage of critics, it has withstood numerous assaults because of its resiliency and popularity among policy-makers.

Proponents of utilitarianism argue that men engage in rational decision-making according to the principle of utility, which holds that people always seek the greatest happiness, or the greatest pleasure, from a choice among alternatives. The English philosopher Jeremy Bentham developed this philosophy based on David Hume's theory of moral sentiments, which asserted that human beings have an instinctive understanding of which acts are useful and therefore appropriately undertaken. Bentham's godson, John Stuart Mill, writing in the mid-nineteenth century, refined Bentham's justification of utilitarianism by suggesting that it is intuitively obvious that human beings seek pleasure in their day-to-day lives in the real world. The wisdom of individual choices is dictated by the character of the people who make decisions. People often set aside their own short-term happiness to advance a larger goal, such as their future happiness. Evidence of this insight is visible everyday when people choose to attend school in lieu of pursuing leisure activities, or they place money in a savings account instead of spending it today. More to the point, a person of good character often chooses a course of action that is not pleasurable; he chooses "higher" pleasures based on his past experiences with pleasure and pain.[3]

Critics of utilitarianism argue that ethics based on maximizing a person's individual preferences is base and undermines society by encouraging appetite-driven human beings to consider their selfish proclivities above all else. Mill's rejoinder is that a proper utilitarian considers the happiness of other persons—the greatest amount of happiness in society as an aggregate collection of individual preferences. Utilitarianism, therefore, is not solely concerned with the individual as the appropriate unit of analysis. The philosophy requires persons to calculate happiness based on an impartial judgment divorced from self-interest. A genuine utilitarian calculation occasionally requires an individual to sacrifice his own happiness for the happiness of a larger group. According to Mill, this is the philosophical basis for democratic government and majority rule. Public policy is most appropriately determined by discovering the greatest good for the greatest number of people and acting accordingly.[4]

Utilitarianism's detractors contend that this numbers-based theory highlights the deficiencies of democratic government. A majority of people seek pleasure instead of pain—this insight is hardly astonishing—but pleasure-seeking does not necessarily form a justifiable basis for government or, for that matter, public sector ethics. Avoidance of pain in pursuit of pleasure is a base calculation that can lead to a base society. Concepts such as "just" or "right" do not depend on the desires of a majority. The tyranny of a majority can lead to oppressive public policy and abhorrent personal conduct all in the name of the higher good or the greatest good for the greatest number. In addition, utilitarianism presupposes that ethical choices are a matter of calculating costs and benefits and selecting a policy that maximizes benefits and minimizes costs. Would that calculating costs and benefits were a simple matter, but utilitarianism provides no workable mechanisms for judging among and between complex calculations where the choices are not always obvious.[5]

Consider a common public policy issue: industrial development versus environmental preservation. Developers argue that an increasing population and the rise of the middle class throughout the world require aggressive policies allowing them to clear away forests and consume natural resources at an advanced rate. In the absence of such consumption, they contend, the infrastructure for supporting the citizenry will be absent, and extreme shortages will result. For their part, environmentalists contend that aggressive resource consumption without careful natural resource protection will exacerbate a variety of ecological problems, including soil erosion, water shortages, and global warming.

Utilitarianism, the champion of rational cost-benefit calculations, can be used to justify either position. Developers can calculate the resources necessary to sustain a growing population in the short term and leave it to future generations to handle subsequent environmental problems. After all, who knows what technological advances and scientific tools will be available to citizens a century from now? To worry about problems and issues in the distant future is to magnify the enormity of problems that scream out for resolution today. A strict weighing of pros and cons is difficult when the possibly negative consequences are not likely to occur, or the probability of their occurrence is so far removed that the consequences cannot be tabulated accurately. Environmentalists can take issue with this calculation and argue that based on their own cost-benefit analysis, prudent resource management is needed now so that resources are not exhausted. In short, the problems of future generations are problems to be dealt with now because without wise environmental protection in the present, there will be no resources available for those persons who come after the current generation passes.

This question of consequences is similar to the distinction between a direct cause and a proximate cause in the law. Because the question of liability often turns on the damages occasioned by a defendant, it is helpful to determine what exactly flowed or resulted from the actions of the defendant. If he or she swings her fist and connects with another person, the injuries that occur are a direct consequence of the assault. The defendant is the direct cause of the damages and must be held accountable for this action. If the defendant swings his or her fist and the person ducks to avoid the contact but, in so ducking, knocks over a bucket that was precariously balanced on a ladder, causing the bucket to strike someone else, the question of causation is much more difficult. The crucial question in that situation is whether the ultimate damage was foreseeable at the time the defendant swung his or her fist. We need not extend the legal analysis too far here; the point is that cause and effect is not always a straightforward calculation. Utilitarianism lacks precision and does not provide a mechanism for resolving this type of conundrum.[6]

Moreover, utilitarianism assumes that individuals are capable of reaching decisions based on rationality, yet understanding the many reasons that an individual decided on a course of action, much less a group of individuals, is difficult. People make decisions for many reasons, some of which may be irrational. In some situations, it is possible that persons would willingly sacrifice their liberty on the altar of the greatest good. In a totalitarian state, individuals might be willing to endure horrible abuses and surrender their civil liberties in hopes that the overall society will be improved. Moreover, different depths of preferences exist; some people desire a particular good a great deal, whereas others are disinterested. Utility calculations generally afford each person's preferences the same unit value. Depths of preferences are not adequately considered.[7]

Despite these attacks, over time utilitarianism has been the predominant philosophical justification for the liberal democratic state. G. E. Moore continued the trend but also signaled a new direction toward evaluating and advancing utilitarianism in his landmark work, *Principia*

Ethica, first published in 1903. In that work he foreshadowed the importance of linguistic analysis that would define much of the philosophy that
followed. According to Moore, previous ethical theorists had developed
elaborate meta-theories without adequately defining their terms at the
outset. Initially, this insight may sound jejune, but it actually raises a pro-
found, if subtle, point. Utilitarians, including Jeremy Bentham and John
Stuart Mill, argue in favor of the greatest good for the greatest number,
but they do not explain what they mean by "good" except to assume that
"goodness" refers to "pleasurable" without arguing the point. In some
cases, pleasure and good may be identical, but this is not necessarily the
case. Moore suggested that "good" is unique; it exists separate and apart
from notions of pleasure. In fact, the "good" is such a simple, fundamental concept that it cannot be defined outside of itself; to do so is to miss
the nuances inherent in the term. People can speak of the good, but they
can never quite pinpoint all facets of the concept.

The difficulty in defining the good means that any system of ethical
reasoning can only approximate the good. Different circumstances, different backgrounds, and different levels of understanding or access to information mean that individuals are always guessing at what choices and
actions are ethical. What constitutes the good can only be judged through
a glass darkly. Because the good cannot be known firsthand, "good" acts
must be judged by examining consequences and determining whether
they are the hoped-for outcome. In short, the principle of utility requires
someone asking the question "what should I do?" to base a decision on
whether the action will cause or contribute to a desired outcome. With
this analysis, Moore shifted the field of ethics from a concern about the
right or wrong nature of certain actions (normative ethics) to a concern
about the meaning or desirability of the terms "right," "wrong," "good,"
"bad," and so forth (metaethics).[8]

INTRINSIC VERSUS INSTRUMENTAL GOOD

Building on Moore's insights, another theme in twentieth-century ethical theory was a concern with goodness and value. Stated in its most ele-
mental terms, the question is whether something is intrinsically good,
that is, good for its own sake, or instrumentally good because it accom-
plishes another underlying, more important goal. Determining whether
something is an end or the means to an end determines, to some extent,

how one approaches goodness as a concept. If goodness is an end in itself, a moral agent must act in ways consistent with the good, even if the consequences that result might be personally disadvantageous. Such a position recalls Kant's emphasis on absolute moral duty. In contrast, approaching the good as the means to an end shifts the focus to consequences, just as the English Utilitarians emphasized the consequences of an action as a crucial consideration.[9]

To understand the debate, it is helpful to understand the debate between two eighteenth-century philosophers, David Hume and Immanuel Kant, concerning relative and absolute value. According to Hume, nothing can ever be known with absolute certainty; therefore, skepticism is the only logical response based on the "narrow capacity of human understanding." Hume was ruthless in his desire to avoid any metaphysical presuppositions that would taint the usefulness of philosophy. In his opinion, aside from mathematics and "experimental reasoning concerning matter of fact and existence," all philosophical inquiry into questions, such as whether a thing is good in and of itself or whether God exists, is simply "sophistry and illusion" and must be "committed to the flames." Hume recognized the utility of abstract concepts such as "good" and "bad" and "right" and "wrong," but not because he thought they were universal truths. Instead, they were ordering principles of society and, therefore, were useful in ensuring that people behaved in socially useful ways. "The inner and outer aspects of human life are unified in morality," Hume wrote.[10]

Hume's relativistic philosophy means that ethical decisions cannot be considered "good" except to the extent that they serve man's purposes. Conversely, a decision is "bad" if it has limited or no utility. Ethics can be useful if social control and individual responsibility result from commonly derived principles, but absolute rules applicable across space and time do not exist. The ethical standards the ancient Greeks found useful do not necessarily apply to modern times because the world of the Greeks was far different than the world of their successors. In short, a code of conduct must be adapted to its time and place.

According to Hume, utilitarian calculation alone is a necessary but insufficient means for grounding ethics. Feeling, or taste, is necessary because rational knowledge alone will not suffice to assign moral blame. Utility and feeling together influence the manner in which individuals arrive at ethical judgments. If human beings were not naturally benevolent—if they did not exhibit sympathy—they would not make ethical judgments because such judgments would be of no value. Hume's utilitarian view of ethics can be thought of as a philosophy of "modified self-interest and a confined benevolence."[11]

His rejection of metaphysics did not prevent Hume from identifying qualities that lead to benevolence. He specified qualities of virtue, including justice, generosity, beneficence, and honesty, which are useful to everyone. Other qualities, including prudence, frugality, industry, and temperance, are useful primarily to the person who possesses them. A third category of qualities—which includes modesty, wit, and decency—are agreeable to others. Self-esteem, love of glory, and magnanimity are agreeable to the person possessing those qualities. Again, these virtues serve a purpose to improve human life—they are lubricants that allow individuals to appreciate their self-worth and the worth of other people—but their value clearly is instrumental, not intrinsic.

Hume's philosophy contains the same deficiencies that all utilitarian-based ethical theory must confront. If the utility of the philosophy determines its value, the standards are different for different cultures and people It is difficult to establish guidelines for behavior because the standards constantly change over time. Hume's relativism triggered a reaction among philosophers who believed that philosophical and ethical standards must be absolute.[12]

The German philosopher Immanuel Kant sought to reconcile Christian religious beliefs with the intellectual state of Western culture, and he viewed Hume as his primary theoretical opponent. In arguing that human beings are obligated to act as rational, autonomous moral agents, Kant set the stage for nineteenth-century ethics and philosophy. He famously wrote that he was awakened from his "dogmatic slumbers" by Hume's skepticism and especially Hume's view of morals as a matter of opinion. For Kant, the logical implications of Hume's "hypothetical imperative" were to reduce standards of conduct to merely a hypothetical discussion of the behavior expected to bring about happiness. Hume's ethical theory was a moral sophistry that permitted individuals to rationalize their behavior according to the situation. By grounding ethics in utility, Hume was allowing individuals to justify any behavior, no matter how egregious, as useful, hence "ethical." In Kant's view, if man is to be free to act as a rational, moral agent, he must obey absolute rules of conduct. In a world where a hypothetical imperative exists, man is little more than an animal because he can undertake actions to fulfill a basic need without reflection or analysis.[13]

In *Fundamental Principles of the Metaphysics of Morals*, Kant theorized that a universal moral law exists, which he labeled the "categorical imperative." The imperative is a standard of behavior for free, rational, moral agents under all circumstances without respect to space and time, as discussed in the Introduction. "Act only on that maxim whereby thou canst at the same time will that it should become a universal law," he wrote. The categorical imperative is the Golden Rule, where a person should do unto others as he would have them do unto him. If a person chooses to undertake an action, he must ask himself a question—"would I want to live in a society where everyone acts in this manner?" If the answer is "no," the person must refrain from acting. If the answer is "yes," the person should act. Utilitarian calculations are not a factor because the categorical imperative applies in all instances, regardless of intervening factors.[14]

The Hume-Kant debate between utility and duty has been at the center of ethical debate for centuries, and each generation of theorists must confront the question of instrumental versus intrinsic value. In 1930, Sir William David Ross published *The Right and the Good*, a work that took up the mantle of Kantianism and attempted to resolve the fundamental dilemma in Kant's philosophy. When two moral imperatives conflict and are mutually exclusive, the difficulty lies in deciding which imperative to honor. Ross called these imperatives "prima facie duties." If two prima facie duties clash, and it is not immediately apparent how these duties should be reconciled, must the Kantian system be rejected altogether? Consequentialists argue that it should. Ross contends that a middle approach is available.

Prima facie duties such as "human life is precious" and "never tell a lie" may conflict, for example, in the case discussed in the Introduction where the knife-wielding marauder asks for information on the whereabouts of his intended victim. Rather than struggle with the moral imperative of two irreconcilable duties, Ross argues that a moral agent can weigh the duties and suspend one duty in this instance. Because lying to an intended murderer is relatively trivial while preserving the life of the would-be victim is far from trivial, lying is justified because it serves a higher purpose. Although it is true that the moral agent has now moved from Kant's insistence on the universality of moral imperatives to a consideration of consequences, it is also true that the compromise in this case does not necessarily apply in other cases. Once the clash of prima facie duties has ended, the original universality of the Kantian maxims remains intact.[15]

A useful analogy is to think of legal prohibitions on trespass. It is a well-settled principle that a person must not enter upon his neighbor's lands unless he is invited. Otherwise, he has infringed on the neighbor's legally protected right to enjoy his property free from encumbrance. In situations where an emergency occurs, however, the doctrine of necessity suggests that a person can temporarily suspend the prohibition on trespass. The quintessential example involves a neighbor's boat dock. I am not allowed to tie up my boat to that dock unless the neighbor specifically invites me to do so. Let us say, however, that one day I am sailing along in my boat and a storm arises before I can navigate back to my property. In my hour of peril, I make it safely to my neighbor's dock, but I cannot make it to my own dock. In this scenario, I am justified by necessity in using my neighbor's dock despite the absence of express permission. The alternative—that I set sail and probably perish in the storm in the interests of preserving a property right—is weighed against the trespass. Similarly, compromising two prima facie duties in cases where exigencies require a compromise is viewed as morally defensible.[16]

ECONOMIC INDIVIDUALISM: EFFICIENCY VERSUS EQUITY

Underlying much of the contemporary ethics literature, at least insofar as it pertains to the American situation, is a presupposition of economic individualism. The American Founders, classical liberals and proponents of laissez-faire economics to the end, famously heralded the idea of "that government is best which governs least." This focus on economic individualism places the interests of the individual higher than the interests of the collectivity. In fact, the purpose of establishing a collectivity in the first place is to provide a mechanism for protecting the individual. When the collectivity becomes too powerful or infringes on the liberties of the individual, the collectivity has become oppressive. Although this idea has changed over time, it remains a significant topic of discussion, especially as political theorists and elected officials have grappled with what it means for a collectivity to be "too powerful."[17]

The question has come to be framed as a tug-of-war between efficiency and equity. Should policies be developed and implemented using the fewest resources in the shortest amount of time, which is the typical definition of efficiency, or should the goal be to treat like cases alike—that is, in an equitable manner—even if such treatment is inefficient? The standard debate casts these concepts as antithetical values so that an increase in one value necessarily requires a corresponding decrease in the other. The state exists to serve the ends of the people, not vice versa, but what does that mean in practice? The efficient use of resources by government means that individuals do not have to support a large, wasteful government through excessive tax revenues. Yet, tax revenues can be used by government to help the less fortunate in society. This tradeoff between efficiency and equity has been considered a key point of contention between political parties in the United States.[18]

At the risk of overgeneralizing, political conservatives, especially prominent members of the Republican Party, argue that efficiency is the paramount value in American society. When the private sector is left to its own devices, and government champions policies that ensure the operation of stable, free markets, the resultant efficiency benefits everyone. Business owners can receive a healthy return on investment, which allows them to invest capital in increasing machinery and production, which in turn provides expanded jobs and an increasing tax base. The old adage "a rising tide raises all boats" reflects the conservative ideology that efficiency will eventually lead to equity, albeit in a roundabout way as wealth trickles down through the economic system from the top.[19]

Political liberals, especially those Democrats who hearken back to the 1960s, contend that equity must be promoted above efficiency. Although efficiency is a laudable goal, promoting efficiency for its own sake without considering the potentially devastating effect it can have on the disadvantaged in a society leads to a divided nation of very few "haves" and a multitude of "have-nots." Political liberals denounce the conservative ideology and "trickle-down economics" as poor justification for abandoning government's affirmative obligation to help its citizens. To ensure a fair and just society, government must step in and regulate markets so a "level playing field" exists and everyone enjoys an equal opportunity to participate in American life. If this may require slightly higher tax rates and more government intrusion into the marketplace, even at the expense of some measure of efficiency, political liberals believe this result is worth the price that must be paid.[20]

Although in many cases such a tradeoff exists, efficiency and equity need not be competing values. Efficiency and equity sometimes can be balanced. To understand this point, it is instructive to think of a continuum between individual liberty and state authority. At one end of the spectrum is absolute liberty, which can be defined as a complete absence of constraints on individual behavior. In a state of absolute liberty, no government exists. A person can do whatever he or she wants, and no entity can step in to curb the behavior. Some extreme libertarians have argued that a state of complete liberty is blissful, a veritable Garden of Eden, but a majority of mainstream Western thinkers since the Enlightenment have viewed a state of absolute liberty with horror, for it dissolves into licentiousness. Thomas Hobbes, a strong supporter of the social contract theory of government, denounced life in a "state of nature" as "nasty, brutish, and short." Subsequent theorists spoke of "nature red in tooth and claw." Rational men willingly surrender some of their individual liberty in exchange for the authority of a state to protect them and to meet basic needs. After people have agreed to surrender a measure of liberty to create a state, the question becomes how much individual liberty should be surrendered in exchange for how much government authority. An increase in one, by definition, decreases the other.[21]

Concerned about the misuse of political power, the American Founders adopted a state with little authority in the Articles of Confederation in 1781. Their first attempt at a constitution proved to be seriously flawed because they emphasized liberty at the expense of a powerful state that could promote a certain measure of efficiency. Popular opinion in the eighteenth century was that the newly liberated Americans needed a state with very few powers so that citizens could enjoy maximum individual liberty. A majority of political leaders subscribed to the libertarian creed: That government is best which governs least; don't tread on me. Government should serve as a kind of night watchman but essentially not interfere in the lives of yeomen farmers. Because a state that has very little authority must continually surrender to the will of the masses, and the masses are constantly in turmoil, the state simply cannot function effectively. After only eight years, American statesmen rejected the classical liberal state established by the Articles of Confederation and replaced it with a stronger system—the federal government found in the new U.S. Constitution.[22]

At the other extreme end of the spectrum, a totalitarian state undermines individual liberty because all political and economic decisions are made by government with a ruthless equality of outcomes enforced by the state. Unlike a condition of absolute liberty, where people may starve to death because there is no one to provide for them and life becomes a Hobbessian war of all-against-all where only the strong and/or cunning survive, a state with absolute authority can ensure that no one starves. The problem is that subjects of a totalitarian regime risk brutalization if a totalitarian regime abuses power and aggrandizes its leaders. This insight was dramatically illustrated by the former Soviet Union and in many other totalitarian states throughout history. Mainstream theorists have rejected a state possessing absolute authority because it invariably degenerates into a dictatorship regardless of the benevolent motives of the regime's founders.[23]

A possible compromise between too much liberty and too much state authority is to embrace socialism. Socialism, according to the theorist Sidney Webb, is not a clearly developed set of doctrines or precisely identified tenets. At its core, socialism is the idea that individuals should be provided with a small measure of liberty, but the state provides essential goods and services when they are necessary. Private enterprise is not prohibited, but it is strictly regulated, and large companies can be nationalized if it is in the public interest to do so. The justification that socialists cite for the extensive use of government controls is that there are so many powerful, consolidated forces amassed against the individual that only government possesses the resources and structure to challenge those forces and ensure that the individual can compete on a level playing field. Different socialist regimes provide different levels of individual liberty; some western European nations are labeled "democratic-socialist" states in recognition of their desire to protect the individual, where necessary, but allow liberty, where possible. In some cultures and traditions where individual liberty is not as highly valued as it is in the United States, a democratic-socialist state is gratefully accepted. In the United States, however, the idea that government controls most of the means of production and makes major economic decisions for the public and private sectors as part of a planned economy is dismissed as too intrusive and potentially oppressive. Anything that appears reminiscent of socialism, regardless of its other virtues, will be rejected by a large percentage of Americans.[24]

This menu of choices means that Americans look to a mixed polity—that is, a regime where people, acting through elected representatives, make some political decisions but unelected experts also make decisions within their areas of expertise—as the preferred form of government for a people who embrace individual liberty but also desire a strong state that meets many needs, especially for national defense, protecting free markets, and ensuring equality of opportunity for individuals. The U.S. political system calls to mind Winston Churchill's famous comment that a democracy is the worst form of government except, of course, for all the others. Thus, Americans seek to have their cake and eat it, too. They want efficiency, but equity, too.[25]

In the face of this seeming contradiction, an exploration of theories of equity and fairness is appropriate. One theory embraces free markets and the idea that individual liberty is a crucial component of life. Modern free market economists often accept this view. The English Utilitarian John Stuart Mill, author of the classic 1859 book *On Liberty*, argued that government should prevent "other-regarding" actions if they are negative, but "self-regarding" actions should not be subject to government intervention because the choices made by an individual are beyond the purview of government. Neoclassical economists and well-known free market proponents such as Milton Friedman, the Nobel Laureate long associated with the University of Chicago, contend that free markets are far more efficient and effective than governments in meeting the needs and desires of citizens. Irving Kristol and Robert Nozick are two politically conservative theorists who have also presented persuasive and influential arguments about the importance of private property and the freedom of the marketplace.[26]

Using this framework, the standard notion of "efficiency" in the twenty-first century is conceptually simple. It is the idea that a rational person seeks to achieve his or her goals while also using as few resources as possible. To be "efficient," therefore, means that the person achieves the greatest return on an investment of his or her time and/or money. The colloquial expression is that a person gets "the biggest bang for the buck." Ideally, an efficient course of action is also effective, albeit effectiveness is a different concept. To be "effective," as that term generally is understood, means that a person achieves the goal but in doing so may use more resources than necessary. In such a case, an individual accomplished the professed goal, but in doing so, he or she used resources wastefully. Conversely, a person could use very few resources—hence, be efficient—but not be especially effective. The idea is to achieve a maximal goal with minimal use of resources.[27]

"Equity," in contrast with traditional notions of "efficiency," refers to fairness. Philosophers of jurisprudence talk about "treating like cases alike." To be equitable means that distinctions, especially among and between human beings, must be made according to a principle of fairness so that people are not harmed or discriminated against based on factors such as race, ethnicity, gender, or other factors they cannot control. Much of modern American law involves efforts to ensure that legal standards and requirements are equitable, but such efforts raise a key issue for mainstream economists: What is the appropriate role of government in the marketplace? The traditional model of capitalism—stretching back to Adam Smith's idea that an "invisible hand" guides the marketplace—champions free markets. According to this view, choosing efficacious public policy means basing decisions on the desires of consumers. The assumption is that people are self-interested rational maximizers. They may not always maximize their self-interest, and they may not always act rationally because they may be mistaken in what they believe, they may have incomplete information (asymmetric information, in the economists' parlance), or transaction costs may be too high, but, to the extent possible, they attempt to maximize their self-interest in a rational manner.[28]

As long as markets do not fail because of externalities, asymmetric information, or the presence of natural monopolies, for many Americans the marketplace is seen as a more efficient barometer of what people want than any measure devised by governments. Public choice theorists such as Anthony Downs and Elinor Ostrom, for example, contend that the measures used by governments to gauge what the people want—voting results, feedback through political pluralism, public opinion polls, and so forth—are not nearly as precise as free markets for measuring what people want in public policies, especially those with economic ramifications. People vote for many reasons, not all of which are clear. One certainly cannot determine from voting studies how people feel about specific policies, despite the claims of elected officials to enjoy a mandate after they are elected to office. Pluralism—the idea that interest groups compete for political power and that this leads to compromises resulting in effective public policy—helps to discern a little of what people want, but not everyone participates in groups. In fact, according to Robert Putnam's book *Bowling Alone*, group participation may be declining. People also do not follow political affairs closely, so public opinion polls are not an accurate indicator of how they feel about long-term policies. Moreover, because governments are so fragmented, and policies are often complex and difficult to fathom, looking to government mechanisms for understanding the "will of the people" in the policy process is misguided.[29]

For many economists, the condition of markets can help determine when it is appropriate for government to intervene into the marketplace, and when it is inappropriate. A market is highly contestable when there is a large private supply of a good, and ownership is vested in the private sector. In those cases, markets can function efficiently, and government should stay out of the way. In cases where markets are not highly contestable—where supplies are low, and ownership is almost wholly within the public sector—government intervention is appropriate. In other words, government should intervene when there is "market failure."[30]

According to Robert Haveman in *Economics of the Public Sector*, markets fail when there is a goal apart from efficiency in the smooth, orderly transfer of goods and services from one party to another.[31] An example can be found in the Rural Electrification Act, a statute enacted by Congress during Franklin D. Roosevelt's administration in the 1930s. Congress and the president decided, as part of the New Deal policies, that every American should have access to electric service. The problem was that some impoverished peoples living in Appalachia could not afford to pay the market rate for electricity even if it were available. In this kind of situation, a private electric company would not have an economic incentive to invest in building an electric generation plant. This lack of a market response to a perceived need is what economists call a "market failure." In that case, the Roosevelt administration created a government corporation called the Tennessee Valley Authority (TVA). TVA built a plant that supplied electricity to poor people in that area at subsidized rates. The market failed, so the government stepped in to fill the gap, as it were.[32]

Free market economists also see a role for government in leveling the playing field. Thus, Ronald Coase, a 1991 Nobel Laureate in Economics, developed a famous theorem bearing his name to explain the appropriate role of government. The Coase Theorem posits that property resources, absent transaction costs, will end up in the hands of the party that places the highest value on that resource. This phenomenon is one of the reasons that private enterprise is so efficient; people will cut a deal to acquire the resources they believe to be beneficial. When transaction costs are involved, however, this skews the process so that sometimes a party is dissuaded from acquiring a resource because of the costs that have to be incurred in the acquisition. The role of government, according to Coase, is to intervene by adopting public policies that minimize transaction costs. For example, if railroad freight rates significantly impede the ability of buyers and sellers to transact business, government is justified in regulating freight rates through the Interstate Commerce Commission. Coase and free market economists harbor no love for the ICC or other government agencies, but they recognize that if those agencies can help level the playing field, participants in the marketplace can be more efficient.[33]

Another problem in the marketplace occurs when externalities exist. Externalities are unintended or unforeseen consequences of individual behavior that are not factored into the decisions made by individual parties in a given transaction. Externalities can be positive, such as the benefits that accrue when someone is educated. It is difficult to know how much good will come out of a more-or-less straightforward transaction of a school instructing a pupil in exchange for tuition and/or tax monies, but the chances are good that the external benefits will extend in many ways well into the future because an educated person contributes to society in myriad ways. Externalities can be negative, too. The quintessential example is pollution. If a small amount of a hazardous air pollutant is below regulatory concern and, therefore, is allowed, the costs of generating the pollution do not have to be taken into consideration by an individual polluter; however, when hundreds or thousands of firms pollute, the aggregate level of pollution can lead to harmful health effects for everyone.[34]

In cases where negative externalities exist, government generally steps in at some point and regulates those externalities. In some cases, government can impose a tax on the negative externality—a so-called "Pigouvian" tax, named for the influential Cambridge economist A. C. Pigou—or it can impose public programs to clean up the negative externality. The programs can be funded partially by private sector funds and partially through government funding. In any case, the goal is to ensure that the costs of externalities are accounted for so that the marginal social costs equal the marginal social benefits, and a kind of balance is achieved.[35]

The traditional economic view of the efficiency-equity tradeoff associated with public policies and programs is certainly not a universally accepted perspective. One of the strongest critiques of this approach was offered by Deborah Stone in her book, *The Policy Paradox*. Stone viewed the traditional approach to public policy—which she derisively labeled the "rationality project"—as seriously deficient because it assumes that a linear process exists. Mainstream economists and students of the policy process act as though people live independently of each other and make decisions as rational maximizers based on clearly defined goals and work through a clearly defined policy process. Stone argued that this conception of how policies are devised is simplistic.[36]

In her view, we actually live in a constantly evolving political community. To think that the policy process or the system of adopting public policies is somehow static and fixed with stable, ongoing issues and procedures is to mistake what happens in the policy process. As our world changes—new policies are adopted, new leaders come into power, new technologies emerge, people's interests and desires change—the process changes. The effect is that the process of adopting a policy today may or may not be the same as the process will be tomorrow. This insight is analogous to the concept of iron triangles. Political scientists used to talk about the triangular relationship among and between Congress, the bureaucracy, and outside interest groups as though this was a fixed framework. With Hugh Heclo's concept of issue networks—where relationships constantly change and alliances form and dissolve with lightning rapidity—iron triangles seem a bit antiquated.[37] Similarly, Stone's argument suggests that the notion that there is some kind of fixed, linear, unchanging relationship between efficiency and equity, on the one hand, and incontrovertible economic principles, on the other, is simply outdated. There is an inherent paradox in any doctrine that assumes a fixed position, such as the standard economic position on efficiency and equity, because, as positions and relationships change, the idea of a fixed position must change as well. The import of Stone's thesis is that it is theoretically possible to adopt a public policy that has the potential to increase both efficiency and equity. In other words, unlike the standard economic viewpoint, which assumes that a tradeoff between efficiency and equity is unavoidable, a policy can embrace both values.[38]

PRAGMATISM

The desire of Americans to "have it all" and herald the virtues of efficiency and equity at the same time leads to an important school of thought, pragmatism. Rather than adopt a clear, consistent, precise, elegant rationale for a distinctly American school of thought, pragmatists search for what works even if contradictions exist. It is to this philosophy that we now turn.

Often called the "American philosophy," pragmatism is an idea most closely associated with the thinkers Charles Sanders Peirce, William

James, and John Dewey. The philosophy champions a practical approach to problems, the possibilities inherent in a democratic ethos, the promise of individualism, the efficacy of the scientific method, and optimism for the future. Pragmatism was widely heralded as a valuable addition to Western philosophy during the latter half of the nineteenth century until the end of World War II. In the postwar years, pragmatism was eclipsed by philosophical traditions such as logical empiricism, existentialism, and critical theory. Richard Rorty, a neopragmatist, has attempted to resurrect the pragmatic paradigm in recent years, although it is not the dominant American philosophy it once was.[39]

Pragmatism assumes that the individual is the important unit of analysis. This is not to say that community is unimportant; rather, community service is best realized by encouraging the development of the individual. Just as Friedrich Nietzsche argued that an individual's perspective is crucial toward understanding the potentiality of a human life, the pragmatists contended that perspective is a key component of their philosophy. A person makes choices in life, and the sum of those choices determines whether the person will succeed or fail. Pragmatism is not a consistent ideology that requires adherence to supposedly immutable propositions that must be linked logically through syllogisms. It is an experimental approach to the world. If an individual tries a course of action, and it proves to be ineffective, the individual is well advised to try something else in its stead. Pragmatists are less concerned with constructing an elegant, logically consistent theory than with discovering what works and applying its lessons to the real world.[40]

Consider modern pragmatism through the work of Richard Rorty. Building on the work of the nineteenth-century pragmatists, Rorty suggested that no difference exists between something that is true and something that works as a practical matter. In other words, he argued that it is nonsensical to think that objective, immutable standards exist separate and apart from the real world. Plato's Theory of Forms, which posited an unseen world of eternal truth and omnipresent standards, is impractical and, therefore, of no consequence in resolving real-world problems. Immutable standards that can never be verified or achieved do not figure into human life. An epistemology that depends on such an abstract, esoteric notion becomes irrelevant, akin to the cliché asking how many angels can dance on the head of a pin.

According to this perspective, human beings do not have an "essence" apart from their ability to use language and the socialization they receive as they grow from infancy. Thinkers who argue in favor of an essence of humanity allow individuals to escape responsibility for their actions, in some instances, because bad behavior can be attributed to the essence of man. "Yes, I acted selfishly," a person might admit, "but ultimately it is not my fault. Selfishness is the essence of man, and so I was simply acting in accordance with my nature." For Rorty and other neopragmatists, appeals to an essence are an excuse that cannot be accepted.

The only standards that apply to people are those reached discursively. People build their lives on a foundation constructed from their language use, the rules and mores of society, and their belief in what works and what does not. Human nature can be changed—Rorty labeled it "contingent"—depending on circumstances and the need to adapt to situations. This is a radical departure from theories that assume human nature is a given and proceed from that point forward. If human nature is contingent on time, place, and circumstances, all manner of creative solutions to human problems are available.

As a materialist, Rorty contended that human beings construct their world. They engage in "sentence uttering" as a means of coping with the world, but he does not believe that human frailties, weaknesses, or shortcomings are rooted in any essential human condition. Rorty's philosophy was designed to be liberating to the individual. So much of philosophical and ethical thinking has been focused on discovering immutable principles that cannot be shown to exist. In Rorty's view, when individuals realize that no laws of God or nature are responsible for the structure or operation of human society and mores, they will recognize that human community is the result of individual achievement. Human beings built these institutions; therefore, human beings can modify and improve institutions. Rather than undermine the human search for meaning in the world, Rorty contended that the realization that human institutions are not external to human beings will cast aside "metaphysical comfort" and imbue human beings with a desire to make sense of the world themselves.[41]

Although not strictly a neopragmatist, the twentieth-century philosopher Jurgen Habermas relied on some aspects of pragmatism in his philosophy. Habermas is best known for his theory of communicative rationality, which moves beyond the traditional concept of rationality rooted in the Enlightenment. In Habermas's interpretation of rationality, linguistic communication is the crucial component of reason as opposed to an outside, omnipotent source of reason. Despite this emphasis on a pragmatic, nonmetaphysical approach to human problems, Habermas also believed in universal pragmatics, namely that all speech has a telos (end) of mutual understanding. Human beings possess the communicative abilities to participate in human discourse, and these abilities hold the key to resolving human problems.

Habermas argued that the Enlightenment that had influenced much of the Western intellectual tradition for centuries was an "unfinished project" that ought to be revised and not rejected. He was especially critical of the postmodernists who undermined the Enlightenment by arguing against the development of recognizable, eternal standards. In Habermas's conception, the world can be made more humane, just, and egalitarian through discourse. In fact, communication is central to humanity. Over time, man's ability to communicate evolves, which allows the human animal to evolve and improve. Unfortunately, man's ability to communicate is impeded by a variety of socially constructed institutions such as organizations, the market, and the nation-state. To the extent that social constructions interfere with people's ability to communicate and interact, these constructions are a threat to human advancement. Habermas's brand of pragmatism is an attempt to map out ways by which communicative rationality can be preserved and augmented.[42]

Pragmatism offers a great deal of guidance for decision-makers working inside government agencies. Rather than search for an elegant, comprehensive, logically nuanced philosophy that might be difficult to apply in practice, it emphasizes the importance of practical applications above all else. The problem is that by emphasizing what works, pragmatism risks becoming a means by which decision-makers reach a decision based on flawed reasoning, which is then justified on the basis of its pragmatic outcome. Without some kind of rules for calculating an outcome, a philosophy can become a hodgepodge of theories and parts of theories that rationalizes any behavior.

ETHICAL EGOISM

Ethical egoism has been another major trend in twentieth-century ethical thought, and it seeks to provide rules for calculating an outcome. This theory is similar to utilitarianism; it suggests that human beings ought to act in ways that advance their own self-interest, calculating costs and benefits, and acting in ways that maximize benefits while minimizing costs.

The calculation might involve economic costs, but it can include intangible considerations of pleasure and pain. Individuals may accept some short-term pain in anticipation of long-term pleasure. This trade-off was central to Epicureanism, an ancient theory of ethical egoism that indicated man's desire to pursue "higher pleasures" (intellectual pursuits and aesthetic appreciation) in lieu of "lower pleasures" (food and sex). Stoics were ethical egoists as well, although their view of self-interest was to adopt an attitude of apatheia (indifference to adverse fortune).

Ethical egoism initially appears identical to the kinds of cost-benefit calculations found in utilitarianism, and in many ways, the two philosophies resemble each other. Ethical egoism, however, seeks to go beyond utilitarianism; it offers an explanation for all human motivation. Everything that people do in their lives ultimately is because they believe it is in their self-interest. Even when they seem to be performing altruistic acts, people have calculated risk and reward and determined that this act will advance their self-interest. Even Christianity and altruistic philosophies that apparently deemphasize individual interests to advance the whole can be attributed to a desire to advance self-interest. The noble Christian who fears Jesus is attempting to win over a vengeful God and secure a place in heaven. The altruistic Mother Teresa secretly longs for the approval of others that comes from supposedly selfless devotion to the downtrodden.[43]

The major distinction between utilitarianism and ethical egoism is that the latter focuses on the self at the exclusion of others. Utilitarianism allows for the possibility that other people have their own interests, needs, and desires, and an individual might selflessly make room for the needs of others. For the committed utilitarian, interests and desires can be quantified, weighed, and compared. Moreover, in some instances, a person may sacrifice his or her interests with no promise of future gain because the well-being of others is important to the person. If I pull a victim from a burning automobile, I might risk my life with no expectation of gain except the satisfaction of knowing that I helped my fellow man. If I slip into the uniform of my country's armed services and head off to war, I risk the possibility that I could be injured or killed in combat. The act of saving another human being in distress or serving in the military can be said to be selfless. I might receive some tangential benefit—an award for heroism or the approbation of my fellow man, true enough—but mostly I am acting in ways that are unlikely to be fully compensated; therefore, it is not the likelihood of compensation and a rational calculation of what it gets him or her that motivates every human being. A utilitarian believes that people are driven by calculations, but they can step beyond themselves upon occasion.[44]

Ethical egoism emphasizes the needs of the self at the exclusion of all else. It is not possible, nor desirable, to step beyond ourselves. Others exist, and are valued only insofar as they can meet the needs of the self. Accordingly, critics of ethical egoism contend that this concept forecloses the possibility of selfless acts. How does a proponent of ethical egoism account for acts of heroism when a person sacrifices his or her life to save the lives of others? The heroism and self-sacrifice are calculations made in the expectation of future benefits. If from time to time, the expectations do not materialize or if the price one pays is too high—I was injured or killed trying to help another person—the result is caused not by selflessness; it was caused by poor judgment and a flawed calculation. The hero thought he could save the damsel in distress and thereby garner praise and public acclaim. He was killed in the process, so he gambled and came up short. He made a bad bargain.

Even if ethical egoism accurately describes human motivations and behavior—and this is by no means an uncontested proposition—the question remains whether it ought to be a standard of conduct. A standard that urges individuals to place their own good above the good of others is a recipe for eroding community and the common good. If people constantly look out for number one, they are prone to cut corners and harm their fellow man in the name of expediency.

The rejoinder to this position is to argue that self-interest is a concrete, easily grasped concept whereas the amorphous "common good" is so vague as to be virtually meaningless. Human nature dictates that a person protect and promote his or her own good and the good of one's family. Any philosophy that ignores human nature is fundamentally flawed. To promote self-interest is not the same as promoting selfishness. A person can be self-interested and still seek to step outside his or her own circumstances to perform altruistic acts. The choice need not be either/or— either completely, unalterably self-interested or selfless and altruistic. A happy median is possible.[45]

RIGHTS

Another major school of thought involves the issue of individual rights. Although definitions of "rights" differ, a mainstream view is the idea that an individual has a claim against other individuals and against government that cannot be abridged absent consent or an orderly process. Similarly, a right is seen as an entitlement to do an act or have the act done on one's behalf.[46]

The source of rights is contested. For much of Western history, kings ruled their regimes based on divine right. The Divine Right of Kings was a principle that allowed a monarch to justify his or her reign because of consanguinity, tracing the king's lineage back to Adam. The monarch was God's emissary on earth; therefore, to go against the king was to go against God. Such a conception of government-granted rights all but foreclosed the possibility of natural rights or democratic government because the king determined the nature of individual rights. English philosopher John Locke offered the possibility of democratic government by arguing that natural rights were granted by God to human beings prior to the establishment of government. Human beings choose to surrender a portion of their natural, God-given rights in exchange for a government. If government abridges individual rights and a majority of citizens believes government should be altered or abolished, the democratic process, at least in theory, allows for such change.[47]

Locke's perspective on rights is rooted in a concept of human worth regardless of birth or lineage. Because human beings are equal to each other by virtue of their humanity, no one human being is more intrinsically valuable than any other human being. An alternative view is to base rights on rationality. Locke's predecessor, Thomas Hobbes, argued that rational beings create governments and move away from a state of nature because they realize, unlike lower animals and other forms of life, the advantages to constructing a society filled with legally sanctioned rules. Rational beings make many decisions that result in an artificially constructed society, including the decision to recognize that each human being enjoys rights and responsibilities. Because human beings are more rational than other forms of life, humans are justified in exercising dominion over lower animals. The difficulty, of course, is that the idea of "rationality" is never clearly defined. Because some humans are more rational than others and because even rational beings are capable of irrationally inflicting enormous pain and suffering on other beings, this view of rights seems deficient.[48]

Aside from the confusion in determining the basis of rights, the term also has different, sometimes overlapping or contradictory, meanings.

"Negative rights" refer to the idea that a person should be free to enjoy his or her life without interference, especially from a powerful government. "Positive rights," however, suggest that people are entitled to certain minimal protections, such as decent working conditions, a minimal standard of health care, and other mutually agreed-upon features.[49]

In addition, "rights" can refer to moral rights and legal rights. The former are personal rights that ought to be honored and respected and may or may not be enforced through the force and effect of law. Legal rights are those rights that are protected through positivist law, that is, the authoritative pronouncements of governmental entities. The virtue of a concept of legal rights is that they are reasonably well-defined, whereas moral rights are less precise and not always recognized by positivist law.[50]

Any discussion of rights, however they are defined, revolves around whether rights should be inviolable or whether they should be compromised in the interests of a higher purpose. Consider John Rawls's argument in *A Theory of Justice*, discussed in detail in Chapter 1. Rawls's conception of rights reflects his view of justice. Because society ought to be constructed so that no collective action harms the least advantaged in the society, individual rights may be constrained by government so that this concept is honored. Pareto Optimality, a related concept, suggests that public policy should be designed to encourage a kind of efficiency equilibrium where economic resources are in balance, and no one can be made better off without at least one person being made worse off. For Rawls, if the person being made worse off is among the least advantaged, public policy would dictate that action not be taken unless the least advantaged are compensated.[51]

For philosopher Robert Nozick, the Rawlsian conception of rights represented a severe infringement on individualism. According to Nozick, either rights are protected by government and cannot be infringed absent due process, or they are not legitimately identified as "rights." For something to be considered a "right," it must be legally recognizable and enforceable, even in situations that persons might consider anathema. If an affluent individual enjoys a fortune and lives in a large mansion, whereas others are starving in the streets, we might wish that the well-to-do citizen would assist the less fortunate. If the well-to-do person legally acquires his or her property and chooses for whatever reasons not to assist the less fortunate, that is an individual choice that the law recognizes and protects, as distasteful as it might appear. Government is not justified in intervening to redistribute incomes simply because the legal protection of individual rights is unpleasant under certain circumstances. If rights are taken seriously, they must be preserved and protected.[52]

The subject of rights would take hundreds of pages to explicate fully. In fact, many books and articles have been written on this subject, especially in response to the Rawls and Nozick debate. The crucial component for ethical theory is to understand that rights involve fundamental questions that go to the core of humanity. What claims can I assert against my fellow man or against the state that allow me to exist and move through my society more or less unfettered? How will and should my rights be protected by the regime? When one right conflicts with another right, how should the conflict be resolved?[53]

David Held, author of a landmark 1995 work, *Democracy and the Global Order*, was concerned that globalization, among other things, undermines traditional Western conceptions of rights. Countries such as the United Kingdom and the United States generally have adhered to the Lockean view that rights are inviolable absent due process. Indeed, for dedicated Lockeans, the primacy of private property rights is the hallmark of the moral, legal, and political code. In Held's view, however, "critical disjunctions" are readily apparent as globalization occurs. Traditional boundaries that divided "incommensurate value systems" are rapidly disappearing, and the rate of change is unprecedented. In the past, totalitarian regimes imposed almost insurmountable barriers to trade and the free exchange of ideas, but many of those regimes have crumbled. Even in formerly totalitarian countries such as the People's Republic of China, where the last vestiges of the Communist empire ostensibly continue to exist, globalization is chipping away at the foundations of the old order. In other nations such as North Korea and Cuba, authoritarian rulers that enjoyed a long tenure will soon pass from the scene. Revolutions in transportation and communications technology ensure that the world will change in ways never imagined by previous generations.

Although clearly such change has its benefits, especially for businesses anxious to pursue global markets, a downside exists. As the world becomes more interconnected, diverse cultures and societies must interact even though they share "no common global pool of memories; no common global way of thinking; and no 'universal history' in and through which people can unite."[54] Each culture approaches societal challenges with a specific worldview that may not translate well, particularly when that view is challenged by long-held prejudices and fundamentally differ-ent values. Held was worried that the Western view of rights cannot hold fast against the onslaught.

The analysis of rights is, and likely will remain, one of the most impor-tant areas of ethical concern for theorists. The difficulties will continue to revolve around the different conceptions of rights, of course, but the work will continue. For ethical theory in the United States, especially as it per-tains to public administration, this will be a crucial, ongoing debate.

ETHICAL RELATIVISM

The question of whether values are absolute or relative to time and place stretches back to antiquity. Plato's attack on the Sophists empha-sized the fixed, eternal nature of ethics. What is right at one point in time is right at all points in time. In a sense, if ethics is not a fixed position regardless of time and place, what will prevent all manner of misconduct from being perpetrated with an explanation, "I did what was necessary under the circumstances"? Humanity loses the possibility of talking about crucial moral issues when ethics depends on the situation. In such a uni-verse, or so the argument goes, Plato may have had much wisdom to impart to the thinkers of his generation, but he has little to say to people of a distant era and presents only a mildly interesting historical case.[55]

Ethical relativism in its most extreme form presents enormous prob-lems, not the least of which is the reductio ad absurdum observation that if the call for relativism is relative, why should anyone heed the call? If everything is relative, the conclusion that everything is relative is an abso-lute, which is therefore nonsensical. Relativism fails its first test of meaning.

The rejoinder is to argue that this absolute/relative dichotomy takes the point too far. Ethical relativism suggests that moral principles do not apply equally to everyone because circumstances differ among people. This is not to say that everything is permissible and, therefore, everything loses meaning. Rather, it suggests that rules of conduct differ according to the needs of a society. For example, it might be considered unethical or illegal to waste water in a desert nation, whereas such wastage is permissi-ble in a nation where water is plentiful. Some behavior that is taboo in one society is treasured in other societies. Thus, some people eat pork, whereas others argue it is against their religious beliefs.[56]

Although these points are well taken, they do not get to the essential nature of ethics. For many observers, prohibitions on eating pork or wasting water, while they are guidelines on appropriate conduct, do not rise to the level of ethical precepts any more than which side of the road one drives on holds a moral component. Whether I drive on the left side of the road or on the right side of the road is a choice, but it does not contain a moral component (assuming I consciously drive on the same side of the road as everyone else in the regime). Rules that societies and governments adopt to govern behavior sometimes trigger moral repercussions—think of racial segregation or laws that once forced mentally challenged patients to be sterilized—but they need not do so.[57]

LINGUISTIC ANALYSIS AND POSTMODERNISM

One of the most creative twentieth-century developments in moral philosophy is the development of linguistic analysis, which sometimes has been lumped together with other creative new theories under the label of "postmodernism." This concept is related to ethical relativism in that it has come to mean different things, depending on the context, but, ultimately, it refers to the belief that society and its rules constrict human freedom. Postmodernists seek to step beyond the rules and reclaim that freedom, although their methods for accomplishing this admittedly amorphous goal are eclectic and not always coherent. Moreover, whether the term "postmodernism" applies, or should apply, is a point of contention, but the idea requires no small measure of attention.[58]

Postmodernism, in general terms, is a rebellion against the rigid confines of nineteenth-century philosophy that was typified by the German philosophers G. W. F. Hegel and Immanuel Kant. Hegel and Kant sought precision and order in a chaotic world. In the case of Hegel, he sought to develop rules for understanding how the broad sweep of history operated across time. Hegel was a systematic thinker who believed that the behavior of individual human beings could be understood as part of a larger process that moved as a kind of geist, or spirit, across the ages. Kant, as discussed previously, posited that immutable laws of morality existed and were not subject to the vagaries of historical epochs. Right was right today, in the past, in the future, and for all time. His emphasis on eternal duties provided an ordered structure for late-eighteenth-century thinkers.[59]

For the philosophers who came of age after Hegel and Kant, especially the pragmatists, existentialists, and postmodernists, these rigid ideas were so abstract and disconnected from human life, so coldly rational while simultaneously smacking of pie-in-the-sky morality that was lacking in any verifiable foundation, they threatened to undermine human creativity. The rules that Hegel and Kant claimed to have uncovered were little more than their own moralizing disguised as universal principles of conduct.[60]

Friedrich Nietzsche was one of "old Kant's" most vociferous critics. More than almost any other Western philosopher except possibly Kierkegaard, Nietzsche championed the individual absent the constraints imposed by society or religion. In many of his masterworks, especially *Beyond Good and Evil*, he insisted that men must move beyond traditional values or rules of morality and recognize, indeed revel in, their individuality. The notion of an absolute virtue advanced by post-Socratic classical philosophers was tantamount to embracing homilies, for it urged human beings to act in moderation based on conventional societal rules and oppressive religious dogma.

Any doctrine that requires man to restrict his will and creativity is oppressive, Nietzsche argued. When man realizes that philosophical "principles," arbitrarily created and staunchly defended despite any lack of credible evidence for their existence, are stifling to the human spirit and should be overcome, he will exercise his own will to power. Appeals to other men or God or the state to save oneself or impose systematic order as Kant tried to do are nothing but desperate acts of self-delusion. Instead, an individual must live creatively without imposing artificial barriers that impede human achievement. This is the virtue in a human life. A man must live each day as valuable, as though he would be willing to live that day again endlessly, as though that day would recur eternally. When a man can do this—when he can stand as a man free of oppression and fear and constraints—he will live a fulfilled human life.[61]

Fast forward to the twentieth century. What seems to unite this diverse group of writers and thinkers who operate under Jean Francois Lyotard's appellation "Postmodern" is the contention that the old methods of interpreting the world are based on strict dogma that bears little or no relation to reality. A philosophy of public service must necessarily consider "real-world" conditions that do not depend on abstractions. Thus, for all the influence modern philosophy wields in the academy, it must be concrete and well-established if it is to serve as the basis for a workable system of ethics.

Linguistic analysis suggests that the world is made through language. Just as the pragmatists recognized, the idea that mankind has an essence or that certain behavioral characteristics are inherently part of the human fabric is absurd. Over time, human beings have created these concepts through language as a means of making sense of the world. Unfortunately, instead of serving as tools for ordering the world and making sense of phenomena, the concepts have been seen as reality. When people fail to see that ideas such as "human nature," "essence," and "behavioral impulses or instincts" are socially constructed through language, they adjust their behavior and assume that these fabricated concepts are limitations on the possibilities open to human beings. The tragedy of modernism is that philosophy, which was supposed to enrich human life, came to restrict human freedom of thought and action.[62]

Whichever approach is most appealing, a public administrator quickly realizes that all schools of thought provide compelling arguments, but few if any provide specific, practical guidance the way a list of rules at least establishes a focal point for making decisions. In and of itself, this observation may not be significant—the purpose of a philosophy, after all, is to provide richness of thought, which is not necessarily geared to practical application—but it suggests that something more than philosophy is needed to develop a workable approach to ethics.[63]

For public administrators, the implications of postmodernism are that the traditional understanding of government administration has developed because decision-makers have a vested interest in structuring society and the institutions of government so that some groups benefit, and others do not. Built into the structure of government are implicit ideas of "right," "wrong," "good," "bad," and other value judgments that supposedly undermine human freedom. Women, people of color, and activists outside the mainstream of thinking on public administration largely have been excluded from taking part in administrative decisions because they were deemed unsuitable for posts inside the bureaucracy. They did not fit in with the modern conception of "merit" in public personnel administration. If a new generation of administrators would reject the tired old ideas of the past and allow a new paradigm of public administration to emerge, the field would move in new, possibly surprising directions— directions that could overcome seemingly insurmountable problems of the past. In an era where people seek more efficient and effective service from their government, allowing for a postmodern approach to government holds great promise.[64]

CONCLUSION: THE FRAGMENTED NATURE OF MODERN ETHICS

Determining an appropriate course of action, at least from a philosophical perspective, was a relatively simple matter when the ancients developed their theories. They lived at a time when little was known of the world and few theories existed to explain human behavior. Over time, as theorists proposed conflicting and occasionally contradictory notions of ethics, discerning appropriate standards became more difficult. In the modern era, especially, choosing from among the competing theories and explanations is problematic. Yet, a choice must be made. The act of choosing or not choosing is in itself an ethical act.

Public administrators may not always have the time or inclination to sift through various schools of thought to discern an appropriate source of ethics. Nonetheless, an administrator will confront a variety of issues requiring the use of administrative discretion in one or more areas of public administration; accordingly, he or she will need to understand at least basic ethical precepts. The theories discussed in this chapter, whether an administrator realizes it or not, form the basis for many of the attempts to develop ethical rules and codes for public administration.

Unlike an individual who works outside the public sector, an administrator serves in a position of trust that ideally reflects the public will. Therefore, when he or she exercises discretion, it holds repercussions for the citizenry. Depending on how the administrator uses discretion, it may be antithetical to democracy because formal checks and balances do not always exist to ensure that decisions relying on discretion are made in accordance with the values of the republic. To use discretion in a responsible manner, a public administrator should understand at least something about ethical theory.

The issue of bureaucratic discretion and its potential damage to democratic accountability will remain a problem for public administration. It is a perennial issue that is unlikely to be fully resolved. For that reason, it must be continually addressed by practitioners, scholars, and students of public administration. In addition to becoming informed on contemporary literature about ethics, an administrator should understand the goals of the organization and its place within a republican form of government. In most cases, a public sector organization will adopt goals compatible with the goals of the republic, but, in those cases where the goals are antithetical, the public administrator must recognize that accountability, due process, and the need for a participatory government are the appropriate goals around which the practice of public administration should be formed. The ultimate objective is to transcend the base needs and desires of private and special interests to embrace higher and broader public interests.[65]

3

THE ROLE OF THE PUBLIC ADMINISTRATOR IN AN ORGANIZATION

At first blush, it might be natural to ask whether an organization—that is, a large, complex structure comprised of individuals working toward a common goal or purpose—is the proper unit of analysis for discussing ethics. Until the twentieth century, the unique features of organizations were largely ignored; most stories of group endeavors focused on the exploits of bold leaders who set the tone for those who would follow. The assumption was that groups were merely an amalgamation of individuals. What was good for a single individual must necessarily apply to a group of individuals only to a greater extent as the number increased. Ethical considerations applied to organizations only because they also applied to individuals, but the dynamics of the organization apart from the individuals laboring inside the organization were only dimly understood and, therefore, largely ignored.[1]

One of the difficulties in discussing administrative ethics inside organizations is that defining and understanding the term "organizations" is not as simple as it might appear. The general textbook definition cites an organization as a collection of individuals engaged in interdependent, specialized activity in furtherance of a specific mission or goal. The definition can be expanded to specify dynamic large, complex organizations. The definition grows ever more complicated when one realizes that exceptions exist; for every organization that relies on specialization, another organization deemphasizes this feature. Some organizations are not large or complex. In any case, the core insight is that organizations involve multiple individuals in pursuit of a common purpose.[2]

Private organizations are those groups that pursue private interests such as profit maximization in the case of a for-profit business or the achievement of an objective such as providing goods and service to targeted populations in the case of a nonprofit institution. Private firms and nonprofit organizations are accountable to a board of directors or shareholders who make strategic decisions about the performance of the organization. In contrast, a public organization is an agency of government at the local, state, or federal level designed to achieve a specified public policy goal. The public nature of the organization and its role within the framework of the American system of government differentiate it from a private firm. In this chapter, administrative ethics is understood in the context of a public organization, although some of the same concerns and troubling problems associated with developing an ethical system also apply to a private-sector organization. Dwight Waldo summarized it best when he wrote, "*Public* and *private* are not categories of nature; they are categories of history, culture, and law."[3]

Students of American bureaucracy study public organizations through a variety of theoretical schools. As the fields of public administration and organizational theory began to evolve toward the end of the nineteenth century, theorists realized that the behavior of organizations was not identical to the behavior of individuals or even groups of individuals. Organizations such as corporations are fictional entities with legal responsibilities that differ in many respects from individual responsibilities, but the differences between organizations and individuals go much deeper. Organizations are created, have goals, acquire and use resources, make decisions, and act in ways that differ from the behavior of individuals. By the twenty-first century, virtually every organization development researcher recognized that organizations and individuals have different identities and needs. With these different identities and needs come questions about the ethics of organizations and individuals.[4]

MORAL NEUTRALITY

One school of thought suggests that large, impersonal structures are not subject to the moral quandaries that confront individuals on an almost daily basis. Organizational theory is an appropriate subject of academic inquiry in schools of business and public administration, but it seems incongruous to consider ethical issues in the context of a fictional entity such as a corporation. According to this perspective, individuals are the moral actors that need guidance on acting appropriately; consequently, ethical issues should be explored though psychology, sociology, or personnel management, not through organizational theory and development.[5]

The vision of a morally neutral organizational structure gradually has changed. Most modern organizational theorists contend that value judgments are necessary in any organization. An organization has a purpose, a set of values it was designed to advance. Often those values are reflected in a mission statement. Although an organization may exist as a fictional entity, it nonetheless reflects the values of those individuals who manage the organization's activities; however, it also has its own distinct circumstances apart from the individual.[6]

Consider the relationship of a corporate officer to the corporation as an example, recognizing that not all organizations are corporations. Presumably, if everything the corporation stands for is antithetical to the corporate officer's values, he or she would not choose to work there. Nonetheless, despite the possibility that the officer and the corporate entity share certain values and interests, their values and interests need not be identical. A corporate officer has a fiduciary obligation to act in the best interests of the corporation, even if the interests of the corporation are detrimental to the officer's interests, and even if the officer does not personally subscribe to the values of the corporation upon occasion.[7]

In this example, a corporate officer may be called upon to act on behalf of the corporation in a situation contrary to the underlying values or interests of the individual. In this instance, the individual's ethical standards may not be applicable to the corporation's actions, or at least they may not be integral to the outcome. A corporation that makes a decision to landfill waste because it is economically efficient may conflict with an individual's personal desire to reduce, reuse, or recycle waste. Because sending waste to a landfill is not illegal or unethical, the corporation's decision is legitimate and defensible, despite a corporate officer's personal desire to pursue another course of action. In this example, the individual's decision-making process differs from the organization's decision-making process. As distasteful as it may be for an individual, he or she must set aside personal feelings and perform on behalf of the organization.[8]

Just as the corporate officer must act in accordance with the corporation's values and interests in this example, an individual public administrator's ethical duties depend on his or her role within an organization. A decision-maker vested with a great deal of discretion situated near the top of the organization has a greater responsibility to practice superior public sector ethics than a lower-level employee who has little discretion or decision-making authority. Despite different roles and responsibilities, all individuals should be aware of the underlying values of the regime, the mission of the organization, and their role inside the organization.[9]

ORGANIZATIONAL STRUCTURE AND
THE ADMINISTRATIVE SCIENCE SCHOOL

Because the traditional understanding of organizational theory and behavior has been assailed, and this broadened perspective on the link between organizations and administrative ethics has been explicated, ethical questions have been raised with greater frequency. In rejecting the idea that an organization can be structured or operated independently of ethical considerations, the new theorists have acknowledged—sometimes explicitly, sometimes not—that ethics is an integral component of organizational theory.[10]

The public administration literature stretches back to the early days of the field when impersonal decision-making in service of efficiency was the goal. Efficiency was hailed as the prescription for what ailed the body politic because it seemed so far removed from the flawed, corrupt practices of patronage, the usual regimen in the Age of Spoils. If cronyism and waste had infected the American national government, the cure could be found in cutting waste and eliminating favoritism. No one seriously argued that efficiency as a goal possessed inherent presuppositions requiring additional scrutiny and debate. Efficiency was hailed as an unassailable good for all citizens of the regime, and what better way to ensure efficient outcomes than to design a government on universal organizational principles?[11]

According to the Administrative Science School of thought, if universal principles of structure could be discerned and applied, successful management would be the necessary result. The renowned German sociologist Max Weber was probably the most famous theorist to search for universal principles in positing the existence of "ideal types" of organizational structure. Among other things, Weber's typology identified an ideal type of bureaucracy, which featured hierarchy, specialization or a division of labor, and the delimited authority of officials working inside the organization.[12]

Each of Weber's three features provided benefits to an organization's stability and, hence, longevity. A hierarchy presumes that an officer at the top rank of an organization has ultimate responsibility for the work of the organization and the performance of the subordinates beneath him or her. For their part, the subordinates are tasked with responsibility for operations within their span of control. They also must report regularly and accurately up the chain of command to ensure an efficient flow of information. The hierarchy is designed so that every individual working inside the organization is cognizant of his or her authority and responsibility and that no favoritism or inequality is allowed to influence the operation of the organization. It is the job position within the hierarchical rank and not the personality of the individuals involved that theoretically determines the efficient function and operation of the whole.[13]

Specialization of labor allows the individual working in a particular position to become highly conversant with the task at hand through repetition. In addition to the development of expertise, as a laborer continually works in a specific area, he or she necessarily learns what works and what does not, which increases the speed of production. This factory model was championed most notably by management theorist Frederick Taylor who, writing early in the twentieth century, examined the activities of individual workers to determine the most efficient method of working. A leader in what came to be called the "scientific management" school, Taylor contended that each task could be assigned to the appropriate worker based on that worker's skills, and each task could be reduced to its essential elements so that no movements were wasted in meeting the stated objectives of the work.[14]

Orthodox public administration theorists came to view the delimited authority of an official inside an organization as a positive feature of a bureaucracy. If each worker knows precisely the nature and scope of the duties assigned to the position, this ensures that a manager can act to fulfill the goals of the organization free from ambiguity and doubt. Moreover, because he or she knows exactly what is expected, accountability is enhanced because a manager cannot say, "I did not know what was required of me in this position." The result is that an organization operates efficiently, with minimal waste and with no regard to the vagaries of politics.[15]

Over time, the organizational structure described by Weber and propounded by the Administrative Science School came to be viewed as the blueprint for efficient, effective design. Other features of the Administrative Science School include the idea of unity of command, a notion that suggests that an administrator should have a clear understanding of his or her superiors within the hierarchy so that confusion, divided loyalties, and unreasonable expectations that arise from serving as a "servant of two masters" are lessened or avoided. In addition, the Administrative Science School identified line staff as those administrators within the chain of command who have responsibility for reporting up to superior officers while simultaneously directing the activities of subordinates beneath them in the chain. In addition, administrators must be given a responsibility for a certain number of employees—generally, about half a dozen—and an administrator's span of control should not be so large that he or she cannot provide effective management within the chain of command. Administrators accepted Weber's and the Administrative Science School's prescriptions without argument or debate as the most appropriate manner of structuring an organization; so total was this acceptance that Herbert Simon later referred to the tenets of this approach as the "proverbs of administration."[16]

It is little wonder that early public administration theorists championed this mechanistic approach to organizational structure. Government administration during most of the nineteenth century had been characterized by the spoils system, which emphasized personal relationships above knowledge or effective management. The Pendleton Act, which created the federal civil service system after its passage in 1883, shifted the focus to neutral competence, the notion that government service required a knowledge base and dedicated employees who were not tied to patronage. Thereafter, public administration was grounded on the assumption that efficiency was the paramount concern, and public administrators were tasked with the responsibility for carrying out the will of a legislative body.[17] In a famous 1887 essay, Woodrow Wilson contended that public administration, like business administration, should be studied and practiced using a scientific methodology. Wilson sought to place the business of operating public agencies on equal footing with other empirically grounded disciplines. If he could identify the scientific principles of public administration, he could subject the discipline to the precise, exacting standards and empirical research required of "hard" sciences such as chemistry, physics, and biology.[18]

In the new era of meritorious service based on education and experience in lieu of favoritism, equity became an important value. Civil service examinations and merit-based competition became the paramount considerations in determining who would become a public servant. Treating like cases alike meant that impersonality was a virtue to be embraced and spread throughout all agencies of the federal government. It was important to separate out the "pure" science of administration from the taint of partisan politics so that public administrators could rise above the fray.[19]

Frank Goodnow, an early innovator in the development of administrative law, emphasized the distinction between politics and administration in his well-known works *Politics and Administration* and *The Principles of the Administrative Law of the United States*. According to Goodnow, the business of government should be separated into two distinct functions, namely the expression of a political will by the people and the implementation of policies that fulfill the expression of that will. The citizenry articulates its goals for a regime through regular elections. After they are elected, legislators develop policies, presumably in accordance with the will of the voters. Afterward, legislators communicate the policy to unelected managers within a public organization so the latter can work out the necessary details and design appropriate programs to accomplish the stated goals.[20]

Leonard D. White built on this insight, arguing that public administration should be understood as a single, ongoing process that, once mastered, would apply to all organizations in all situations. The "correct" structure for a public agency in the United States is correct for a public agency at any level of government or in any country. In this way, public administration could exist as a "scientific" discipline with replicable principles just as other scientific disciplines identify principles and practices that can be applied everywhere.[21] Commenting on this argument, Herbert Storing observed that, "Leonard D. White did not plant the seeds from which the field of public administration grew; but for four decades he tended the garden with unexcelled devotion."[22]

Perhaps the high point of this mechanistic view of administration came in 1937 in a book titled *Papers on the Science of Administration*. Edited by Luther Gulick and Lyndall Urwick, the work famously employed a mnemonic device—POSDCORB (planning, organizing, staffing, directing, coordinating, reporting, and budgeting)—to explain how a chief executive can divide work within a department to maximize efficiency. POSDCORB ensured that "scientific" principles of management were implemented within a public organization. "POSDCORB is, of course, a made-up word designed to call attention to the various functional elements of the work of a chief executive because 'administration' and 'management' have lost all specific content. If these seven elements may be accepted as the major duties of the chief executive," Gulick wrote, "it follows that they *may* be separately organized as subdivisions of the executive."[23]

This perspective on the appropriate role of a public organization greatly affected administrative ethics. An "ethical" public administrator should not be concerned about exercising discretion because discretion is not an issue. The ethical administrator must follow orders as efficiently and effectively as possible. Legislators answer to the will of the people and compete in the political arena; therefore, they are the decision-makers. Public administrators are unelected officials, experts in their fields, and immune to political pressure. They are to demonstrate morally neutral competence in the performance of their duties. Policy formulation, the province of elected legislators, differs markedly from policy implementation, the province of administrators, according to this view. Formulation requires discretion, and implementation does not.[24]

The prevailing view of public administration gradually changed, especially with the rise of the administrative state beginning in the 1940s and the realization that public servants exercise considerable discretion in implementing policy. With a change in the prevailing view came a change in administrative ethics. The suggestion that unelected officials serving inside an administrative agency should exercise discretion and thereby undertake a significant policy-making role would have been dismissed as anathema to proponents of the Administrative Science School. Yet, with a new perspective comes a new understanding of political responsibilities. The new perspective hailed administrators as specialists who must employ their expertise to reach decisions that frequently trigger political repercussions. Policy formulation and implementation are part of a continuous process; to divide the two based on the use of discretion in the former but not the latter is nonsensical and just plain wrong.[25]

As an example, consider a complex law involving the regulations of hazardous air pollutants (HAPs). Congress, which is composed of generalists, may decide because of pressure from constituents and interest groups that a group of HAPs must be regulated to mitigate the negative effects of pollutants on persons with respiratory illnesses, especially young children, the elderly, and persons with compromised immune systems. Based on testimony from leading scientists, environmentalists, and public health experts, Congress enacts a bill, which the president duly signs, to limit the production of dozens of HAPs, except in tightly controlled situations.

The law passed by Congress generally would not set the specific standards required to ensure that the HAPs are regulated at a level appropriate to protect public health. Generalists who are not trained in atmospheric chemistry or biological systems do not possess the necessary specialization or expertise to determine appropriate standards. Accordingly, Congress delegates authority to the appropriate specialists in the appropriate federal executive branch agency, in this case the U.S. Environmental Protection Agency (EPA). EPA scientists are trained in the scientific disciplines necessary to review the congressional goals, research the issue, and determine an appropriate scientific standard to carry out the will of Congress.[26]

Career civil servants inside the agency research the literature on appropriate scientific standards and, if necessary, commission studies to fill in gaps in the data. After the results of their explorations have been gathered and assessed, the civil servants formulate a plan that is publicized in the *Federal Register*. The public announcement of the plan can trigger comments and possible revisions to the plan, but ultimately, the civil servants establish specific criteria by which the will of Congress, at least theoretically, is fulfilled. In this manner, the bureaucracy supports the legislative process.[27]

The image of the public administrator that emerges with the changing perspective on organizations is an autonomous actor who is not immune from the political process but is immersed in policy-making details. When legislators abdicate their responsibilities by delegating considerable authority to administrators to work out the details of policies and conduct little or no oversight afterward, the political process changes. Far from acting as automatons who execute political will, administrators develop policies that augment political will. That elected officials retain ultimate authority for overseeing and correcting policies they disapprove of cannot be denied. That elected officials possess the gumption or desire to intervene except in cases where their constituents are outraged remains an open question.[28]

As for ethical considerations, it was a relatively simple matter to develop ethical rules under the paradigm of the Administrative Science School. An ethical administrator was the person who responded to direction from those higher in the hierarchy who passed down orders from the legislative branch. To act in an ethical manner was to execute the policy as efficiently as possible, and accountability was measured by how well an administrator followed orders. Some discretion existed in determining what constituted "following orders," but ambiguity could be resolved by asking for clarification and precision when the orders were handed down.[29]

In the new frontier of the discretionary public administrator, ethics became more intricate. If an unelected official was charged with developing a policy based on broad guidelines that were vague, ambiguous, or outright opaque, the old admonition to act efficiently and report back with as much speed as possible was little more than a homily. A more specific framework was needed. One way to develop the framework was to provide guidance on the appropriate core values of the American regime by explicating the political theory of the republic. However, this, too, presented a problem that proved to be far more complex than it initially appeared.[30]

In his widely heralded work *The Administrative State*, Dwight Waldo observed that public administration contains a "consequential" political theory based on pragmatic ideas and concepts developed through trial and error, as opposed to a systematic, well-grounded theoretical framework developed by theorists logically outlining clear, consistent political principles. In Waldo's view, this consequential political theory in public administration is grounded on an incoherent patchwork of "beliefs and sentiments" borrowed from "liberal-democratic ideology" and remnants of "eighteenth-century rationalism, infusions of business authoritarianism and paternalism, borrowings from various varieties of academic-scientific psychology."[31] If administrative ethics are to be identified, according to Waldo, the field of public administration first must have an improved political theory. Moreover, if Waldo's description of the political theory behind public administration sounds remarkably similar to pragmatism, as discussed in Chapter 2, it is because the principles of pragmatism are similar to the principles of public administration. The emphasis is on finding what works and applying it to administrative agencies.[32]

Stated broadly, the patchwork political theory of the regime might be thought of as adherence to pluralism, faith in democratic institutions, the desire to safeguard minority rights through "mitigated democracy" created and maintained via institutional controls such as checks and balances, separated powers, federalism, and a republican form of government, and the relative sovereignty of citizens who participate in consensual self-government. Although some theorists might add or modify certain aspects of this list, they generally would agree that these are hallmarks of the American political system.[33]

The difficulty is that this grouping of values is not tantamount to a coherent political theory. Even if it were a political theory, it would be little more than a statement of political principles. Principles are surely important. They serve as an expression of the ideas and concepts that are integral to the structure and operation of a political regime; they are similar to mission statements that guide private organizations in their work. Yet, mission statements and political principles alone are not enough to guide human behavior except in the most general sense. Principles are necessary, but insufficient, to provide ethical guidance. Principles are vague and general, whereas rules, if they are crafted appropriately, are precise and specific.[34]

Consider a further distinction between principles and rules. The former are broad statements of a general philosophy designed to set the stage for the greater specificity that rules provide. Perhaps a concrete example will illustrate the point; this is the classic explanation for why principles alone are insufficient guidance for human behavior. As discussed previously in this text, Kant posited through his categorical imperative that some values are true anytime, anyplace, anywhere. In keeping with Kant's insight, most Americans would probably agree that human life is precious and ought to be preserved and protected to the extent possible, all things being equal. In addition, most Americans probably would agree that it is important to tell the truth. Society cannot function when people habitually lie for any reason, big or small, or for no reason at all. Kant would likely agree that these core principles are immutable and exist across time. The difficulty occurs when these principles conflict, in which case rules are necessary.

Rules are specific statements tied to concrete situations that guide behavior with more precision than statements of principle allow. A rule is therefore more context-specific than a principle, which is broad and open to multiple interpretations. A political theory, when properly developed and explicated, can bridge the gap between principles and rules and can help an individual administrator appreciate what is expected while he or she works inside an organization.[35]

If Waldo is correct that an improved political theory is needed, the next step is to ask how public servants can be held accountable in accordance with the theory. Stated another way, how can the polity ensure that public servants behave in ways that support the work of a regime given the diverse work performed in public agencies and the lack of a centralized profession of public administration? What mechanisms exist, or need to exist, to ensure ethical behavior?[36]

ACCOUNTABILITY AND NEW PUBLIC MANAGEMENT

Beginning in the 1990s, some theorists began to speak of accountability through market mechanisms. New public management, in some ways, focuses on the traditional value of efficiency, ensuring greater productivity with fewer resources so that bureaucracy is a "lean, mean, efficiency-effectiveness machine." Private-sector manufacturing companies speak of "lean manufacturing technologies" and "smart growth," buzzwords for industry's desire to manufacture the same number—or more, if possible—of products using an ever smaller labor force. Proponents of government performance reform argue that the same ideals that apply to the private sector—emphasizing customer service while relying on market mechanisms to increase performance efficiencies and ensure greater accountability—should be applied to the public sector.[37]

In a traditional, stable bureaucracy where lines of authority are clear and change seldom occurs, high-level managers make decisions and are held accountable to their superiors within the hierarchy or in the legislative branch, as appropriate. Administrative discretion is used only at relatively high levels inside the organization. Lower-level employees are expected to perform their duties in accordance with directions from their superiors, in effect shifting accountability to the organization's upper echelon. These organizations are staid and often resistant to change, but they are fairly predictable and can be evaluated in accordance with a series of rules set forth ahead of time. Effective leaders know the rules, theoretically follow them, and occasionally adapt them to changing needs and circumstances.[38]

In contrast, a more decentralized organization that subscribes to the new organizational development theory is more fluid and far less hierarchical than a traditional bureaucracy. The behavior of these organizations is dictated by events that occur in the marketplace or by external actions that affect the organization's context. Effective leaders are risk takers who value intuitive knowledge, flexibility, and adaptive skills. Teams are important, as is creative problem-solving, and administrative discretion is exercised by virtually every employee at every level. Accountability is a question of function, not a person's title or placement within the hierarchy. In industry parlance, each person working toward a solution to a problem takes ownership of the issue instead of deferring to others with ostensibly more institutional authority.[39]

The accountability expectations and values embraced by centralized and decentralized organizations are markedly different. It is axiomatic that both a traditional organization and a modern, fluid organization seek an organizational structure and operational plan that avoid egregious cases of maladministration resulting from fraud and corruption. More commonly, both types of organizations also can be subject to what Van Wort and Denhardt refer to as "muladministration ... due to organizational dysfunction." Organizational dysfunction occurs when an organization is structured in a manner that makes it difficult, if not impossible, to achieve its goals. Sometimes this happens when rigid conformity to the rules displaces the underlying goals of the organization so that agency officials slavishly uphold the letter of the law or policy without adequately considering its spirit or intent. In other instances, an agency adheres to a "command-and-control" mentality that emphasizes the power of the organization and its officers with little or no regard for an appropriate course of action to achieve the desired ends.[40]

The new type of fluid or "flat" hierarchy holds great promise for expanding the accountability of public employees and ensuring that an individual public administrator cannot hide behind the excuse of "I was just following orders. Don't blame me." When every employee at every level of an organization is expected to take ownership of an issue, he or she must be willing and able to answer for decision-making. A difficulty arises when employees are empowered to assume greater responsibility but fail to do so because of inability, negligence, or outright hostility toward shouldering a heavy burden. In such situations, managers will be called upon to ensure that change occurs in an orderly way and that training programs clarify the new expectations placed on employees. A failure to act appropriately, of course, can occur in any organization, however it is organized.[41]

Another difficulty is that leaner, "flat" organizations may be more in line with external market forces, but an emphasis on efficiency and quality may ignore or insufficiently consider issues surrounding representation and democracy. If the new public manager in a modern organization places efficiency ahead of equity and the right of constituents to be heard and protected through due process mechanisms—which often increase the time and money spent on public safeguards, thereby decreasing efficiency—the change may be detrimental to larger societal values. Ironically, this bifurcation between the efficiency of the marketplace and the needs and desires of the citizenry to participate in government decisions seems tantamount to a return to the old politics and administration dichotomy prevalent in the early years of American public administration.[42]

The idea of properly structuring an organization suggests that value judgments are inherent in any enterprise involving organizations. Public organizations reflect social values regardless of whether those values are stated explicitly. In establishing a public agency, for example, Congress can choose to create mechanisms for effective legislative oversight, public participation in rulemaking activities, and transparent policy-making procedures. Such values determine in no small measure how individuals who staff the organization will perform their roles. Strict organizational controls help to ensure that an organization performs in accordance with the values underlying the creation of the organization in the first place. In short, there is always an ethical component to organizational development and operation even if this component is not readily apparent at the outset.[43]

ORGANIZATIONAL CHANGE

The primary insight behind New Public Management is that government, especially in the federal executive branch, has become too big, bloated, and unresponsive to citizens. When government is maladministered in this manner, it loses accountability, and it ceases to perform well. If the ultimate purpose of government is to meet the needs of its citizens, and it fails to meet those needs, fundamental change is needed.[44]

Maladministration is manifested typically through outright corruption or serious abuse because of sloth, inattention, or incompetence. Stories of government abuses abound. The human mind is endlessly inventive and can be used for all purposes, good and ill. Because government administration reflects human actions, it is little wonder that graft, fraud, corruption, nepotism, and misuse of funds and property occur upon occasion. A properly functioning organization will never prevent or correct all abuses, but it can establish procedures and an organizational ethic that discourages a majority of abuses and mitigates the damage in cases where prevention was not possible.[45]

More often, however, maladministration occurs because an organization does not function as well as it ought. Sometimes labeled "bureaupathologies," these are instances in which an organization does not work well because of fundamental problems inherent in any organization. For example, some theorists speak of the Peter Principle, which suggests that people are promoted to their level of incompetence. If a worker performs well as a technician, for example, he or she might be promoted into a management position in recognition of fine work. The problem is that managing people requires different skills than working as a technician. In organizations where a person is promoted to the point at which he or she is no longer competent to perform the assigned tasks, the resultant dysfunction reduces the effectiveness of the organization and frustrates an individual who seeks to perform competently.[46]

An organization that performs well and avoids dysfunction, to the extent possible, is one that incorporates ethics into all parts of the organization. Ethical conduct inside an organization is influenced by a variety of forces: the beliefs and values, moral development, and ethical framework of individuals developed over a lifetime and shaped by numerous experiences; the organizational culture (i.e., rituals, language, traditions, symbols) of the organization; the organizational structure (i.e., policies, rules, and training) of the organization; and external stakeholders (i.e., customers, interest groups, regulatory environment, and market forces). It is instructive to explore each of these forces in turn.[47]

The role of an individual's personal beliefs and values cannot be overstated. Personal values and moral reasoning are the foundation of any system of ethics; therefore, some attention must be given to understanding individual moral development. All individuals pass through stages of development as they age. As children, they learn values from their families, social networks, peers, religious beliefs, and schools. Over time, they act on these values in ways that demonstrate the individual's commitment, or lack thereof, to all that has been learned. Children must be taught right conduct through a consistent, proportional system of punishment and reward. Eventually, the values reinforced through repetition and habituation become the basis for the moral choices that an individual will make throughout his or her life.[48]

Despite the importance of personal beliefs on ethics, an organization's culture and traditions also influence the behavior of persons who labor inside the organization. Leaders within the organization set the tone and establish what they deem to be appropriate business practices. Some organizations conscientiously develop a code of ethics and train workers on performance expectations based on the code. Other organizations are less formal, but they still expect their workers to adhere to certain standards of behavior. Even when the organization's traditions are not written down or formalized, most employees know what is considered appropriate behavior and what is deemed impermissible.[49]

The way an organization is structured can, and frequently does, influence how the organization operates. Some large organizations employ an ombudsman to provide guidance to employees and to investigate instances of inappropriate behavior. In a hierarchical organization, employees can be instructed on the proper method of communicating their concerns about the organization's conduct to selected officials that rank higher in the hierarchy. A "hotline" can be established so employees can anonymously report malfeasance without fear of reprisal. Employee handbooks can be disseminated to spell out the behavior expected of employees and the sanctions to be applied for misbehavior.[50]

Organizations also perform in accordance with the expectations of external stakeholders. If an organization exists in a field that it tightly regulated, employees will respond by attempting to comply with applicable regulations. A sales organization responds to pressure from customers; in some instances, the organization may have to choose between remaining true to the organization's sense of propriety and the demands of its customers for goods and services at the quickest time and with the least cost. Often, an organization is forced to maneuver around multiple external stakeholder expectations, many of which are conflicting or contradictory. In other cases, officials inside an organization may seek to bargain and negotiate with external stakeholders to modify their demands.[51]

Effective leadership is essential if an organization is to prosper in the long run because leaders set the tone and direction for the organization.

Much has been written about the relationship between leadership and ethics, and virtually all theorists agree that leaders at the top of an organization shape the manner in which the organization operates. Leaders create and sustain a culture that focuses on the centrality of ethical behavior. When a top leader engages in unethical behavior or fails to demonstrate by example that ethical practices are the norm, this attitude permeates every corner of the organization. Codes of ethics and training programs in ethical rules and procedures are essentially meaningless if leaders do not set a high standard and practice what they preach.[52]

The values of an organization are shaped through what sometimes is known as "values-based leadership." The relationship between a leader and followers inside an organization is based on shared, internalized values that the leader must articulate and act upon for all to see and emulate. The most effective manner of communicating values of leaders is through everyday behavior, organized rituals, public ceremonies, the use of symbols, and the establishment of formal policies and codes of ethics. Employees carefully follow the statements and activities of the organization's leaders for clues about expected behavior. An organization whose leaders say they value ethics but actually engage in "success-at-any-price" behavior by cutting corners to gain an advantage in achieving their goals sends a powerful message to its employees that ethical behavior is not valued. In contrast, leaders who say they value ethical behavior and act in an ethical manner, rewarding such behavior and punishing unethical behavior, send a signal that the organization stands for ethics at all levels and in every transaction.[53]

CONCLUSION

This quick review of the literature and thinking on public organizations suggests that administrative ethics largely depends on the values, structure, and operation of an organization. Individuals influence, and in turn are influenced by, the organizations in which they work. For an organization to engage in ethical practices, it must be designed so that ethical behavior is allowed and encouraged, its leaders and employees must understand expectations for ethical behavior, and everyone must work together to ensure that ethical behavior is an integral part of the whole.

The difficulty is that public organizations differ in size, scope, mission, funding, and responsibilities. The individuals who work inside organizations also differ; they have different backgrounds, levels of experience and education, expectations, and predilections. It is relatively easy to state that organizations affect individuals and vice versa; it is an altogether different matter to set forth a standard view of ethics that applies to all administrators across all organizations. Requiring a senior executive in a federal intelligence agency to adhere to the same ethical standards as a street-level administrator in a state motor vehicle department seems nonsensical because the duties of the organizations and individuals vary widely.

Despite differences in the scenarios, the cases possess similar characteristics, not the least of which is the role of the administrator as a moral agent. A moral agent is someone who can act independently to assess the potential ethical pitfalls and act on that assessment whether the agent works in a high-level position inside a large federal agency or in a low-level position inside a state or local agency. It is this issue that we now turn to in Chapter 4.[54]

4

THE ROLE OF THE PUBLIC ADMINISTRATOR AS A MORAL AGENT

Having discussed the literature on public administration ethics (Chapter 1) and other contemporary literature on ethics (Chapter 2) and having reviewed the evolving role of the American public administrator within a larger organization (Chapter 3), the task now is to chart a path for the individual public administrator to practice "better ethics." This is not to suggest that public administrators engage in unethical conduct or deliberately turn a blind eye to moral issues, although these things may happen occasionally. Rather, many administrators need to identify an appropriate standard for ethical behavior and act accordingly.

The starting point for improving ethics is to cast the public administrator as a moral agent. This is a more difficult issue than it might seem initially. The American system of public administration was designed to be morally neutral and to avoid assigning individual responsibility for collective action. As discussed in Chapter 3, the Administrative Science School contended that administration was a science with clearly discernible principles analogous to a practical field of endeavor such as engineering. By eschewing the vagaries of personality and favoritism in favor of immutable principles that could be applied under multiple scenarios, government could be established and operated on a sound basis that emphasized equitable treatment of citizens and efficiency in outputs. Subsequent theorists debunked the myth of the morally neutral organization staffed with automatons who checked their biases at the door and instead focused on ways to ensure democratic administration with at least a modicum of efficiency.

Despite the passing of the Administrative Science School, many citizens adhere to the notion of "good government" as that government which expends the least amount of resources for the most return on investment. This kind of de facto cost-benefit analysis holds enormous appeal for people who are struggling to meet their own needs and who believe that government must be held accountable on a similar basis. The difficulty is that accountability is thought to be a collective value that applies to an organization as a whole when, at it core, accountability is a concept that applies to individuals.

As discussed earlier in this book, organizations are only as effective or as accountable as the individuals who staff the organization. Because an organization is a fictional entity and does not exist apart from the individuals who design its operations, staff its offices, and carry out its mission, the individual is the proper source of ethical conduct. The Administrative Science School may have sought to discount the eccentricities and limitations of the individual, but this wholesale rejection of the varieties of individual behavior is not possible. Whether an organization is comprised of a handful of individuals or tens of thousands of individuals, the individual must remain the unit of analysis in developing a system of ethics.

In her book *The Ethics of Public Service*, Kathryn G. Denhardt summarized the task succinctly by suggesting that "the ethical administrator is one who examines in a critical and independent manner the standards by which decisions are made, attempting to reflect the morality of society as well as acting in consideration of the administrators' commitments, obligations, and responsibilities to the organization, and to other individuals and groups to whom the administrator is accountable."[1] The definition is a good one, but it requires considerable explanation. To understand how an administrator can fulfill Denhardt's assignment, a public administrator's domain must be identified, the content of moral standards must be identified, and a process by which deliberations occur must be established.

ORGANIZATIONAL DOMAIN AND BUREAUCRATIC POLITICS

The problem, of course, is that it is difficult to identify a domain with precision. In Denhardt's summary of the task, considering an administrator's "commitments, obligations, and responsibilities to the organization" is not as straightforward as it initially sounds. The Administrative Science School set forth a model of an administrator's obligations as singular and more or less uncontested. Under this model, the administrator is told that his or her superiors have decided on a course of action, and the administrator is expected to act with dispatch to implement the course of action. The harbinger of success under this model is how well the administrator understands what has been communicated and how skillfully the administrator can act. With the demise of the Administrative Science School, a variety of factors influence the commitments, responsibilities, and obligations of the organization.

It is axiomatic that a public organization charged with undertaking a series of tasks must act to fulfill its duty. In many instances, the assignment of duty is open-ended, ambiguous, or open to interpretation. Moreover, organizations are not static. The world constantly changes, and with it the context in which organizations operate evolves. An agency that is important at one period of time may fall out of favor or become obsolete as priorities change. Administrators know this, of course, and they seek to protect and even enhance the power and prestige of their organizations.[2]

Complex, purposive organizations, public or private, must establish a domain, which consists of claims that an organization stakes out for itself against competing organizations. A domain can be thought of as the organization's raison d'être. To justify its existence, an organization must make a case in terms of programs covered, populations served, or services rendered. Without a domain, an organization loses its purpose and cannot explain its existence to its members, client groups, or third parties. Simply saying that the organization has a domain does not suffice; establishing a domain, in the words of one researcher, cannot be "an arbitrary, unilateral action," but "the organization's claims to a domain must be recognized by those who can provide needed support by the task environment." An organization needs to possess a specialized knowledge base that unequivocally supports the existence of the domain. Thus, the U.S. Department of Justice must employ attorneys with sufficient skill and training to represent the legal interests of the United States. The U.S. Department of Transportation employs staffers trained in urban planning, construction engineering, and other fields related to the orderly maintenance of the transportation infrastructure. If an organization fails to make a case that it can provide expertise unavailable elsewhere, the organization is unlikely to survive, much less thrive. Consequently, it is not an exaggeration to conclude that establishing and maintaining a domain is a crucial, fundamental goal for any organization.[3]

After the demise of the Administrative Science School, detailed in Chapter 3, the concept of bureaucratic politics was seen as an integral feature of a career in the civil service, as counterintuitive as it may initially appear. The concept of "bureaucratic politics" presents ethical problems for a public administrator who seeks to honor his or her "commitments, obligations, and responsibilities to the organization" while simultaneously acting as an autonomous moral agent. Because the United States was founded on principles that allow for consent of the governed, political power exercised by elected officials who earn their authority via free elections is considered legitimate because it is based on periodic review by the electorate. If voters are dissatisfied with their elected representatives, they have the opportunity to make changes in the next electoral cycle. Elected officials are held accountable, to some extent, to voters for their choices, which ideally reflect the will of the people, although this concept in itself has been much criticized. Although this model of the relationship between elected officials and voters is problematic, it reflects an accountability principle absent from the bureaucracy. Except in rare cases, public administrators are not elected; they are either political appointees or they secure their positions through the civil service or a similar competitive hiring process.[4]

The direct correctives that ensure the continued responsiveness of elected officials are not present in the bureaucracy, although indirect accountability exists because of bureaucratic oversight by elected officials. Nonetheless, oversight takes time and expertise that are often in short supply among elected officials. Public administrators, who are never required to face voters, with some exceptions below the federal level, mostly are left to their own devices in a majority of situations. Such wide-ranging discretion with little direct accountability naturally worries some observers because it means that public administrators generally do not have to factor public accountability into their decision-making process.[5]

What, then, motivates public administrators? Unlike the private sector, public servants generally do not have a profit motive, except in rare, egregious instances where a rogue administrator embezzles public funds for private gain. Although some administrators act from a sense of public spiritedness or for purely personal reasons (e.g., they are true believers in the cause of the agency), for many administrators, the ability to wield power or influence events is a powerful motivator. Power in the public sector is a function of how much responsibility an agency has, how many clients it serves, the importance of its mission to the functioning of the nation, and the size of the agency's budget. In an effort to secure and sometimes even expand their domain, public administrators engage in political infighting. Increased power is the reward that accrues to an agency that creates a strong domain.[6]

In the political arena where many organizations seek to establish and maintain a domain, participants compete for scarce resources and constantly seek to outperform competing agencies. This competition among agencies can be healthy if recognized rules and norms are followed, but the temptation to cut corners can be strong. In light of a scarcity of resources and the possibility of intergovernmental competition, political concerns are never far from the forefront when public organizations compete in the policy-making arena to establish and maintain a policy domain. Aside from working inside the agency, public administrators also cater to clientele groups in an effort to ensure their support. These groups appeal to the agency to respond to the interests of the groups; in turn, they provide knowledge and **information** to public administrators. This happens in virtually every agency at all levels of the bureaucracy. As an example, defense contractors seek to meet the needs of U.S. defense agencies, and defense agency personnel continuously look to their contractors for validation and support.[7]

Researcher D. D. Riley argues that public administrators must be politically astute, not merely policy specialists or technocrats. "If bureaucrats are going to enter the political arena they will need to bring some coin of the realm—that is, they will need power," he writes. "Knowledge provides some, but not enough, so bureaucrats must find an expressly political base of power."[8]

Because public organizations are populated with personnel who seek to establish a domain, distinguish the agency from its competition, and develop effective political strategies for maintaining and possibly expanding the agency's domain, the existence of the administrator as an independent moral agent becomes more important than ever, but it becomes more difficult as well. Denhardt suggests that an administrator acts ethically when he or she "examines in a critical and independent manner the standards by which decisions are made," but this examination is never easy.[9] A "critical and independent manner" is open to interpretation. Blindly following orders is to close one's eyes to ethical problems, but challenging every decision on suspected ethical grounds is to risk insubordination and needless argument. A happy medium must be found.

The ethical public administrator recognizes that he or she must engage in political infighting, to some extent, if the agency is to retain and perhaps expand its domain. Playing the game, however, does not obviate the need for rules of engagement—quite the contrary. The ethical public administrator realizes that power must not be an end in itself but a means toward accomplishing the objectives of the organization. To say the ends justify the means it to mistake the ultimate "public interest" of providing goods and services to citizens in a fair and equitable manner with expediency in increasing the political power of a particular public agency.[10]

IDENTIFYING THE "CLIENT"

Let us suppose that the proverbial midlevel career administrator has a concern that someone inside the agency—perhaps a superior—has behaved unethically. The issue is far from clear; in fact, the behavior may be explained by someone with access to more information than the lowly administrator. If this were a clear, unequivocal violation of the public trust, the administrator could blow the whistle and retain a reasonable sense of security at having exposed graft or corruption of a high magnitude. In this instance, the matter can be interpreted as ethical or unethical because transparency is lacking, and it is the transparency that will determine the nature of the deed. Without the authority to investigate further or compel production of additional documentation that would resolve the matter, the administrator is at a crossroads. What is to be done?

An analogy may clarify the administrator's dilemma. It is well known that attorneys have a duty to represent their client's interests above all else, save an ongoing duty not to perpetuate fraud against the court. Sometimes, this duty requires an attorney to represent positions and ideas that he or she finds personally distasteful. In any event, the duty to protect the client is relatively straightforward in most instances. The exception that proves the rule is when the attorney represents a corporate entity or an organization because, unlike an individual, the client is a fictional person.

The question of identifying the client is murky because a corporation is more than the sum of its parts. It is natural to assume that the client is the chief executive officer, the organization's general counsel, or the person who hired the attorney and/or pays the invoices. In many cases, determining the specific person or interest who serves as the client is academic because the needs of the organization and the individuals who make up the organization are identical. In egregious cases, however, the attorney may discover that one or more officers are acting in ways that harm the organization's interests. The malfeasance may be corruption—a high-ranking officer of the organization is embezzling funds or hiring unqualified friends and family despite regulations against nepotism—or it may be less severe, such as extravagant spending or extremely poor judgment because of inattention or perhaps gross negligence. The ultimate issue is the duty of the attorney. In virtually all instances, the duty of the attorney is to safeguard the interests of the fictional entity, even if those interests are contrary to the interests of one or all of the current officers of the organization.[11]

Set aside the obvious fallacy in this example—an administrator does not share the attorney's legally enforceable obligation to a client—and consider the administrator's plight. Although public administrators do not enjoy an attorney-client privilege protected by law and custom, they do have a similar fiduciary duty to protect the interests of the agency. Even more important than the specific agency, however, is the administrator's duty to safeguard the "public interest," however that is defined. As an independent moral agent, the administrator seeks to behave in a rational, ethical manner. What is needed is guidance that is clear, direct, and sets forth a reasonable path toward resolution of the conflict.

In several works, Dwight Waldo suggested that a public administrator has a variety of duties depending on the unit of analysis. To the nation, he or she has a responsibility to adhere to the U.S. Constitution. To the agency or the profession, the public administrator owes a duty to understand bureaucratic rules and norms of behavior, and to family and friends, he or she must act according to the dictates of religion or a personal code of ethics.[12]

In most cases, adhering to the Constitution will not be an issue. Unless the administrator is a highly placed political appointee or charged with a sensitive assignment involving classified information or material related to a criminal investigation, it is unlikely that a street-level administrator will be called upon to interpret the Constitution. Exceptions may exist to prove the rule, but generally, an administrator can assume that the routine decisions made by members of a public organization pass constitutional muster.

As for a duty to understand and follow bureaucratic rules and norms of behavior, this is probably one of the most straightforward duties exercised by an administrator. He or she will become acclimated to the organization through numerous interactions throughout a given day. Orientation programs, training sessions, and experience working with others inside and outside of the organization will ensure that the expectations of the agency are reasonably clear and understandable. In the majority of cases, questions about the expected level of behavior can be addressed to superiors or other people working in the organization who have been around a long time and are intimately familiar with the rules and norms.

An individual generally has a developed sense of right and wrong even in cases where the person may not be able to articulate the reasons for a certain behavior. The difficult part occurs when the requirements of the Constitution, the public organization's rules and norms, and the administrator's personal sense of ethics seem to be in conflict. Determining which duty is paramount when conflicts exist, and why, is problematic.

Arguably, the public nature of an administrator's position suggests that appreciating one's broad duty to a democratic regime is a crucial duty. In *The Responsible Administrator*, Terry Cooper observed that regime values in a democratic government are broader than an emphasis on constitutional values articulated by the U.S. Supreme Court or other authoritative governmental bodies. Cooper contended that public servants do not need a "substantive ethic" to govern their behavior because they will take their cues on ethical behavior from their respective organizations. This is not to suggest that an individual public servant can avoid individual responsibility for his or her actions by placing blame on the organization. If the organization does not function properly, the public servant owes a higher duty to the public to act in an ethical manner based on the person's private ethical sense. In most cases, however, it is a combination of two concepts— acting in accordance with a properly run organization's central tenets and exercising individual notions of ethical behavior—that results in a responsible public servant. The organization, an external control, sets the standard of behavior, and the individual seeks to understand and comply with that standard. If the standard is deficient, in the individual's opinion, then he or she has a duty as a citizen—a secondary, internal control—to ensure that the organization does not undermine democratic principles.[13]

As discussed in Chapter 3, personal responsibility does not always seem compatible with organizational controls. The embattled administrator might contend that ethical questions are misplaced inside a bureaucracy because such organizations are large, impersonal structures, and individuals who work inside a bureaucracy must comply with instructions from officials placed higher inside the hierarchy. According to this perspective, the nature of the modern organization makes personal responsibility a superfluous proposition. If anyone is to be held accountable according to ethical rules establishing personal responsibility for the structure and operation of the organization, the most appropriate place to look is in the upper echelon of management. Leaders set the tone, establish the rules, and set an example of organization expectations.[14]

Undoubtedly, leadership is a crucial concept, but the effectiveness, or lack thereof, of an organization or its leaders still does not relieve an administrator from personal responsibility. As the traditional understanding of an organization as an impersonal monolith where automatons labor anonymously has been modified, this broadened perspective changes the nature of administrative ethics and the role of an individual administrator as a moral agent. "I was just doing my job" and "I was just following orders" are inappropriate responses when an administrator exercises discretion and has options for acting on directions from superiors.

Make no mistake; an administrator occasionally will face enormous pressure, directly or indirectly, to "get with the program." The rate-buster or whistleblower often is viewed as a troublemaker because he or she upsets the time-tested way of doing things in the organization. The desire to please superiors, to say nothing of the objective of avoiding poor conduct reports, sanctions, or discharge for supposed dereliction of duty are powerful disincentives to take on the organization, especially if the suspected ethical lapse is perpetuated by the administrator's direct superior, and the allegation is unclear or difficult to prove.

Complicating the administrator's task are trends in government operations and management. In recent years, the field of public administration has seen a renewed push to use market forces as a mechanism for improving government service. As discussed previously, the New Public Management and Reinventing Government movements became popular in the 1990s as citizens clamoring for a government that costs less and performs better argued that markets are more reliable indicators of high-performance organizations than the traditional bureaucratic model that originated with the Administrative Science School.

When public organizations are restructured to ensure a more entrepreneurial focus and greater decentralization of authority, the resultant organization is less accountable to a legislative body or an authority placed higher in an administrative hierarchy. Although less rigid organizational control may be beneficial, especially when the organization needs to respond quickly to changing dynamics, entrepreneurial organizations present a new set of challenges. A hierarchical structure helps to ensure stability and control, which vests a great deal of authority in the hands of high-ranking leaders inside the organization. In contrast, a more fluid, decentralized organization helps to ensure flexibility and change by, among other things, empowering individuals acting at lower levels inside the organization to act on their own initiative. Thus, whatever else reorganization does, it rearranges the values of the new organization.

The worrisome feature of a market model is that it assumes efficiency in the delivery of goods and services is the end of all organizations, public and private. For the administrator concerned about ethical behavior, following markets can lead to results that may not be consistent with a democratic government. Many of the guarantees found in the Bill of Rights to the U.S. Constitution are inefficient from a purely market perspective, but they have long been deemed integral to the operation of a republican form of government. From a market perspective, devoting a disproportionately high share of government resources to Social Security, Medicare, and programs that assist the infirm may be inefficient given actuarial predictions of life expectancy and the value of work performed for the polity, yet from a political perspective, these programs are close to sacrosanct. A market model may be efficient—and even this point is not beyond debate—but efficiency does not satisfy all the demands of a democratic government. In short, a market model does not cure all that ails a poorly performing regime, to say nothing of the message it sends to the lowly administrator seeking guidance on a proper course of conduct.[15]

Regardless of the size or structure of an organization, administrative ethics must focus on the role of the individual as an independent moral agent first and foremost. When it comes to ethics, an organization is equal to the sum of its parts. History teaches that a society that allows individuals to avoid personal responsibility for their actions breeds a professional class of amoral automatons. If the individual is allowed to plead that he or she should be absolved from blame because the organization was the appropriate unit of analysis, the game is over before it begins. Everyone inside the organization, even those at the top who make the crucial decisions and theoretically provide leadership, will blame the collectivity. The embattled chief executive officer will argue that he was unaware of the details because his ethically challenged staff failed to keep him informed. The midlevel managers will contend they were pressured from on high based on the old chestnut "that's the way we have always done things," and, besides, "everybody does it." The street-level administrator will explain that he or she is but a lowly cog in a huge machine, and the machine cannot be resisted.

When personal responsibility is checked at the door in the field of public administration, "the organization" is the culprit in every situation where an ethical lapse occurs, even though the organization is a fictional entity. Without personal responsibility, ethics is a fictional concept, devoid of genuine meaning or application. It is a theoretical concept with no practical use in the modern organization. It might as well be Plato's "forms," a useful philosophical ideal designed to stimulate thought and debate, but unworkable in practice.

To illustrate the need for personal responsibility in public organizations, consider three admittedly extreme examples of individuals who attempted to escape personal responsibility because they were part of a larger organization that, to some extent, imposed its values on them and overrode their personal responsibility—at least that was the argument. A rejoinder, as we shall see, is that they had options available to be true to their own set of values, and they chose to follow orders, as a fourth example makes clear. The examples of ethical lapses involve Nathan Bedford Forrest and the Fort Pillow Massacre during the American Civil War, William Calley and the My Lai incident during the Vietnam War, and Adolf Eichmann and the Holocaust during World War II. All three examples are drawn from wartime exigencies because it is in extreme circumstances such as war that ethical precepts are put to the test. The fourth example, the case of Mary Ann Wright, a career civil servant who resigned from the State Department to protest the Bush administration's decision to invade Iraq, illustrates the challenges of following ethical principles and the price that sometimes must be paid.

FOUR TALES OF ETHICAL CHOICES
AND THEIR CONSEQUENCES

Participants in war often argue that exigent circumstances require that they set aside their normal set of values and step beyond what civilization deems to be acceptable conduct or perish in service to "pie-in-the-sky" ideals. The problem with this line of reasoning is that setting aside values in times of crisis can be tantamount to having no values at all. Ethical reasoning must apply in bad times and good. In fact, one might argue that it is precisely when times are hard and exigencies exist that ethical precepts are most needed.

Confederate General Nathan Bedford Forrest remains today, as he was in an earlier era, a controversial, polarizing figure. Unlike many general officers on both sides of the Civil War, Forrest was not a graduate of the U.S. Military Academy at West Point. He was self-taught, an untutored, fearless, profane, enthusiastic warrior who had amassed a fortune in the slave trade during the antebellum years. When war erupted, Forrest joined the Confederate States Army and rose through the ranks to be widely regarded as one of the most effective soldiers to emerge from the conflict. A friend and confidant of Union General Ulysses S. Grant once remarked that "that devil Forrest" was the only Confederate cavalryman to alarm the famously stoic U.S. commander. In the postwar years, Forrest briefly served as the Grand Wizard of the Ku Klux Klan, a white supremacist group that formed during Reconstruction to terrorize newly emancipated slaves and prevent them from exercising their hard-won political rights.[16]

Forrest was in command of a group of Confederate forces in the spring of 1864 when a horrific episode occurred at Fort Pillow, a small Union Tennessee outpost situated on a bluff overlooking the Mississippi River approximately 75 miles north of Memphis. The fort was not an important strategic vantage point. It probably would have been a minor incident in the annals of the war had it not become a symbol for the brutality of the American Civil War, especially the mistreatment of black troops serving in the Northern army.

More than anything, it was the presence of black troops that infuriated Forrest's men during and after the Fort Pillow assault. The Union's decision to recruit, train, and use black soldiers was widely condemned in the South, where slavery was considered by many to be a cornerstone of society. The Confederates believed that allowing black men to enlist in military service was little better than aiding and abetting armed slave insurrection. If blacks proved to be good soldiers, the entire structure of Southern society was open to criticism and possibly reevaluation. Similar to many of his contemporaries, Forrest was known to regard the use of black soldiers as illegitimate and not subject to the normal rules of war and engagement among civilized nations; hence, captured blacks in the uniform of a Federal soldier either were sold into bondage or dealt with brutally. Against this backdrop, the troops under Forrest's command assailed Fort Pillow as part of the Confederate effort to disrupt Union communications.[17]

Garrisoned by 550 Union soldiers, about half of whom were newly recruited blacks, Fort Pillow was no match for an attack led by 1,500 seasoned Confederate cavalrymen. In short order, on the morning of April 12, 1864, the Confederates surrounded the fort. That afternoon, Forrest rode onto the battlefield under a flag of truce and demanded that the Union troops inside the fortification unconditionally surrender. The harsh language of his written demand, although hardly unique, has been greatly scrutinized in the years since the incident, and his detractors contend that the general's intent, although admittedly somewhat oblique, was to brutalize black Union soldiers. Promising fair treatment if the Union occupiers of the fort laid down their arms without further bloodshed, Forrest warned that "Should my demand be refused, I cannot be responsible for the fate of your command."[18]

The Union commander requested an hour to consult with his staff. Forrest agreed to 20 minutes. Ultimately, after the Union soldiers refused to capitulate, Forrest ordered an attack. In little time, the Confederates swept over the parapets and drove the Union soldiers down the bluff onto the banks of the Mississippi River.

What happened next has been fiercely debated. According to General Forrest and his men, the defenders refused to surrender their weapons. Although they were fleeing and in disarray, they continued firing their guns and posing a threat to the Confederates. If this account is to be believed, the victorious Confederates were well within their rights to fire upon the enemy and take all measures to carry the day.

Union survivors painted a different picture of events. They later said that virtually all the defenders, recognizing they had lost and were routed beyond all hope of recovery, surrendered their weapons. No sooner had they laid down their arms than they were bayoneted by the enraged Confederates, who repeatedly screamed "no quarter!" Although it is possible in the fog of war that the account provided by Forrest and his men was accurate, the large, disproportionate number of blacks killed hints at a far more sinister scenario.

Some accounts indicate that Forrest ordered his men to slaughter the offending black soldiers. Still others recall that the general ordered his men to cease firing their weapons when it became clear that the Union soldiers had been routed and no longer represented a threat. In all likelihood, the question of whether Nathan Bedford Forrest ordered the Fort Pillow Massacre will never be answered to the satisfaction of everyone. What is clear is that Forrest, intentionally or otherwise, set into motion a series of events that resulted in gratuitous slaughter, and he attempted to avoid responsibility by laying blame on the fort's Union commander.[19]

Forrest's culpability is a muddled question, although a central tenet of military command is that an officer is responsible for the conduct of his men. More to the point, Forrest's note that "Should my demand be refused, I cannot be responsible for the fate of your command," suggests that he understood at least the possibility of a massacre taking place if the Union troops refused to capitulate. Throughout his career, not simply at Fort Pillow, Forrest unleashed violent forces and afterward sought to avoid responsibility by arguing that he did not specifically countenance the actions of his men. (If a modern public administrator practiced such a "hands-off" approach to ethical quandaries, the public sector would be far worse off for the supposed indifference.)

A similar moral dilemma for a U.S. military officer occurred more than one hundred years later during the Vietnam War, although the direct participation of the commanding officer was more direct in this second example than it was with Forrest. William L. Calley, Jr., according to most accounts, was a substandard soldier with an undistinguished military record, a virtual ne'er-do-well who stumbled into a military career. A junior college dropout, Calley seemed to drift through his life without purpose. Eventually, he enlisted in the U.S. Army as the conflict in Vietnam began to escalate. By 1968, two years into his enlistment, he had advanced through the ranks to become a lieutenant, junior grade, in command of a platoon in Charlie Company, 1st Battalion, 20th Infantry Regiment, 11th Brigade, Americal Division. His unit was stationed in the Quang Ngai Province of South Vietnam.[20]

Calley and his men were frustrated and angry in the wake of the Tet Offense, the Viet Cong–sponsored movement to strike at civilian and military sites in the Republic of Vietnam and topple the decaying South Vietnamese government. Although tactically the Tet offensive was a defeat for the Viet Cong, who suffered a high number of casualties during the fighting, the episode highlighted the arduous road ahead for the United States and the unpopularity of what many people, North and South Vietnamese, saw as U.S. imperialism. If American troops did not take drastic action to shore up the South Vietnamese government and its military forces, the war probably would be lost in short order.

As American troops pursued Viet Cong guerillas into the countryside, intelligence reports suggested that the enemy was hiding in the Village of Song My, which included the smaller hamlets of My Lai 1, 2, 3, and 4. The problem at Song My, as was often the case on all the battlefields of Southeast Asia, was the difficulty in fighting guerillas who resembled the general population. Distinguishing friend from foe was no easy matter, and so many frustrated American officers decided to strike out without grappling with the niceties of ferreting out the Viet Cong from the citizenry. This thinking drove Captain Ernest Medina, the officer in charge of coordinating an assault on the enemy positions, to issue orders to his subordinates directing them to pursue and stop the enemy at all costs. He later explained that, in fact, his superior officers insisted that he and his soldiers "aggressively" assail the Viet Cong even if innocent women and children were injured or killed.

With the leadership setting a sinister tone and urging enlisted men to root out the enemy above all else, an incident occurred that is still discussed among those concerned about military ethics. At eight o'clock on the morning of 16 March 1968, Charlie Company stormed the village of My Lai with guns drawn. As with the Fort Pillow Massacre, eyewitness accounts vary. Whatever the particulars, in slightly over three hours, the Americans butchered between 350 and 500 civilians, most of whom were women, children, the old, and the infirm. Although some of the dead may have been Viet Cong guerilla fighters or sympathizers, the platoon did not distinguish between the guilty and the innocent as they rounded up their captives and summarily shot them.

The sordid episode might have been covered up were it not for a soldier named Ronald L. Ridenhouer. A year after the massacre, Ridenhouer sent a letter to the president and military leaders at the Pentagon detailing secondhand reports that were common knowledge among many American troops. Ridenhouer had overheard rumors spreading among the soldiers in Charlie Company, and he believed that the massacre ought to be investigated. The army had already completed a perfunctory inquiry, but Ridenhouer's letter exposed the army's investigation as pro forma and wholly inadequate. The investigation triggered by the letter became far more public than the first, and it revealed that Charlie Company had executed civilians at My Lai with little regard for the safety or well-being of noncombatants.

The report generated after the conclusion of the second investigation underscored a lack of leadership by officers on the ground at My Lai. Unlike Nathan Bedford Forrest, who could argue somewhat plausibly that he did not order his men to massacre defenseless men, the officers at My Lai took a more direct role in events. Lieutenant Calley stood out as an enthusiastic and active participant in the carnage. Not only did he fail to discipline his men or refuse to rein them in when the killing began, apparently Calley fired his rifle into a group of at least 80 defenseless civilians. He also ordered his men to herd civilians into a group so they could be shot and their bodies discarded in nearby ditches.[21]

In light of the media scrutiny and high visibility of the My Lai incident, Calley's case became emblematic of the atrocities perpetuated against civilians during the Vietnam War. The young lieutenant was charged with premeditated murder in September 1969, although other officers were named as codefendants on lesser charges. As part of his defense strategy, Calley's attorneys argued that he was following orders from his superiors and should not be made a scapegoat for acting in a manner that, if not officially condoned, was accepted practice. In fact, if Calley had not followed orders that day at My Lai, his defense team contended, he would have been court-martialed. Despite this line of argument, Calley was found guilty and dishonorably discharged from the army. He also received a life sentence in prison. The sentence was later reduced, and Calley was paroled in 1974 after serving three and a half years behind bars.[22]

Although Calley's actions at My Lai are better documented than Forrest's actions at Fort Pillow, both commanders faced ethical choices in the field. They could argue they were acting in accordance with unofficially sanctioned policy within their respective military units. Aside from the veracity of this argument, each man could conclude he was making explicit a course of action that was implicit in the organizational culture in which he operated. In each case, the commander evinced a serious lapse of ethical judgment because he failed to acknowledge that he had a moral choice to make. Instead of acting because "everyone else does it," these commanders could have served as moral exemplars for their subordinates by refusing to bow to pressure to reject personal responsibility for morally repugnant acts.

Adolf Eichmann presents an even more intriguing case than Forrest or Calley because he was acting on the express orders of his superiors. He had no need to conceal his behavior beneath a façade of respectability; he was unequivocally carrying out the policy of his regime. A high-ranking German officer during World War II, Eichmann was recognized for his organizational skills early in his career. After he joined the Nazi Party in the early 1930s, he became the chief overseer of the mass deportation and extermination of millions of Jews when Reinhard Heydrich, the architect of the "final solution" to the "Jewish problem," selected the young officer as a key subordinate. Eichmann was not a rabid Nazi who displayed a zeal for persecuting Jews; he was a mild-mannered public administrator who went about his business as though he were an engineer calmly solving a logistical problem that carried no moral repercussions.

Despite his moral obtuseness, the "desk murderer," as he came to be known, realized at war's end that the victorious Allies would be searching for responsible parties to stand trial for war crimes. Realizing that he might face execution, Eichmann methodically planned his escape. Unlike the leaders who were apprehended or committed suicide, the desk murderer quietly slipped out of the country undetected and traveled on falsified passports until he landed in Argentina, where he lived into the 1950s. He might have died incognito except that the Mossad, the Israeli intelligence agency, discovered his whereabouts. In a dramatic scene, Mossad agents kidnapped the desk murderer and smuggled him into Israel, where he was tried for his starring role in perpetuating the Holocaust. After a highly publicized trial, he was found guilty and executed in 1962.[23]

During the proceedings, Eichmann argued that he should not be punished because he was obeying the orders of a totalitarian regime. Even if he recognized his ethical choices, he had no free will to obey. Disobedience would not have stopped or even slowed the killing. If he had taken a principled stance and died, someone else would have taken his place. "When the state leadership is good, the subordinate is lucky," Eichmann famously said in his defense. "I was unlucky because the head of state at that time issued the order to exterminate the Jews."[24]

Eichmann's situation is in many ways the easiest of the three cases to assess. On one hand, his culpability seems assured; he was not acting in the heat of battle, nor was he possibly under fire by enemy soldiers. He was carefully, deliberately sending men, women, and children to their deaths. His actions in this regard were unambiguous. On the other hand, he was part of a vast organization, tightly controlled, and subject to brutal reprisals if he failed to implement his orders with the appropriate zeal and dispatch.

The Forrest, Calley, and Eichmann cases, and many less dramatic examples, highlight the need to provide individuals who act as part of a larger organization with a process by which ethical choices can be made. The cases have been presented in order of severity. In the first case, Forrest may or may not have known that his men would slay fleeing Confederates, especially blacks who wore the Union colors, although his detractors believe this assessment is far too kind. Be that as it may, the fact is that history may never know what really happened at Fort Pillow that day in 1864. Forrest may have ordered the slaughter, or he may simply have set into motion a series of events that resulted in the execution of the prisoners. He can avoid some measure of personal responsibility by arguing that he did not know his men would act with such alacrity in the fog of war. That this excuse is not completely convincing is hardly surprising; that it would be offered by way of explanation is even less surprising. Even the most brazen of men fears the sting of opprobrium from his peers, to say nothing of his progeny or of history.

Calley was more directly involved in the killing at My Lai than Forrest was at Fort Pillow. By some accounts, the lieutenant gleefully pulled the trigger. He could not plead ignorance to the circumstances. Nonetheless, just as his defense claimed he was following orders, Calley could argue that his personal responsibility, although undeniable, was mitigated by other factors beyond his control. The ethical failure came from the top of the organization where his superiors, in their frustration at the elusive nature of the Viet Cong and the public relations success of the Tet Offensive, chose to cut a swath of destruction through the countryside in retaliation for the enemy's attacks. Calley's crime, his defenders intimated, was that he was too enthusiastic in carrying out his orders, but he was no more culpable than the leaders who ordered him to wage war against old men, women, and children.

As mentioned above, in some ways, Eichmann's argument against personal responsibility is even stronger than Forrest's or Calley's. He exercised little discretion inside the Nazi bureaucracy, whereas Forrest and Calley at least could choose within the narrow confines of their organizations whether to act in a certain manner. Eichmann was but a small part of a political system that terrorized Jews as part of government policy. If he had not actively worked to exterminate the offending group, he would have been replaced and, depending on the circumstances, possibly forfeited his own life as a consequence of his failure. He was not guessing at what his superiors wanted and getting carried away in the heat of the moment. Adolf Eichmann did not cross a line; he efficiently carried out his orders with no regard for the consequences or collateral damage caused by those actions. He was an instrument of his masters, a cog in a larger machine. Eichmann repulses the reader because he was so nonchalant in carrying out his duties. The political theorist Hannah Arendt famously identified this little man who seemed ordinary and unassuming as the embodiment of the "banality of evil."[25]

Forrest and Calley repulse those who read of their exploits because we can read between the lines: Forrest detested blacks, and Calley detested Vietnamese. Consciously or unconsciously, they did not view their opponents empathically. In fighting the "other," they objectified the people they victimized. Examined another way, Nathan Bedford Forrest and William Calley acted with little regard for the consequences at the time, although after the fact, they sought to conceal their behavior from public scrutiny. Recognizing that not everyone would agree with their moral choices, they were concerned enough about how their actions would be perceived that they couched their conduct behind superficial rationalizations. Eichmann did not need to conceal his actions until the Nazis were defeated and the Allies were in control, at which time he fled Germany to avoid prosecution.

Consider a different example of what happens when an individual laboring inside of an organization chooses to stand on an ethical principle. In 2003, Mary Ann Wright was a civil servant working in the U.S. Department of State. During a long career that included a stint in the U.S. military and positions as deputy chief of mission in the embassies in Afghanistan, Sierra Leone, Micronesia, and Mongolia, and service in Uzbekistan, Kyrgyzstan, Grenada, and Nicaragua, Wright had distinguished herself as a dedicated public official. In 1997, she received the State Department's Award for Heroism for her assistance in evacuating 2,500 people from the Sierra Leone civil war zone. According to F. Allen

"Tex" Harris, a retired senior foreign service officer who worked with Wright and knew her well, "as a diplomat, Ann had an absolutely phenomenal career. She had abilities, background, and luck. The luck is that she served in several posts where things went crazy, and she was given an opportunity to show her capability."[26]

Aside from her long record of service in many far-flung outposts, Wright was known as a vehement critic of American policies that she believed to be misguided. Most notably, she protested U.S. bombing tactics in Somalia, but she also, by her own account, "held her nose" on numerous occasions throughout her career. Unlike some career State Department officials, she believed that a major part of her job was to call attention to departmental mistakes that threatened the long-term security interests of the United States.[27]

Of all the incidents that caused her concern, Wright was especially alarmed when she realized that the administration of U.S. President George W. Bush intended to invade Iraq in March 2003. "There was no doubt that Saddam Hussein was a despicable dictator and had done incredible damage to the Iraqi people and to others in the region," she later wrote in a book chapter explaining her actions. "I believed, however, the United States should not use military force without United Nations Security Council (UNSC) agreement." If this had been merely her opinion, Wright probably would have held her nose once again, but the nature of the disagreement transcended her own personal predilections. The use of U.S. military force created "deep chasms in the international community." Moreover, the administration's decision to engage in a unilateral military operation "alienated many of our allies and created ill will in much of the world, particularly the Arab world."[28]

Wright's dilemma reflects the Hobson's choice that confronts any public administrator that must choose between his or her personal and professional roles. If an individual believes that the organization is acting inappropriately, should he or she "get with the program," as Forrest, Calley, and Eichmann did—albeit with varying levels of support and enthusiasm—or should the administrator take a principled stand and oppose the organization's plans? The answer to this age-old question depends on how the administrator views the issue and his or her role. If the dilemma amounts to a policy disagreement, and the moral implications are muddled or nonexistent, obeying orders and holding one's nose may be an acceptable choice. If the disagreement concerns a fundamental principle of right or wrong, acquiescing may be tantamount to "following orders," à la Calley and Eichmann. As will be discussed in greater detail in Chapter 5, in egregious cases, the administrator may feel compelled to resign in protest rather than continue serving in an organization that engages in morally suspect actions.

Mary Ann Wright wrestled with her conscience as she struggled to determine an appropriate course of action in 2003. She had dedicated a substantial portion of her life to serving her country, and she did not want to walk away from her career without considerable thought and reflection. The immediacy of her internal debate was underscored by her official position; she was the administration's voice in the Mongolian embassy—in effect, second in command—so she would bear the burden of defending the Iraqi invasion. If the issue had been a simple policy disagreement, she later explained, she would not have felt a moral duty to protest the invasion. In the final analysis, however, she felt she must voice her strongly held beliefs. "I felt it was my professional obligation to put my concerns on record with senior policymakers," especially after Secretary of State Colin Powell presented the administration's evidence to the UNSC in February 2003. After the secretary's speech, Wright sent a dissenting cable to the State Department in Washington, DC, because "the dissent channel was the only on-the-record procedure available to make my concerns known...."[29]

The State Department did not reply, but the department's public position was unsatisfactory, amounting to little more than the standard administration line that Iraqi dictator Saddam Hussein had undermined the stability of the region because he possessed weapons of mass destruction and had repeatedly refused to curtail his dangerous activities. Wright believed that this explanation was a convenient rationale, in effect a smokescreen, for the administration's decision to invade Iraq well before the September 11, 2001 terrorist attacks had heightened the awareness of citizens to international threats. Because the administration had plotted a course of action ahead of time and afterward had constructed an explanation that was deliberately ambiguous at best—and an outright fabrication at worst—Wright believed that she had few options; she must support the administration or leave government service.[30]

Lacking any other recourse, Wright chose to resign her position. In her letter of resignation to Secretary Powell dated 21 March 2003, she said, "I wrote this letter five weeks ago and held it hoping that the Administration would not go to war against Iraq at this time without United Nations

Security Council agreement." When it became clear that the war would commence, Wright believed she had no choice but to act. "This is the only time in my many years of serving America that I have felt I cannot represent the policies of an Administration of the United States." As a result, "I feel obligated morally and professionally to set out my deep and firm concerns on these policies and to resign from government service as I cannot defend or implement them."[31] She was the third senior diplomat to resign in protest over the U.S. invasion of Iraq.[32]

"When one disagrees so strongly with an important policy of any administration," she explained later, "in my view, resignation is the honorable action to take." Realizing that her action might be dismissed as "insubordinate, even unpatriotic," she cited her twenty-six-year career serving in the active military and the reserves to demonstrate her loyalty to the nation. In Wright's opinion, her choice of resignation in protest was a moral decision. "All actions have consequences and nations, like individuals, ultimately are held accountable for their actions. I felt the action of the Bush administration in waging war in Iraq would have the consequence of harming America, not making America safer, both in the short and long terms."[33]

Had she stopped at that point, Mary Ann Wright would have remained a controversial figure but perhaps not a divisive one. Nonetheless, she became a well-known peace activist in the years after her resignation. In addition to attending meetings and conferences to speak out against the war and accepting more than 180 speaking engagements a year, Wright took part in numerous demonstrations against the U.S. policy in Iraq, most notably joining antiwar activist Cindy Sheehan in the August 2005 demonstration outside of President Bush's ranch in Crawford, Texas. She also picketed at Guantánamo Bay, Cuba, during a month-long fast. Because she was arrested more than a dozen times, Wright became unpopular with U.S. authorities. In October 2007, border guards refused to allow her to enter Canada after her name appeared on a Federal Bureau of Investigation database that tracked potential terrorists, fugitives, and felons.[34] The Canadian episode was hardly unique; in the years after she left the State Department, Wright was severely criticized and challenged, especially by conservatives who viewed her outspoken, high-profile activism as an unpatriotic betrayal of U.S. interests.[35]

The Wright case illustrates the other side of the Forrest-Calley-Eichmann dilemma, namely the repercussions of taking a stand against the organization. The administrator who seeks an easy answer to an ethical quandary will be sorely disappointed, for seldom are easy answers available. Even in cases where the administrator's actions are considered praiseworthy, a price must be paid. The question is when and where the price will be paid. Forrest, Calley, and Eichmann chose to ignore ethics and risk in the short term but found themselves excoriated by history in the long run. Wright refused to compromise in the short term, although it would have been the path of least resistance and probably a means to advance her career. It remains to be seen whether her actions will be viewed favorably in the future.

THE NEED FOR "MORAL AUTONOMY"

Each of these examples dramatically illustrates the ethical problems inherent in public administration, albeit the street-level administrator may not be called on to make such odious choices in the course of his or her career. When does an individual assume personal responsibility for his or her actions and when is the organization the responsible entity? Clearly, in the public sector, organizational structure, culture, and formal rules play an important part in determining the choices that are made, but ultimately, the individual must make a choice. An ethical system can never work if it fails to assign final responsibility to the individual.

In the cases involving Forrest, Calley, and Eichmann, all three men, when put to the test, attributed their actions, at least in part, to someone or something else. Perhaps in normal times, each of the three would have made different choices that would not have visited harm on their fellow man, but the exigencies of war and the requirements of their respective institutions required that they sacrifice their free will to service a higher goal, namely the organization and its goals. In contrast, Mary Ann Wright, recognizing that the institutions of government would not change, exercised what little authority she had and left her post rather than be a party to a course of action she deemed to be unjustified and unethical.

The problem with rationalizations that relieve an individual from responsibility for his or her choices is that outside factors almost always affect a person's choices. Inside an organization, an individual can always claim to have been following orders. Outside of an organization, numerous mitigating factors may constrain the menu of choices available to a person. If the individual is permitted to avoid responsibility in this manner, a system of ethics does not exist because responsibility can always be avoided. "The devil made me do it" becomes a one-size-fits-all means of discounting a person's moral autonomy.[36]

The law recognizes mitigating factors, but ethical duties require a higher standard. Generally, the law consists of a series of rules that prescribe the duties that individuals owe to third parties and provide sanctions for a failure to fulfill those duties. Ethics, however, involves the duties that an individual owes to himself or herself and to third parties. Because ethical lapses do not necessarily involve breaches of contract, the peace, or rules of engagement, an offender's property or liberty rights generally are not forfeited (unless the ethical lapse occurs within the context of a positivist code of ethics that prescribes penalties for violations). Without the possible forfeiture of rights, the individual who violates one or more ethical precepts can say that the harm occasioned by the ethical lapse is localized and does not spread to others within the society in the same way that everyone in the polity is harmed when a person violates a criminal law.[37]

The difficulty occurs when the individual who acted unethically is a public administrator because he or she, to some extent, is engaged in the public's business. Although an ethical lapse by a public administrator may not violate the criminal law, the offense may nonetheless affect the public. In short, ethical standards are, and ought to be, higher than legal standards. Moreover, administrative ethics ought to be higher still because of the public nature of the administrator's role.

Individuals assume a reasonably well-defined role within an organization, and in no small measure, that role affects the person's ethical duty. Despite the need for individual personal responsibility as the ultimate check on the behavior of public servants, the more decision-making responsibility a person assumes within his or her organizational role, generally, the more responsibility the individual retains. A small cog working in a large machine may seem powerless to act against the organization, but such apparent powerlessness does not allow the ethical administrator to plead ignorance of, or indifference to, ethical quandaries.

At the same time, it is important not to transform every disagreement over policy into an ethical dilemma. This tendency takes the matter too far and makes a mockery of legitimate ethical concerns. An administrator who believes that his agency's decision to pursue a course of action that appears foolhardy, unnecessarily expensive, or contrary to agency policies and procedures naturally should call attention to his or her concerns through the established chain of command. Even if the policy is adopted in the face of these concerns, the administrator does not have grounds for an objection based on ethics. The pursuit of bad policies is not tantamount to an ethical lapse; if it were, no government that has ever existed could be said to meet our lofty standards of ethical excellence.

If an administrator objects to a policy because it violates the law, compromises the public's right to know, deceives the public or elected officials with oversight authority, or hides some important fact that might cause direct harm to others, the administrator is justified in blowing the whistle. In situations where the objection is based on strongly felt opinions that do not raise issues of honesty of integrity, the administrator is obliged to support the policy or leave the organization. Distinguishing between legitimate disputes over public policy and ethical lapses is not always an easy task, but it is a necessary one.[38]

The difficulty in resolving questions of administrative ethics is that ethical precepts are not precise. Even a well-crafted, diligently compiled code of ethics does not possess the same clearly delineated, relatively well articulated standards that positivist law exhibits. Ethical administrators are faced with the daunting task of identifying their duties from a variety of sources, some of which may not be readily apparent or free from vagueness or ambiguity. Although ethics standards may or may not be written down and publicized, they are still lived and practiced. Ethical administrators constantly strive to "do the right thing," even if it is not always clear what that is in a given context.[39]

This book is about the problem of developing a standard of administrative ethics in light of the vagueness and ambiguity of ethics. Administrators can, of course, read applicable statutes, case law, and regulations to discern the requirements that must be met and thereby act in accordance with applicable external sources. Internal sources are important as well. Instilling values into administrators is an ongoing, never-ending process. Parents, friends, social and civic organizations, schools, peers, and governmental organizations all play an important role in inculcating the values of a democratic society into a person who may one day serve the public interest. When an administrator who has been schooled in the ways of the regime confronts an ethical dilemma in decision-making, for example, he or she must look to external sources for guidance, if possible, but the first line of defense is a well-developed internal sense of right and wrong.[40]

The next chapter will present a model for administrative ethics that can apply within the context of various schools of thought and approaches to the subject. It is probably impossible to reconcile the divergent perspectives, and perhaps it is not desirable to do so even if it were possible, but the model at least will provide guidance on making ethical decisions despite the variety of approaches to ethical concerns. This book certainly will not end the debate over an appropriate means of approaching administrative ethics, but if it can provide a road map for the journey, the mission will be accomplished.

5

TOWARD A PROCESS THEORY
OF ADMINISTRATIVE ETHICS

This book is about developing an effective decision-making process for public administrators to make justifiable ethical choices. Reconciling the five theoretical approaches discussed in Chapter 1 is daunting, and probably not possible. The myriad approaches—ethics as virtue; regime values, constitutional theory, and founding thought; citizenship; social equity; or the public interest—have much to recommend them, but they represent different conceptions of the same issue. Beyond the field of public administration, the varieties of ethical theories that have been developed and debated in the twentieth and twenty-first centuries complicate the quest for an overarching metanarrative. One school of thought—postmodernism—rejects the viability of a grand narrative in the first place, whereas another school of thought—pragmatism—suggests that doing what works is preferable to the search for an elegant, logically consistent ethical theory. It is probably a cliché to say that no one approach is "correct" at the expense of the others—or the "correct" approach would no doubt have beat out its competitors by this stage of the game—but neither can they all be fused together into a coherent and satisfying unified theory. To fuse the myriad approaches together is to ignore the blatant contradictions that would have to be papered over or reconciled through tortured means. Moreover, as discussed in Chapter 2, different ethical theories and approaches have been developed because legitimate discourse can lead to different emphases and conclusions. In the face of such a morass of theories and approaches, how does one begin to put together a credible model of administrative ethics?

On top of the philosophical problems, a major difficulty in developing a workable model for administrative ethics is that the field of public administration is extremely diverse and exists at all levels of government. Generalizing about ethical behavior that would pertain to all, or substantially all, of the bureaucracy is challenging. Public administrators, to a large extent, do not share an understanding of their place in the public sector, nor are individual administrators similarly situated from one agency to the next. Unlike professions such as law and medicine, where authoritative entities exercise a gatekeeping function, the field of public administration, if it can be called that, is heterogeneous. It is diverse and exists at multiple levels of government. Public administration is ubiquitous, but apart from the widespread existence of public organizations—the bureaucracy exists across many fields of endeavor—administrators juggle multiple responsibilities that are remarkably dissimilar depending on the levels and job positions scrutinized. Generalizing about the work of a hypothetical administrator reveals many fissures and incongruities that complicate the search for a single source or content of administrative ethics.

The field of public administration poses another enormous challenge to the scholar who seeks to reconcile approaches. A quick perusal of a standard textbook or an authoritative source of mainstream public administration theory and practice reveals the extent to which the field is comprised of many other fields and theories. Part of this developmental schizophrenia is because public administration was developed in the early years through an emphasis on pragmatic organization and management, focusing on what works as opposed to striving for intellectual consistency or theoretical niceties. A political theory that develops over decades or centuries can be refined and modified with little regard for the practical consequences; public administration, however, is where "the rubber meets the road." Administrators must administer service and programs, distribute goods, and ensure the continuing, day-to-day operations of government. If a theory of public administration does not work or proves to be deficient in some fundamental manner, it must be jettisoned as soon as a suitable replacement can be found, even if that replacement is far from ideal.

Stated succinctly, public administrators do not enjoy a shared notion of the "good." In the quest for a workable system of government administration, scholars frequently have ignored or undervalued theory-building.

For the ancient Greeks, the good was thought to be something abstract but more or less agreed upon, a universal concept that applied to everyone. For this reason, Plato had no qualms about seeking out rules, principles, laws, and virtues that would rely on common values and shared expectations among all in society. In the centuries since the ancients lived and died, the notion that universals exist and are applicable in the gritty world of man has been assailed from all quarters. Occasionally, a thinker such as Kant will revitalize universals, but even proponents of idealism recognize that applying universals to the particularities of government administration is a poor fit. Accordingly, when philosophy has been applied to public administration, it has seemed incongruous, to say the least. As Charles J. Fox of Texas Tech wrote in 2001, "Since public administration has always been *eclectic*, borrowing from several disciplines including political science, sociology, social-psychology, and business administration, there was little compunction against picking out a hodge-podge of ideas, norms, and concepts from other more integrated literatures." The problem, of course, is that such cherry-picking can lead to unintended consequences. "In misplacement," Fox continued, "concepts take on entirely different and skewed meanings when deprived of the context in which they were originally developed and to which they originally spoke."[1]

Let us state a central thesis for what is to follow in this chapter: Reconciling administrative theories is not possible. Just as modern philosophers, including Publius and the thinkers who established the government of the United States, recognized that "the nature of faction is sown into the nature of man," we must recognize the factions that exist in the realm of administrative ethics. Unlike the ancients, who sought to convince skeptics that a universal system could exist for all, Publius made a virtue of necessity: If an immutable, universal notion of the good could not be discovered or created, the next best thing was needed. A system would be put into place that would recognize and allow for the diversity in opinion and behavior without struggling to reconcile the irreconcilable. If the causes of factions could not be prevented short of indoctrination or coercion, the effects must be mitigated.[2]

If a universal theory of administrative ethics cannot be developed, a system for making choices among competing theories and approaches must be developed. An individual administrator may decide that he or she subscribes to the "ethics as regime values, constitutional theory, and founding thought" school, whereas another administrator may believe the "ethics of citizenship" school offers the most promise. Rather than squabble over the source and content of ethics—because it is unlikely that the dispute will ever be resolved to the satisfaction of the parties—it is preferable to provide each decision-maker with the means by which an ethical decision can be made and justified. This is not a situational ethic; rather, it is a system that can accommodate a multiplicity of views and opinions, much as Publius argued in favor of a government that could get things done even if its denizens fundamentally disagreed about the values and aims of the regime.

In the spirit of Publius and his intellectual brethren, let us say that this book cannot "pick the winner" among Terry L. Cooper's approaches to administrative ethics. No approach is so obviously superior to its rivals that a consensus of mainstream theorists will find safe harbor in its embrace. It is important to recognize at the outset, therefore, that no theory, no approach, no reconciliation will resolve all issues to the satisfaction of all who seek to find a universal ethical theory. Individuals practice ethical behavior; they do not perfect it. No book or article can claim to have "solved the problem" of ethics because there is not one problem. There are many problems. Ethics in its own way is as diverse and multifaceted as public administration. Unlike mathematics or a hard science where time-tested methodologies generally lead to more or less uncontested results, ethics remains an amorphous, loosely structured, complex web of ideas and concepts related to the human desire to "do the right thing."

DEVELOPING AN "ETHICAL ROADMAP"

An "ethical roadmap," for want of a better term, is needed. It must not be just any roadmap. First, it must be practical. For all of the benefits of asking administrators to study up on regime values and the rationale behind black letter law and well-articulated public policy, in reality, this search for the source of administrative values is unlikely to occur except perhaps among highly placed administrators or those with special skills or academic prowess. Even then, the wide variety of materials available on ethics and the competing theories do not ensure that specific ethical questions will be resolved in a timely manner or that they will be resolved in a way that is markedly different from, or preferable to, the way they would have been resolved in the absence of a concerted effort to find an appropriately authoritative source.

An ethics roadmap will need to provide guidance in resolving critical questions without relying on administrators to launch a full-scale litera- ture review. This is not to say that a code of ethics or ethics pamphlet is the panacea, nor is it to suggest that there is no value in encouraging administrators to delve into readings on administrative ethics or pro- nouncements of authoritative governmental bodies. It recognizes that bright-line guidelines are desirable to ensure the accessibility of an ethical model to substantially all who seek guidance on right conduct.

Warning bells reverberate at this point; a five-alarm conflagration is in progress. Bright-line guidelines have their drawbacks, of course. No mat- ter how many rules are developed and painstakingly explained, invariably a situation arises that is not covered by the guidelines. Human behavior and motivations may be similar across time and space, but the variety of human experience in all its intricate detail is infinite. It might be desirable to develop bright-line guidelines to govern general categories of conduct, but specific rules are no substitute for a model that provides an individual with decision-making tools and strategies for resolving ethical dilemmas.[3]

The inherent difficulty in developing a model of right conduct for all, or substantially all, situations does not obviate the need to develop a model. Indeed, the difficulty suggests that work is desperately needed. A caveat is in order here. A model is a representation of the world and how it works, but a model is only as useful as the assumptions it relies on to explain reality. In many of the models developed by theorists seeking to reconcile the divergent perspectives among and between public adminis- tration researchers, the assumptions either have not been clearly stated, or they have been woefully inadequate. Even when the assumptions have been stated clearly and seem to be well-developed, different schools of thought have focused on different aspects of the issue; they have talked past each other.

A model can be as simple as a series of steps to be taken at key decision points and/or a decision tree with branches indicating possible avenues of resolution. Each branch, of course, must include enough detail to ensure that even the uninitiated can discern the appropriate course of action and the reasons this course is preferable to the universe of alternatives. Indeed, later in this chapter a series of steps and several figures with possible out- comes will be presented as a graphic depiction of the appropriate analytical course. The danger is that the figures will substitute for critical judgment and a thoughtful analysis of the myriad alternatives. Perhaps this criticism is valid, but such criticism is true in any mind-mapping exercise. It is preferable to develop a roadmap that risks oversimplifying the situation than to have no roadmap at all.[4]

The objective is to provide a framework for developing a process theory of administrative ethics that can apply across the board to all agencies and the personnel within the agencies regardless of their position. This is no mean feat; indeed, simply suggesting that such a process or roadmap is even possible risks the label of "hubris" by scholars who have spent their careers delving into administrative ethics. The point is well taken. Thus, with advance apologies to the Paul Applebys, Dwight Waldos, Terry Coopers, John Rohrs, Kathryn Denhardts, and Ralph Clark Chandlers of the world, let the task begin and the risk be undertaken.

PERSONAL RESPONSIBILITY

A useful model must begin with one basic assumption: Ultimately, the question of personal responsibility is at the heart of administrative ethics. The statement, although it is perhaps trite, is nonetheless crucial. As discussed in Chapter 4, without a requirement for a sense of personal responsibility, no system of ethics can work because an individual always has a means of escape. Without the ability to accept personal responsibility, a convenient rationale—"it's not my fault; blame another!"—exists to undermine an ethical framework. The examples of Nathan Bedford Forrest, William Calley, and Adolf Eichmann in the preceding chapter, although admittedly dramatic and extreme, certainly set forth the difficulties that occur when personal responsibility is absent from a system of administrative ethics. Exercising personal responsibility is not for the faint of heart, however; Mary Ann Wright's case illustrates the difficulties that occur when personal responsibility is the foundation of an individual's decision-making process.

Consider child-rearing as an example of the centrality of personal responsibility. For many parents in earlier generations, the twin pillars of self-esteem—shame and pride—served as effective tools for instilling values in the young. Setting aside the negative connotations of these attributes, it is not difficult to understand how parents employ these tools.

If the child acts in a socially unacceptable manner, the parent says, "you should be ashamed of yourself. That is not the proper way to behave in this setting." Under circumstances when the child has behaved in a socially acceptable manner, the parent says, "you should be proud of your accomplishments. You worked hard, played by the rules, and it paid off for you. This is a model for future behavior." As the child grows, he or she begins to see the universe of behavior that will generate feelings of shame or pride and becomes habituated to these modes of behavior. Assuming that the child is not suffering from medical or behavioral disorders, he or she accepts these values and gradually assumes personal responsibility for his or her actions.

The parent is not the only source of values for the child, although obviously the inculcation of values begins in the home from an early age. The church, school, social institutions, civic organizations, television, the Internet, other electronic media, and peers also help to shape the child's values. The older the child becomes, the more he or she is expected to assume personal responsibility for acting in certain ways. A child of five is provided more leeway to make mistakes and poor choices than is a child of ten. By the time the child is an adult, he or she is expected to possess a fully formed moral sense. When he or she repeatedly makes poor choices at an advanced age, we no longer attribute the lapse merely to the inexperience and inattentiveness of youth. We say the person has a bad character. Conversely, a person who possesses a strong sense of ethics and acts on that well-developed moral code is said to be a person of good character, especially when actions are undertaken at great personal risk or sacrifice.[5]

Personal responsibility does not cease when the child, once grown to adulthood, is employed by a public organization. The administrator must understand the role he or she plays inside the organization, but personal responsibility is always part of the role. If an administrator exercises little or no personal autonomy or administrative discretion, he or she might argue against the assumption of personal responsibility for decisions he or she made while working within an organization. Arguing that the "organization made me do it" is a logical argument, especially for persons who work in the lower echelon of an organization. The lowly street-level administrator may have little personal autonomy when it comes to deciding agency policy, directing the work of others, or even determining when and how claims will be processed. The organization is much larger and more powerful than the individual, and it is governed by rules that override a person's freedom of choice. This insight raises a fundamental question: How can an administrator be assigned responsibility when his or her choices were limited or nonexistent because of organizational rules or norms? Even if the administrator adopts a principled stand and rails against the result in a particular case, it is unlikely that the result will change. If he or she presses the point, the probable outcome is that the administrator will be reassigned or possibly fired if he or she does not have civil service protection, or if the protest is viewed as misconduct.

In another sense, if an individual can avoid responsibility because "I was just following orders," managers at the top of the organization can decide what constitutes appropriate behavior, however unethical it may appear to the outside world, and individuals lower in the hierarchy must obey. Dissent will be treated as disloyalty, and disloyalty cannot be tolerated indefinitely. The entire organization becomes dysfunctional. In good times, when the leadership of this dysfunctional organization works well, subordinates still cannot be relied upon to take independent action and accept the consequences because they require direction from above. If the purpose of designing and operating a public organization is to conduct business as effectively and efficiently as possible—and this always was the stated objective of the Administrative Science School—it is not effective or efficient to shield administrators from the consequences of their decisions. In bad times, of course, leaders engage in unethical conduct, and it filters down to subordinates that right conduct is a superfluous luxury for the organization. Allowing the individual to escape responsibility on the grounds that an exterior source has determined what constitutes right conduct beforehand can lead to a moral blindness that harms both the individual and the organization.

In situations where individual responsibility is secondary to organizational ethos, the excuses offered by Nathan Bedford Forrest, William Calley, and Adolf Eichmann are valid. Situational ethics of this sort undermines a serious attempt to articulate a workable model of administrative ethics. Any model of administrative ethics must include at its core a place for the individual public administrator to make decisions based on his or her sense of individual responsibility, which is developed over time from many internal and external sources. See Figure 5.1, on the next page.[6]

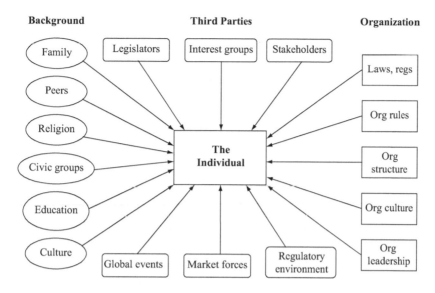

Figure 5.1 Factors Affecting Personal Responsibility.

INSTILLING PERSONAL RESPONSIBILITY THROUGH EDUCATION

Let us use another analogy regarding attorneys to make a point, this time about the role of education. Lawyers are taught the eggshell skull doctrine, which states that a tortfeasor must take a plaintiff as he finds him or her; in other words, if a more robust person would not have received an injury, but this plaintiff was especially fragile, the person who occasioned the injury is still held liable. Similarly, it would be helpful if every individual who worked in the public sector had been taught to work hard, act in an honest and forthright manner, and protect the values of the democratic regime. Unfortunately, not every individual shares such values. Thus, the public sector must take its employees as they are, not as we might wish them to be. The values of an individual are influenced by factors beyond the control of all but the most oppressive, totalitarian regimes, and even then the cure for factions is worse than the disease, to paraphrase Publius.[7] In light of this realization, of all the ways in which an individual's ethical development can be encouraged outside of family and peer influences, formal education arguably is the most promising.

It is not an exaggeration to suggest that personal responsibility begins with the education and upbringing of the individuals who eventually will work in public organizations. Because a sense of personal responsibility develops through multiple channels, few of the background factors can be controlled except for the educational curricula, and even then the control and influence are limited. Unlike the ancient Greeks, who strongly adhered to the notion of values-based instruction, the modern Western paradigm has been to eschew overt expressions of religious or moral values, especially for young children, because of concerns about institutions manipulating young minds into mirroring the values of their teachers, especially in cases where the beliefs of the parents are opposed to the values of the teacher. Of course, indirect instruction and the influence of a moral exemplar cannot, and perhaps should not, be avoided, but the desire for moral neutrality in the content of instruction, particularly in public schools at the pre-college level, has been a cornerstone of modern educational approaches.

Exceptions exist, of course. Some groups have championed the rise of parochial academies and schools that stress one set of values in opposition to what some moral and political conservatives view as the moral degradation and ubiquitous, corrosive influence of modern society and the mass media. Although some of these educational reforms have been designed to promote a broad, liberal education—witness former Secretary of Education William Bennett's call for values instruction in education—a large number have been designed to replace the predominant biases of mainstream society with a competing set of biases. Some question exists whether the new biases are inferior or superior to the biases they are designed to replace.

Despite the difficulty in promoting ethics instruction, frequent attempts have been made. In 1991, for example, the Section on Public Administration Research of the American Society for Public Administration and the Public Administration Ethics Network, recognizing the difficulty in incorporating abstract ethical values into a concrete field of endeavor, sponsored the National Conference on Government Ethics Research to facilitate an exchange of ideas among scholars that study philosophical ethics and scholars involved in empirical research. Meeting participants were divided on many issues, but they concurred on the importance of ethics education. The nature and scope of that education proved to be divisive, but the need for ethics instruction and a clear sense of administrative right conduct was hailed as essential by virtually all participants.[8]

As William D. Richardson has written, "Historically, one usually finds considerable disagreement as to what a proper education should be for the people who would govern in any regime." Researchers have agreed educational programs should "seek to hone rationality at the same time that they channel the passions and interests of the individual toward higher ends."[9]

As a general statement of the goals of ethics education, or any education, for that matter, Richardson's conclusion is exactly correct. Developing a course of study in ethics is a broad goal and little consensus exists as to how to proceed, but that has not stopped scholars and educators from the attempt. In 1989, the National Association of Schools of Public Administration and Affairs (NASPAA), an accrediting body for academic programs in public administration and public affairs, presented a revised curriculum standard indicating that the curriculum "shall enhance the student's values, knowledge, and skills to act ethically and effectively."[10]

During the 1990s, programs in public administration and public affairs increased the number of courses offered in administrative ethics, although whether this development was a result of the NASPAA curriculum standard or for other reasons is not altogether clear. In some cases, the courses were required; in other cases, they were elective. Some courses concentrated on what might be called "practical ethics," an approach that emphasizes case studies and "real world" exercises. Other courses introduced students to the "Great Thinkers" in the Western intellectual tradition—for example, Plato, Aristotle, Immanuel Kant, the English Utilitarians, and so forth—with little or no regard for practical applications. Still other courses provided a mix of several approaches and course materials. Courses also differed on whether to highlight normative issues, empirical issues, or a combination.[11]

The variety of approaches and course offerings is attributable to the different goals in ethics education. Some programs focus on developing analytical skills so that students learn to recognize potential ethical problems and chart an appropriate course of action. Other programs emphasize philosophical issues, "rather than operating as if ethics were a mere matter of technique." What seems clear from the variety of programs is that no one approach eclipses the others. As long as intellectual rigor and a strong analytic component exist, a program can effectively educate students on appropriate ethical constructs.[12]

Assuming common objectives can be developed and assuming agreed-upon standards and measurement criteria can be established, the underlying question remains whether ethics education matters. Can ethics be taught and, if so, to what end? If it does not matter—if students derive no benefit from such courses apart from an easy grade or a break from more rigorous coursework—an argument can be made that ethics has no place in the curriculum. If ethics education does matter, the question arises as to whether ethics education can be improved through superior teaching methods or approaches.

In 1997, Donald C. Menzel published an article in *Public Administration Review* with the provocative title, "Teaching Ethics and Values in Public Administration: Are We Making a Difference?" In that article, he concluded that ethics education was valuable in schools of public administration, but instruction needed to be improved. "Is ethics instruction finding a niche in PA/A schools?" he asked rhetorically. "Unquestionably. Are we making a difference? Yes, so it appears. Are we making a large enough difference? Probably not." In his view, the wide variation in techniques and approaches in ethics education made it difficult to assess the effect of ethics education or to compare one form of instruction with another. As Menzel concluded, "There is probably no one best way to acquire ethics. Still, there is much to learn about both the teaching and learning (or acquiring) of ethics and values in public administration."[13]

The scope and content of a comprehensive program on ethics education easily could be the subject of a stand-alone book or series of articles, as they have been in the past. Suffice it to say in this context that any number of methods and means for mastering and applying ethical concepts in public service exist, and some are more effective than others. However such education is acquired, it is important to stress that right conduct does not occur unless and until individuals understand the expectations for their behavior and can problem solve when faced with ethical choices. The model here presupposes that education is a crucial component of administrative ethics—an "input," if you will—but it is only one facet of a multifaceted approach.

DECISION-MAKING FOR THE ETHICAL ADMINISTRATOR

If the development of an individual administrator's values through his or her lifetime experiences and education can be seen as the inputs, decision-making might be labeled the "throughput" (and the action that results from the decision can be deemed the "output"). Decision-making unquestionably involves an administrator's values and character, but these factors are only part of the equation. A decision-making model of the ethical administrator necessarily involves five related, essential stages. First, the larger context must be identified. Next, the role of an ethical administrator within the context must be identified. Third, the content of the appropriate ethical standards must be defined. Fourth, the nature of the ethical conflict must be identified. Finally, a feasible course of action must be charted, and steps must be taken to resolve the conflict or at least deal with it if the conflict cannot be resolved. These steps are the components of deliberative process that must exist so that a public administrator can appropriately assess the ethical questions and chart a satisfactory means of moving from the recognition of an ethical problem to a decision on how to proceed. It is instructive to examine each of these stages in turn.

Stage One: The Larger Context

As discussed previously, in some ways, administrative ethics is complicated because of the public nature of an administrator's duties. An individual seeking to chart an appropriate course of action generally need not worry about the larger societal implications of the decision, except in rare cases where the individual's decision somehow affects the larger society. A public administrator, however, must be concerned with the larger context by virtue of his or her position within a democratic regime.

Even before an ethical issue arises, an administrator is well served by knowing the context in which he or she operates. In the private sector, an employee working inside a large corporation is well-advised to know the corporation's place in the world, the industry, and its geographical area of operation. If nothing else, following a public company's stock price can be an effective way of determining whether the employee can expect to be laid off or to receive a bonus based on the company's performance. Although a public sector employee typically cannot find such direct and clear measures of organizational performance, he or she would be wise to understand the company's place in the regime and the factors governing performance inside the organization.

As Figure 5.2 graphically illustrates, background experiences influence the administrator before he or she considers the larger context. Because

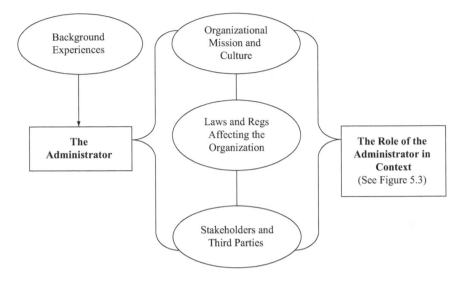

Figure 5.2   The Larger Context of Administrative Decision-Making.

the administrator holds a position of public power and responsibility, he or she must know something about the organization and its context—the organizational mission and culture, laws and regulations affecting the organization, and the stakeholders and third parties that both influence the operation of the organization and, in turn, are influenced by it. The challenge is to locate and delve into credible sources of information.

Many organizations, public and private, have an employee handbook or similar list of expectations related to employee performance. Such a handbook or list is a valuable source of information about the organization. By reviewing the particular list of expectations, the thoroughness (or lack thereof) of the list and the statements regarding the way the organization operates will provide explicit and implicit information about the organization.

Virtually every organization also has a Web site in the twenty-first century. Moreover, if an employee searches via Google for news and information on the organization, generally, a treasure trove of data will emerge within seconds. A few hours devoted to perusing these pages will be time well spent.

Notice the key phrase "credible sources of information." The modern era has provided untold volumes of information at an individual's fingertips. A few key strokes will yield more data than most people can probably sift through in the time available to them. The problem is that some of the data are not reliable. Blogs, rumor and innuendo, and mistakes that occur when information is taken out of context can provide a misleading picture of an organization and its purpose. Accordingly, an administrator must ferret through the information to distinguish between high-quality data and Internet noise. Information supplied by the organization, third-party, peer-reviewed studies, newspaper articles from reputable publications, and information gleaned from online library sources are the most credible, although no single source can be said to be unimpeachable.

An employee over time will come to understand the context in which the organization operates. Aside from outside sources, it will be helpful to talk with more experienced workers and take stock of their advice. Morale is a reasonably reliable indicator of how well an organization functions, although it is by no means infallible. In many cases, however, employees working in an organization where leadership is lacking or ethical shortcuts are the rule rather than the exception will demonstrate their disdain in subtle and not-so-subtle ways. The old adage that a fish rots from the head down is not without a glimmer of truth.

Stage Two: The Scope of a Public Administrator's Duties: Role Morality

Aside from the broader context, to a large extent, a public administrator's world is shaped by his or her place within a specific organization. Many factors influence the operation of an organization. Obviously, the formal procedural rules and statutory requirements determine to no small extent how the organization will conduct its daily business. An organization that is tightly organized and controlled by statutory requirements leaves little room for an individual laboring inside the organization to maneuver beyond what the law or regulation requires. An individual must recognize when a legal requirement exists and discern the standard set by the legal rule so he or she can act appropriately within his or her role.

Even this seemingly straightforward statement of an administrator's duty poses challenges. First, because legal rules contained in statutes and regulations may be incomplete, vague, ambiguous, contradictory, or inexplicable, grasping the appropriate course of action from a positivist legal source may be problematic. For an administrator who is not trained in the law and has neither the expertise nor the time to navigate through rough seas toward understanding, legal requirements can raise more questions than they solve.

More fundamentally, a statute or regulation may be obsolete or so obviously unjust as to present a moral dilemma that calls for an administrator to act in a manner that precludes blind obedience. Although presumably such instances are rare, they are not unique. For decades, American laws and regulations at the federal, state, and local level included provisions not only allowing, but requiring, legal segregation. Today, Americans overwhelmingly reject laws that promote de jure discrimination and segregation, but the demise of these unjust laws required long-term, ongoing commitments by opponents working to amend the laws and those persons who practiced civil disobedience at great personal sacrifice.[14]

Because administrators are the people on the front lines administering laws and regulations, they often have a firsthand view of how well or poorly implementation occurs. Instead of merely following the law because it is a requirement passed down from superiors, an ethical administrator has a continuing obligation to point out deficiencies so that systematic changes can be considered and perhaps adopted. This is not to say that an administrator may take issue with all laws and regulations or raise questions because implementation is inconvenient or personally distasteful. A distinction exists between an individual who prefers a different policy or legal requirement and a policy or legal requirement that can be labeled as morally reprehensible. The sensible administrator will need to ask hard questions about whether an organization's requirements are generally defensible versus clearly unconscionable.[15]

As an example, an employee of a state voter registration office may disagree with a legal requirement that all prospective voters must present a government-issued identification card before voting because this prerequisite may deny a small group of poor and historically disenfranchised peoples the right to vote. Nonetheless, arguments can be made that requiring an identification card reduces the likelihood of voter fraud, certainly a desirable public policy goal. In this situation, the employee may disagree with the policy, but he or she is obligated to act in accordance with the policy; it is defensible. In contrast, a policy that required people of color to present identification cards and exempted whites from the same requirement would not be defensible. In this latter case, the employee who objects to the policy is not simply disagreeing with a policy; he or she is raising a serious constitutional issue about the equal protection of the laws, among other things.

Notice what happens during stage two of this decision-making process. The administrator moves from the general to the particular in his or her understanding of ethical duties. Instead of searching for general information on the larger context of the organization, as suggested in Figure 5.2, now the administrator seeks to understand how the larger context applies to his or her corner of the world. A street-level administrator may be so far down inside the hierarchy of an organization that few occasions arise when detailed knowledge of laws and regulations apply. As long as his or her peers are not openly engaged in theft or other forms of clear, incontrovertibly egregious behavior, knowledge of the larger context may seem esoteric. Appreciating his or her role and the duties associated with that role are more concrete.

Equally as important as understanding legal requirements is the need to master an organization's culture and the individual's role inside that culture. Organizational culture affects virtually all aspects of the organization's performance, including how groups within the organization interact. Combining the individual and the group can provide insight into how organizations operate. In the words of one influential organization theorist, Talcott Parsons, "like any social system, an organization is conceived as having a describable structure. This can be described and analyzed from two points of view, both of which are essential to completeness. The first is the 'cultural-institutional' point of view which uses the values of the system and their institutionalization in different functional contexts as its point of departure. [T]he second is the 'group' or 'role' point of view which takes suborganizations and the roles of individuals participating in the functioning of the organization as its point of departure."[16]

Although the focus in any discussion of ethics invariably must emphasize the importance of the individual, it is important to understand the role of the group and how it affects and is affected by an organization. A formal organization also contains informal organizations composed of groups that form naturally, regardless of the formal, hierarchical structure. Informal organizations influence the perceptions and attitudes of group members and shape behavioral values and norms. As Chester

Barnard once observed, informal groups are an integral part of an organization; they fulfill functions that the formal organization cannot or will not fulfill. Today, some theorists refer to this issue as "group dynamics."[17]

Groups develop values that augment, and sometimes partially supplant, individual values and norms. If a person goes to work in an agency where everyone is expected to perform certain chores or behave in certain ways, an individual is pressured, subtly and not so subtly, to conform. A formal role may be spelled out on an organizational chart, but informal rules of behavior often determine how an individual will perform. In some settings, employees seek guidance and advice from senior members of the group, even if the senior member is a peer. An employee's relationship with peers can determine how well the employee fits into the organization and whether that employee, and other employees as well, enjoy positive experiences and good morale in the workplace.

Groupthink is so powerful and influential that even the most grounded and thoughtful person can succumb to a "mob mentality." Surrounded by peers for much of the day week after week, the individual is immersed in the values, traditions, and customs of the organization and the group. Eventually, without realizing that a change has occurred, the individual conforms. It is an incremental, unseen process. In some cases—for example, when a dysfunctional organization perpetuates unethical conduct because of a failure of leadership at the top—the consequences of groupthink can be insidious, a corrosive force that undermines right conduct. In other instances, the influence of the organization on the individual need not be seen as nefarious; rather, it is a natural evolution as an individual who existed apart from the group is brought into the fold and accepted as an integral member of the team.[18]

Understanding an administrator's scope of duties highlights the difficulties inherent in moving away from individual notions of ethics toward a broader emphasis on institutions. It is not difficult to understand how ethical precepts apply to private individuals acting in a private capacity because accountability is straightforward. Except in rare cases when an individual was acting under duress, mental illness, or diminished capacity, he or she will be held accountable for his or her actions. In contrast, an individual acting as a public employee in an official public capacity must consider a variety of factors apart from personal predilections in making choices. The potential conflict between an individual's desires and his or her duties to the agency and to the public can raise many ethical problems, and the nature of such a conflict complicates administrative ethics.

Despite the complications involved in identifying the scope of an administrator's duties, this task is an important stage in the decision-making process. Some theorists have suggested that the scope, or domain, is broad and extends beyond simply an individual's span of control. As Kathryn G. Denhardt noted in *The Ethics of Public Service*, "The evidence can suggest no other conclusion: the domain of ethical responsibility for the public administrator is very broad and very encompassing. Administrators are intimately involved in the policy-making process, the analyses they use in arriving at decisions have ethically relevant value biases, and organizational structures do not relieve individuals from responsibility for the actions, policies, and decisions in which they take part."[19]

Although Denhardt is correct that "organizational structures do not relieve individuals from responsibility," it is nonetheless instructive to examine the specific context in which administrators make decisions and face ethical choices. The crucial component of personal responsibility is always present, but the nature and extent of the administrator's role will determine the nature and extent of that personal responsibility. It is absurd to hold a low-level, non-policy-making employee responsible for policy decisions if he or she was only dimly aware of the situation and exercised little or no control over the policy. Even in instances when it is appropriate to assign some measure of responsibility to a lower-level employee, the assignment depends on degrees of responsibility.

Figure 5.3 shows a simplified view of the types of questions that arise when considering the administrator's role within the context of the organization. First, is the administrator a clerical or nonclerical employee? Although a clerical employee exercises some degree of authority, he or she generally is directed to perform tasks with little or no understanding of the big picture. Similarly, distinguishing between a supervisory and nonsupervisory position can determine, to some extent, the responsibility of a particular administrator. Presumably, a supervisor will exercise more control over the structure and content of some decisions inside of a public organization, especially where personnel and administrative matters concerning subordinates are involved.

In some organizations, an administrator exercises statutory authority; that is to say that the employee is authorized by law to undertake

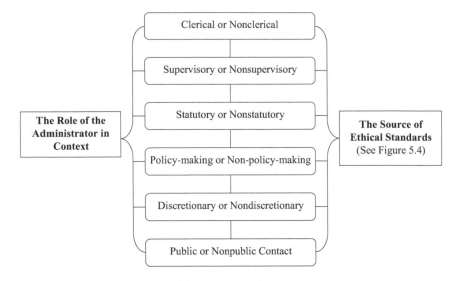

Figure 5.3   The Administrator's Role in an Organizational Context.

certain duties. Although the distinction between law and ethics is not exact, as previously discussed, in many cases, the two concepts overlap and exist in tandem. The paramount virtue of a legal rule is its relative clarity, at least compared with an ethical precept, which often is vague and unclear. When law and ethics overlap, and a public administrator is charged with a specific duty by law, he or she must make a good faith attempt to comply with the law. Failure to do so, aside from the violation of a legal duty and its attendant consequences, amounts to an ethical violation, assuming the failure was deliberate and not the result of a mistake or a similar justifiable excuse. The ethical responsibilities of an administrator charged with a statutory duty can be judged with more precision than an administrator who has no specific statutory responsibilities.

   Other questions that arise with respect to an administrator's role are whether he or she is a policy-maker or a non-policy-maker and whether he or she exercises discretion. Recognizing, of course, that virtually every public employee, even those ensconced in the lower levels of an agency, are vested with some small measure of policy-making or discretionary author-ity, it is axiomatic that the more policy-making or discretionary authority an administrator has, the more responsibility he or she assumes. If respon-sibility rests on the concept of free will, the more free will an administrator has, the more he or she will exercise responsibility for the content of a decision made inside a public organization.

Last but certainly not least is the question of whether the administrator comes into contact with the public. In this context, public contact is not merely counting back change or interacting with a citizen for three minutes at the Department of Motor Vehicles, although it can include these interactions. Instead, the main concern is that the public often knows very little about how government is structured and operates. An administrator who interacts with the public in a friendly, fair, efficient manner will communicate a great deal to the citizen about the responsiveness, of lack thereof, of a democratic regime. If this point sounds trite, that is because it sometimes is trite. Efforts to transform government into a more "customer-responsive" or "consumer-friendly" entity often focus on minor matters, such as requiring government employees to return telephone calls in a timely manner or insisting that they be polite. Being timely and polite may be important, but they are minor in the larger scheme of things. Rather, the essential issue is whether the administrator takes ownership of a problem and deals with the citizen in a way that resolves the issue or at least clearly and accurately communicates the reasons why the issue cannot be resolved. The more contact an administrator has with the public, the heavier the ethical responsibility, at least insofar as handling the interaction is concerned.

Stage Three: The Content of Acceptable Ethical Standards

It is one thing to suggest that individuals accept responsibility for behaving in an ethical manner without hiding behind the accepted values of their respective organizations; it is another matter to identify the content of an ethical code. The devil is in the details. For every professional standard or system or analogous guidelines that can be adopted, discrepancies can be isolated. For every rule or guideline that is identified, exceptions can be found. For every model code of ethical rules that can be established, situations arise where the code is ambiguous or does not apply. The realization that developing ethical content is problematic does not mean the endeavor is fruitless; it does mean the endeavor is ongoing and iterative.

The content of acceptable standards may come from several sources. A particular organization may have its own code of ethics or a handbook that outlines its expectations for employee behavior and performance. In addition, professional associations such as the American Society for Public Administration (ASPA) have sponsored study committees on revamping public service ethics, debated the appropriate components of an ethical system, and passed resolutions urging public administrators to adopt and comply with ethical standards. Formalized codes of ethics such as the ASPA Code of Ethics and Guidelines, the International City Management Code of Ethics with Guidelines, the National Contract Management Association Code of Ethics, and the U.S. Code of Ethics of 1980 can provide templates for how a code can be written and administered.[20]

Professions, especially medicine and law, provide guidance on the construction and operation of codes of ethics, but precedents must not be stretched beyond their breaking point. The professions can be celebrated for having developed "black letter" ethical precepts, for which much credit is deserved, but the field of public administration, if it can even be so designated, differs from the professions. "Public administration" is a term with no fixed, precise meaning. To be a public administrator means that an individual acts in service of a public organization, to be sure, but beyond this broad statement little can be said with confidence. A local public administrator may be tasked with ensuring that streets are kept clean and sidewalks are maintained in good repair. At the other extreme, a federal public administrator might be in charge of American foreign policy in a troubled region of the world through the State Department. Individuals employed in both positions are public administrators, but their duties, budgets, and expectations are widely divergent. To develop a workable, enforceable code of ethics that applies to both with equal vigor is a Herculean task.[21]

Professionals, however, are united by their entry into a particular field of study and practice. Physicians must pass a licensing board and affirm the Hippocratic oath before they are admitted to the profession. Attorneys must pass the bar exam and be certified as fit for the practice of law. Licensure presumably ensures that practitioners possess at least a minimal level of competence, although it remains a debatable point whether this presumption is valid. In any case, licensure serves a gatekeeping function. No one, regardless of his or her prior education or work experience, can be a duly authorized physician or attorney in the United States without gaining a license. Licensure substantially reduces the difficulty in developing and enforcing an ethical code.

A physician or an attorney facing a professional dilemma is directed to consult an authoritative source for what constitutes ethics in that profession. Although no code can address all likely scenarios, a well-drafted code of ethics can provide reasonable direction about appropriate standards of conduct. Professional codes of ethics also can specify sanctions for noncompliance, an enormously helpful part of the professional code. If a code of ethics is to have teeth and be enforceable, sanctions are integral.[22]

Most codes of ethics apart from the professions have few, if any, sanctions. In a professional setting, if a practitioner violates the code, he or she potentially faces suspension or expulsion from the profession. This severe penalty ensures in all but the most egregious cases that practitioners will ponder their actions prior to engaging in conduct they know or should know is unethical. Without the possibility of sanctions, however, the consequences of noncompliance are negligible. The possibility of opprobrium may serve as a deterrent, but such a deterrent is not as effective as the loss of one's license and livelihood.

A professional code of ethics may be suitable as content for ethical guidance, but theorists worry that a professional might adhere to the profession over and above the larger responsibilities. As an example, an attorney asked to review another attorney's work to determine whether malpractice occurred may be reluctant to find fault with a fellow member of the bar even if it would appear to someone outside the profession that a violation had occurred. In such a case, the reviewing attorney has placed the supposed well-being of the legal profession above the duty to expose malfeasance. Of course, one might argue that a larger duty to the public exists—to expose malpractice whenever and wherever it occurs—and when an attorney exposes a fellow member of the bar as unethical this chore, distasteful though it might be, roots out problems before they grow worse. Despite this observation, the fear is that some members of a profession place their desire to protect the reputation of the profession above the desire to expose ethical lapses.[23]

Aside from a formal code of ethics, individuals also have developed their own internal ethical code based on their family and social ties, education, experience, and religious beliefs. People may be hard-pressed to state how or why they act in certain ways, but even if they do not consciously recognize their own internal checks on behavior, they have developed a sense of right and wrong throughout the course of their lives. Individuals rely on their moral compass to make decisions and determine whether that moral compass is at odds with the requirements of the larger organization. To some extent, an administrator must separate personal feelings from professional responsibility when and if a conflict exists.

Although a particular individual may feel uncomfortable divorcing his or her individual feelings from the role he or she plays as a public servant, society benefits from this division of duties. Social institutions within a democratic regime are designed so that individuals who interact with those institutions promote social values. If an individual working within an institutional setting decides to promote his or her personal values above the values of the institution, this circumvents the democratic processes that created those social values.

An individual has the option to oppose the death penalty on ethical grounds as long as he or she is acting outside the confines of an institution. If that same individual holds a position within a public agency—for example, a state prosecutor's office with responsibility for prosecuting death penalty cases—this role will not necessarily change the individual's personal objections to the death penalty; however, it does require that the individual carry out the prosecutor's mission of prosecuting death penalty cases. If the individual cannot reconcile his or her personal objections to the death penalty with the prosecutor's public responsibility for prosecuting death penalty cases, the individual must leave the prosecutor's office. The individual serves as a public servant because of the division of labor between private individuals and individuals acting as decision-makers within the regime. This public role requires that the individual consider his or her duty as a public servant above his or her individual feelings, except in rare instances. The rare instances involve egregious behavior within the organization, which leads to the next point, namely the need for a deliberative decision-making process for the ethical administrator.[24]

Where, then, does a person find the content of an ethical code? The answer is that no one overarching ethical code exists. Some individuals rely on their long-held personal beliefs, which were formed over time and are based on multiple sources. Others cite the Bible. Professionals may follow the dictates of their professions. Still others may cite the works of famous thinkers or a popular book, such as The Purpose-Driven Life, as a source of guidance.

Individuals frequently are inconsistent in their habits and beliefs. A person may subscribe to closely held beliefs that contradict other closely held beliefs. In some cases, the individual may recognize the contradiction and choose to live with it based on the adage that a foolish consistency is the hobgoblin of little minds. Other individuals may not recognize the contradiction. In any event, even if the content of ethical decisions can be isolated, the possibility of conflicts in reaching a particular determination is not necessarily diminished.[25]

It does not seem possible to identify a specific code of ethics that will apply to every public administrator. What is clear is that individual administrators will search for ethical guidance from a wide variety of sources. Figure 5.4 shows the typical source of ethical standards for public administrators. Moving down the chart from general sources to specific sources, some administrators will search for the guidance in resolving ethical questions by reading great works of philosophy or by searching for regime values, as discussed in Chapter 1. Others will rely on organizational culture to understand how ethical dilemmas should be handled. An employee handbook or other written materials may provide assistance. Direction provided by supervisors is another source of guidance. A professional code of ethics or specific legal requirements found in statutes or regulations can help as well. In all likelihood, an administrator will consult multiple sources for direction.

Much of the literature on ethics cited in Chapters 1 and 2 of this book emphasizes the importance of clearly identifying the source and content

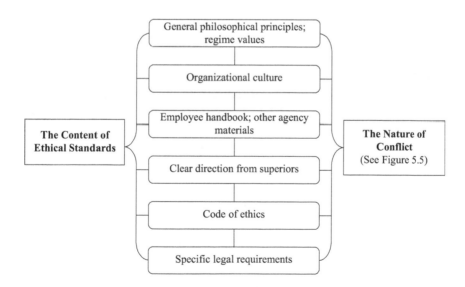

Figure 5.4   The Source of Ethical Standards.

of ethical standards. A major reason that the five theoretical approaches to administrative ethics identified by Terry L. Cooper were developed was because different schools of thought harbored different opinions about the most appropriate method for addressing ethical conundrums. Each approach has its merits and its drawbacks.

The divide among and between the schools of thought will never be bridged, nor should it be. Each administrator must decide for himself or herself what source of guidance is appropriate. This realization means that different people will reach different conclusions, depending on the sources they rely on and the analysis they undertake to determine their ethical responsibility. So be it. The crucial outcome is that an administrator should be able to justify why he or she resolved the ethical dilemma in a certain way. Pointing to the decision-making process after the fact, he or she should be able to say, "I chose to do X because of these five factors." Choosing a pragmatic approach over a specific school of thought allows the administrator maximum freedom of choice, even if it occasionally results in inconsistencies among and between different decisions involving ethical choices.

Stage Four: The Nature of the Ethical Conflict

This pragmatic approach depends in no small measure on the nature of the conflict. An administrator confronting a potential ethical dilemma faces three key decision points. First, is the potential conflict merely a difference of opinion? A superior may favor handling an issue in a manner that the subordinate disagrees with, but the fact that a difference of opinion exists does not mean that an ethical problem has occurred. If the supervisor's preferred approach is not contrary to an ethical standard (see Figure 5.5), the subordinate should recognize that the disagreement does not raise an ethical issue and drop the matter.

If this advice to drop the matter seems ultimately unsatisfying, it is little wonder. A difference of opinion can, in fact, be an ethical issue in disguise. Each individual administrator must decide how far to pursue the matter. Let us say, for example, that a middle manager inside the U.S. Department of Agriculture objects to the rationale of his or her superiors to make crucial decisions behind close doors. A hallmark of the democratic process is the transparency in decision-making, except in rare cases when a person's right to privacy might be compromised or if national

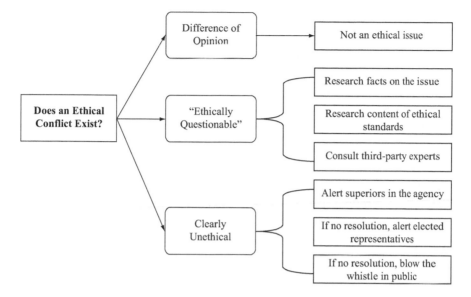

Figure 5.5   The Nature of the Conflict.

security considerations are involved. The subordinate may learn that the superiors are making decisions far away from public scrutiny and decide that this practice, although distasteful to the administrator, is a difference of opinion about the proper method for conducting agency business. Further investigation might reveal, however, that the superiors, in fact, were violating agency policy, to say nothing of the law.

Does the administrator have an obligation to investigate the facts to learn more information and details about the decision-making process? Generally, the answer is no unless the administrator is an ombudsman or someone charged with specific responsibility for investigating potential malfeasance. Recall in Figure 5.3 that an administrator's role determines, to some extent, his or her duties. If it is not the administrator's responsibility to roam the hallways as a roving ethics investigator, he or she should not assume that role. If knowledge of the inappropriate behavior comes to the administrator through the normal course of business, the analysis changes, as will be discussed shortly. Until such time that the administrator knew or should have known of ethical lapses, however, he or she need not shoulder responsibility unnecessarily.

At the other end of the spectrum—namely, actions that are clearly unethical—the administrator's task is much easier to identify, even if actually following through requires an intestinal fortitude that few possess. An action that is clearly and unequivocally unethical presumably is rare—for example, outright violation of a statute or regulation, willful disobedience to an agency policy or directions from a superior, or other unambiguous violations of a known standard of conduct. Typically, the first step in rectifying such abuse is to contact a superior inside the organization and call attention to the abuse. If the abuse continues, it is incumbent upon the administrator to take the complaint to another source, perhaps even a legislator, or, in truly exceptional cases, to third parties outside the organization. These steps are not to be taken lightly. Blowing the whistle can hold negative consequences, especially if the administrator ultimately misconstrued the nature of the act or made public an issue that could have been rectified internally.

As for the middle category, actions labeled "ethically questionable," this is where the greatest degree of conflict and uncertainty occurs. Differences of opinion and clearly unethical activities are relatively easy to identify. Ethically questionable actions are difficult precisely because the situation is not clear. In researching the facts and the content of ethical standards, the potential ethical lapse nonetheless may be partially obscured by the parties involved or simply because the activities naturally have taken place far from public scrutiny. Occasionally, an administrator can seek advice and guidance from third parties, but if the facts are in dispute or may never be known and understood completely, he or she must decide what action, if any, to take. The question of action or inaction in the face of ambiguity will be discussed in connection with Figure 5.6 momentarily.

Stage Five: Taking Action to Resolve an Ethical Conflict

We have come to the heart of the matter. The difficulty in identifying an administrator's role within an organization pales in comparison with the difficulty in resolving the dilemma when legitimate role requirements clash. Competing missions, mandates, legal requirements, and organizational cultures invariably give rise to ethical problems. This is not the public's widely held misperception of lazy bureaucrats who are asleep at the switch or simply do not care when the U.S. Department of Defense purchases tools and toilet seats for hundreds of dollars. Instead, this is the question of how a well-meaning public administrator who genuinely

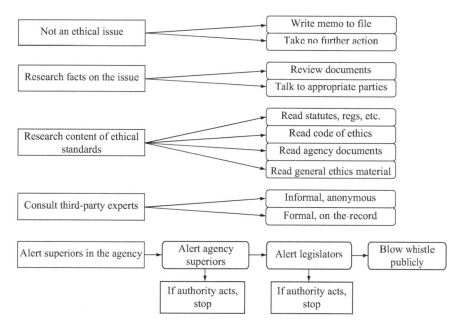

Figure 5.6   Taking Action to Resolve an Ethical Conflict.

seeks to "do the right thing" acts in such a way that the public interest, however it is defined, is protected.[26]

No matter how conscientious and well-meaning an administrator is, if he or she is unwilling to act in the face of an ethical dilemma no decision-making process, regardless of its analytic rigor, will be useful. Thought without deed is pie-in-the-sky, an intellectual exercise that can be valuable, but one that ultimately fails to ensure right conduct in public administration.

Figure 5.6 is a continuation of Figure 5.5 with an added layer of detail. Recall that Figure 5.5 identified the nature of an ethical conflict and offered recommendations on the steps to take in three categories of conflicts, namely when a difference of opinion exists, when ethically questionable activities have occurred, and when clearly unethical actions have been undertaken. Figure 5.6 adds detail to the options facing an administrator in each of these situations.

Moving down the figure, even when an administrator determines that an ethical issue does not exist and further action is unwarranted, it is advisable to add a written memorandum to one's internal file. Perhaps this represents an abundance of caution, but one can envision questions arising months, perhaps years later. A written memorandum to file allows an administrator to recall the events and his or her suspicions without trying to piece together an event years after the fact.

In instances where more facts are needed to determine whether further action is required, reviewing documents and speaking to parties, as appropriate, is prudent. An administrator faced with a decision point will be able to look to past examples and resolve the matter according to the way similar matters were resolved previously. This is what lawyers do when they resolve legal cases. They look at the reasoning in cases that are factually similar and analogize to the present case. Are the facts in the instant case close enough logically to the facts in the previous case to warrant a similar outcome? If the answer is yes—and this is not always an easy conclusion to reach—they explain their actions as justifiable based on the previous decision.[27]

Simultaneously, researching the content of ethical standards through one or more of the sources identified in Figure 5.4 is an important method for combining the facts with advice on right conduct. In rare instances when past examples conflict or simply do not exist, an administrator can seek guidance from a more experienced employee, informally or formally, or from the organization's published guidelines and procedures. Although such processes probably will address more than 90 percent of the cases, almost invariably there will be situations where no previous rule, guideline, or procedure provides a clear resolution. The administrator must first recognize that this case is not covered by preexisting rules and standards. This means that he or she must understand the role of bureaucracy in a democratic society, the specific organization's rules and standards, and/or professional standards developed by outside organizations and the reasoning behind each of these sources. Faced with an unusual situation that must be resolved, the administrator must be able to evaluate the situation and analogize to cases that may not be exactly on point but reflect the underlying values in place within the organization.

After the administrator recognizes the issue and decides to act in accordance with the organization's underlying values, he or she must have the fortitude to move forward even in the face of opposition or indifference from others. This may be as simple as alerting one or more superiors within the agency of the situation and the results of the administrator's research and analysis. If the administrator's superiors take action, even if it is action that the administrator disagrees with, this should end the matter. Assuming the superiors' action is not tantamount to ignoring the issue or participating in a cover-up—which in themselves would raise a host of additional issues—the administrator has discharged his or her duties as a public employee.

If the superiors do not take action, the administrator can alert elected officials, especially those in the legislative branch, as to the issue. This is a bold step, and it is not taken without risk. Moving beyond the agency to alert lawmakers about a possible ethical violation is certain to aggravate agency officials, at a minimum, and can result in disciplinary and possible legal action, especially if the alleged ethical lapse proves to be wrong. An even more aggressive and risky move is to blow the whistle in a public forum. Although whistleblowers have certain legal protections, the reality is that an administrator who goes outside the organization risks losing his or her job and perhaps becoming embroiled in an ongoing legal controversy. For these reasons, acting on suspicions of ethical improprieties is the most difficult, and probably the most important, of all the stages in the decision-making process.[28]

REFINING A MODEL OF ADMINISTRATIVE ETHICS

Recall that this book began with Terry L. Cooper's plea for a more comprehensive approach to administrative ethics. As he saw it, the field of administrative ethics could be divided into at least five approaches: (1) ethics as virtue; (2) ethics as regime values, constitutional theory, and founding thought; (3) ethics as citizenship; (4) ethics as social equity; or (5) ethics as the public interest. He left open the possibility, indeed the likelihood, that other approaches could be added to the list. However the subject is approached, he argued, quite rightly, that an ethical decision-maker must be a person with a well-developed moral compass and an understanding of the requirements inherent in a democratically based regime. How that person comes to develop his or her moral compass and understand the requirements of a democratic regime remain open questions, which explain the different emphases among and between the different approaches.

Some facts must be accepted up front. First, a public organization can do little to promote virtue directly among its employees and the citizenry, which is developed over the course of a human life and is based on many particularized experiences; however, it can ensure that public administrators understand regime values, citizenship requirements, social equity considerations, and the concept of the "public interest," although obviously individual factors will influence how these concepts are understood. As discussed previously, education is the crucial element. From the time students enter elementary school, they should be taught about their rights and responsibilities in a democratic regime. Later, when they enter college and graduate schools of public administration, they should be instructed in the nuances of administrative ethics. As John P. Burke has observed, quoting Terry L. Cooper, administrative ethics must be instilled through "'objective' responsibility to laws, procedures, and the dictates of organizational hierarchies and 'subjective' responsibility to ethical values, shared experiences, and professional training." Any effort to identify and clarify the issues must recognize that a "discussion of administrative ethics is not simply a task of encouraging moral calculation or applying some favored system of ethics but that it involves a more complex understanding" of how each of these approaches interacts with other approaches.[29]

Because of the inherent difficulty in identifying a specific school of thought or conceptual approach that triumphs over its competitors, this text has argued for a process approach to ethical decision-making. The thesis is that individual administrators will differ in their decision-making capabilities. Finding an approach that all, or substantially all, administrators can agree with is virtually impossible. Each school of thought and approach has its defenders and its detractors. Instead of debating how many angels can dance on the head of a pin, the goal of this book has been to develop a process by which ethical decisions can be made and defended.

To my students and others who seek a single source of ethical guidance that cuts through the morass and unifies all theories and approaches, my apologies. It is doubtful that such guidance is possible or, for that matter, even desirable. Perhaps it is the eternal quest for ethical guidance, and not the development of a specific system of ethics, that leads to what Aristotle called "practical wisdom."[30]

NOTES

INTRODUCTION

1. Ralph Clark Chandler, "Deontological Dimensions of Administrative Ethics Revisited," in *Handbook of Administrative Ethics*, 2nd ed., ed. Terry L. Cooper (New York: Marcel Dekker, 2001), 179–93; Gerald M. Pops, "A Teleological Approach to Administrative Ethics," in *Handbook of Administrative Ethics*, 2nd ed., ed. Terry L. Cooper (New York: Marcel Dekker, 2001), 195–206.

2. David E. Cooper, *World Philosophies: An Historical Introduction* (Cambridge, MA: Blackwell, 1996), 295; Pierre Hassner, "Immanuel Kant," in *History of Political Philosophy*, 2nd ed., ed. Leo Strauss and Joseph Cropsey (Chicago: Rand McNally & Company, 1972), 554–94; Immanuel Kant, "The Categorical Imperative," in *Combating Corruption/Encouraging Ethics: A Sourcebook for Public Service Ethics*, ed. William L. Richter, Francis Burke, and Jameson W. Doig (Washington, DC: The American Society for Public Administration, 1990), 27; J. Michael Martinez and William D. Richardson, *Administrative Ethics in the Twenty-first Century* (New York: Peter Lang USA, 2008), 27–28.

3. Immanuel Kant, *Fundamental Principles of the Metaphysics of Morals*, trans. T. Abbott (New York: Prometheus, 1987), 49.

4. Jeffrey S. Luke and David W. Hart, "Character and Conduct in the Public Service: A Review of Historical Perspectives," in *Handbook of Administrative Ethics*, 2nd ed., ed. Terry L. Cooper (New York: Marcel Dekker, 2001), 536–37;

Martinez and Richardson, *Administrative Ethics in the Twenty-first Century*, 27–28.

5. Pops, "A Teleological Approach to Administrative Ethics," 195–96.

6. Mortimer J. Adler and Seymour Cain, *Ethics: The Study of Moral Values* (Chicago: Encyclopedia Britannica, Inc., 1962), 262–63.

7. Terry L. Cooper, "Big Questions in Administrative Ethics: A Need for Focused, Collaborative Effort," *Public Administration Review* 64 (July/August 2004): 395–407. For a discussion of the pros and cons inherent in conflicts in administrative ethics, see F. Neil Brady and David W. Hart, "An Aesthetic Theory of Conflict in Administrative Ethics," *Administration & Society* 38 (March 2006): 113–34; Charles T. Goodsell, "Conflating Forms of Separation in Administrative Ethics," *Administration & Society* 38 (March 2006): 135–41.

CHAPTER 1

1. George D. Cameron III, "Ethics and Equity: Enforcing Ethical Standards in Commercial Relationships," *Journal of Business Ethics* 23 (January 2000): 161–72; Julian Le Grand, "Equity as an Economic Objective," *Journal of Applied Philosophy* 1 (March 1984): 39–51.

2. Terry L. Cooper, "The Emergence of Administrative Ethics as a Field of Study in the United States," in *Handbook of Administrative Ethics*, 2nd ed., ed. Terry L. Cooper (New York: Marcel Dekker, 2001), 1–36.

3. Richard Stillman II, *American Bureaucracy: The Core of Modern Government*, 3rd ed. (Belmont, CA: Wadsworth/Thompson, 2004), 158–59; Leonard D. White, *The Republican Era, 1869–1901* (New York: MacMillan, 1958), 232–56.

4. Martin Diamond, "Ethics and Politics: The American Way," in *The Moral Foundations of the American Republic*, 3rd ed., ed. Robert H. Horwitz (Charlottesville: The University Press of Virginia, 1986), 75–108.

5. Herbert A. Simon, *Administrative Behavior*, 2nd ed. (New York: The Free Press, 1957); Herbert A. Simon, "The Proverbs of Administration," in *Classics of Organization Theory*, 2nd ed., eds. Jay M. Shafritz and J. Steven Ott (Pacific Grove, CA: Brooks/Cole Publishing Company, 1987), 102–18; Dwight Waldo, *The Administrative State*, 2nd ed. (New York: Holmes & Meier, 1984).

6. Cooper, "The Emergence of Administrative Ethics as a Field of Study in the United States," 6–8; Fritz Morstein Marx, "Administrative Ethics and the Rule of Law," *The American Political Science Review* 43 (December 1949): 1119–44.

7. Carl J. Friedrich, "Public Policy and the Nature of Administrative Responsibility," in *Combating Corruption/Encouraging Ethics: A Sourcebook for Public Service Ethics*, eds. William L. Richter, Francis Burke, and Jameson W.

Doig (Washington, DC: The American Society for Public Administration, 1990), 43–44.

8. Luther Gulick and Lyndall F. Urwick, eds., *Papers on the Science of Administration* (New York: Augustus M. Kelley, 1937); D. W. Martin, "The Fading Legacy of Woodrow Wilson," *Public Administration Review* 48 (March/April 1988): 631–36.

9. Herman Finer, "Administrative Responsibility in Democratic Government," in *Combating Corruption/Encouraging Ethics: A Sourcebook for Public Service Ethics*, eds. William L. Richter, Francis Burke, and Jameson W. Doig (Washington, DC: The American Society for Public Administration, 1990), 44.

10. Terry L. Cooper, *The Responsible Administrator: An Approach to Ethics for the Administrative Role*, 3d ed. (San Francisco: Jossey-Bass, 1990), 128–32; Finer, "Administrative Responsibility in Democratic Government," 44.

11. Paul H. Appleby, *Morality and Administration in Democratic Government* (Baton Rouge: Louisiana State University Press, 1952), 56; Dwight Waldo, "Reflections on Public Morality," *Administration & Society* 6 (November 1974): 267–82.

12. See, for example, Cooper, "The Emergence of Administrative Ethics as a Field of Study in the United States," 11–16; J. Michael Martinez, "Law Versus Ethics: Reconciling Two Concepts of Public Service Ethics," *Administration & Society* 29 (January 1998): 707–8; Waldo, "Reflections on Public Morality," 281.

13. Terry L. Cooper, "Big Questions in Administrative Ethics: A Need for Focused, Collaborative Effort," *Public Administration Review* 64 (July/August 2004): 395.

14. See, for example, Ralph Clark Chandler, "The Civil Servant as Trustee: A Reorganization of the Professionalism Discussion," *Dialogue* 5 (Summer 1983): 5–21; Cooper, *The Responsible Administrator*; Patrick J. Dobel; "Integrity in the Public Service," *Public Administration Review* 50 (May/June 1990): 356–199066; Gregory D. Foster, "Law, Morality, and the Public Servant," *Public Administration Review* 41 (January/February 1981): 29–34; Robert T. Golembiewski, *Men, Management and Morality: Toward a New Organizational Ethic* (New York: McGraw-Hill, 1965); Eugene B. McGregor, "Social Equity and the Public Service," *Public Administration Review* 34 (January/February 1974): 18–29; Debra W. Stewart, "Ethics and the Profession of Public Administration: The Moral Responsibility of Individuals in Public Sector Organizations," *Public Administration Review* 45 (Winter 1985): 487–95; Gregory Streib, "Ethics and Expertise in the Public Service: Maintaining Democracy in an Era of Professionalism," *Southeastern Political Review* 20 (Spring 1992): 122–43.

15. Ralph Clark Chandler, "Deontological Dimensions of Administrative Ethics, Revisited," *Public Personnel Management* 28 (Winter 1999): 506–11; W. T. Jones, *The Classical Mind: A History of Western Philosophy*, 2nd ed. (New York: Harcourt Brace Jovanovich, 1970), 108, 215; J. Michael Martinez and

William D. Richardson, *Administrative Ethics in the Twenty-first Century* (New York: Peter Lang USA, 2008), 2–5, 18–22; James D. Wallace, *Virtues and Vices* (Ithaca, NY: Cornell University Press, 1978), 10.

16. David E. Cooper, *World Philosophies: An Historical Introduction* (Cambridge, MA: Blackwell, 1996), 232; Andrew Heywood, *Political Ideas and Concepts: An Introduction* (New York: St. Martin's Press, 1994), 19; Kenneth R. Hoover, *Ideology and Political Life*, 2nd ed. (Belmont, CA: Wadsworth, 1994), 31; Leo Strauss, "Niccolo Machiavelli, 1469–1527," in *History of Political Philosophy*, 2nd ed., ed. Leo Strauss and Joseph Cropsey (Chicago: The University of Chicago Press, 1972), 271–92.

17. Martinez and Richardson, *Administrative Ethics in the Twenty-first Century*, 3–5; Strauss, "Niccolo Machiavelli, 1469–1527," 271–73.

18. Mark T. Lilla, "Ethos, 'Ethics,' and Public Service," *The Public Interest* 63 (Spring 1981): 3–17.

19. Cooper, "Big Questions in Administrative Ethics," 397–98; David K. Hart, "A Partnership in Virtue Among All Citizens: The Public Service and Civic Humanism," *Public Administration Review* 49 (March-April 1989): 101–5; J. Michael Martinez and William D. Richardson, "*The Federalist Papers* and Legal Interpretation," *South Dakota Law Review* 45 (Summer 2000): 320–21; William D. Richardson, *Democracy, Bureaucracy, & Character: Founding Thought* (Lawrence: University Press of Kansas, 1997), 90–93.

20. John A. Rohr, *Ethics for Bureaucrats: An Essay on Law and Values*, 2nd ed. (New York: Marcel Dekker, 1989); Dennis P. Wittmer, "Ethical Decision-Making," in *Handbook of Administrative Ethics*, 2nd ed., ed. Terry L. Cooper (New York: Marcel Dekker, 2001), 493–94.

21. David K. Hart, "A Dream of What We Could Be: The Founding Values, the Oath, and *Homo Virtutis Americanus*," in *Handbook of Administrative Ethics*, 2nd ed., ed. Terry L. Cooper (New York: Marcel Dekker, 2001), 214–16; David K. Hart and P. Artell Smith, "Fame, Fame-Worthiness, and the Public Service," *Administration & Society* 20 (August 1988): 131–51; William D. Richardson and Lloyd G. Nigro, "Administrative Ethics and Founding Thought: Constitutional Correctives, Honor, and Education," *Public Administration Review* 47 (September/October 1987): 367–76; William D. Richardson and Lloyd G. Nigro, "Self-Interest Properly Understood: The American Character and Public Administration," *Administration & Society* 19 (August 1987): 157–77.

22. Alexander Hamilton, James Madison, and John Jay, "Federalist No. 37," in *The Federalist Papers*, ed. Clinton Rossiter (New York: The New American Library, 1961), 229; Michael I. Meyerson, *Liberty's Blueprint: How Madison and Hamilton Wrote the Federalist Papers, Defined the Constitution, and Made Democracy Safe for the World* (New York: Basic Books, 2008), 219–20.

23. Edward S. Corwin, "The 'Higher Law' Background of American Constitutional Law," in *American Government: Readings and Cases*, 3rd ed., ed. Peter Woll (Boston: Little Brown & Company, 1969), 37–54. See also: Robert A. Dahl, *A Preface to Democratic Theory* (Chicago: The University Press of Chicago, 1956); John Patrick Diggins, "Recovering 'First Principles': Critical Perspectives on the Constitution and the Fate of Classical Republicanism," in *Toward a More Perfect Union: Six Essays on the Constitution*, ed. Neil L. York (Provo, UT: Brigham Young University, 1988), 119–43.

24. Rohr, *Ethics for Bureaucrats*, 67–69.

25. Lawrence Baum, *The Supreme Court*, 3rd. ed. (Washington, DC: Congressional Quarterly Press, 1989), 116–21; David M. O'Brien, *Storm Center: The Supreme Court in American Politics* (New York: W. W. Norton, 1986), 213–75.

26. *Plessy v. Ferguson*, 163 U.S. 537 (1896). See also Jack Bass and Walter DeVries, *The Transformation of Southern Politics: Social Change and Political Consequence since 1945* (Athens: University Press of Georgia, 1995), 5–7; N. Lee Cooper, "President's Message—The Harlan Standard: Former Associate Justice Can Teach Us the Value of Reasoned Dissent," *ABA Journal* 83 (June 1997): 8; Cheryl I. Harris, "Symposium: Race Jurisprudence and the Supreme Court: Where Do We Go from Here? In the Shadow of *Plessy*," *University of Pennsylvania Journal of Constitutional Law* 7 (February 2005): 867–901; Frederic Rodgers, "'Our Constitution Is Color Blind': Justice John Marshall Harlan and the *Plessy v. Ferguson* Dissent," *American Bar Association Judges' Journal* 43 (Spring 2004): 15; Robert P. Steed and Laurence W. Moreland, "Southern Politics in Perspective," in *Confederate Symbols in the Contemporary South*, eds. J. Michael Martinez, William D. Richardson, and Ron McNinch-Su (Gainesville: University Press of Florida, 2000), 68–73.

27. *Brown v. Board of Education of Topeka*, 347 U.S. 483 (1954).

28. Bass and DeVries, *The Transformation of Southern Politics*, 5–4; Harris, "Symposium: Race Jurisprudence and the Supreme Court," 889–901.

29. Rohr, *Ethics for Bureaucrats*, 67–68.

30. David H. Rosenbloom, *Public Administration: Understanding Management, Politics, and Law in the Public Sector*, 2nd ed. (New York: Random House, 1989), 483.

31. Ronald C. Moe and Robert S. Gilmour, "Rediscovering Principles of Public Administration: The Neglected Foundation of Public Law," *Public Administration Review* 55 (March/April 1995): 135–36.

32. David H. Rosenbloom, "Retrofitting the Administrative State to the Constitution: Congress and the Judiciary's Twentieth-Century Progress," *Public Administration Review* 60 (January/February 2000): 29–46.

33. Laurence J. O'Toole, Jr. "Doctrines and Developments: Separation of Powers, the Politics-Administration Dichotomy, and the Rise of the Administrative State," *Public Administration Review* 47 (January/February 1987): 18–22.

34. Charles R. Wise, "The Supreme Court's Constitutional Federalism: Implications for Public Administration," *Public Administration Review* 61 (May/June 2001): 343–58.

35. Hart, "A Dream of What We Could Be," 214–19, 222–23.

36. Richard C. Box and Deborah A. Sagen, "Working with Citizens: Breaking Down Barriers to Citizen Self-Governance," in *Government Is Us: Public Administration in an Anti-Government Era*, eds. Cheryl Simrell King and Camilla Stivers (Thousand Oaks, CA: Sage Publications, 1998), 158–74; Dolores Foley, "We Want Your Input: Dilemmas of Citizen Participation," in *Government Is Us: Public Administration in an Anti-Government Era*, eds. Cheryl Simrell King and Camilla Stivers (Thousand Oaks, CA: Sage Publications, 1998), 140–57; Camilla Stivers, "Citizenship Ethics in Public Administration," in *Handbook of Administrative Ethics*, 2nd ed., ed. Terry L. Cooper (New York: Marcel Dekker, 2001), 583–602; Camilla Stivers, "Comments: Some Tensions in the Notion of 'The Public as Citizen': Rejoinder to Frederickson," *Administration & Society* 22 (February 1991): 418–23; Mary M. Timney, "Overcoming Administrative Barriers to Citizen Participation: Citizens as Partners, Not Adversaries," in *Government Is Us: Public Administration in an Anti-Government Era*, eds. Cheryl Simrell King and Camilla Stivers (Thousand Oaks, CA: Sage Publications, 1998), 88–101.

37. Garret Hardin, "The Tragedy of the Commons," *Science* 162 (December 1968): 1243–48.

38. Quoted in Martinez and Richardson, *Administrative Ethics in the Twenty-first Century*, 30.

39. Barry Bozeman, *Public Values and Public Interest: Counterbalancing Economic Individualism* (Washington, DC: Georgetown University Press, 2007), 1–3, 100–12; Terry L. Cooper, *An Ethic of Citizenship for Public Administration* (Englewood Cliffs, NJ: Prentice Hall, 1991), 140–57; Louis C. Gawthrop, "Civis, Civitas, and Civilitas: A New Focus for the Year 2000," *Public Administration Review* 44 (March 1984): 101–7; Kalu N. Kalu, "Of Citizenship, Virtue, and the Administrative Imperative: Deconstructing Aristotelian Civic Republicanism," *Public Administration Review* 63 (July/August 2003): 418–27; Richardson, *Democracy, Bureaucracy, & Character*, 18–26; Camilla Stivers, "The Public Agency as Polis: Active Citizenship in the Administrative State," *Administration & Society* 22 (May 1990): 86–105.

40. Linda de Leon and Robert B. Denhardt, "The Political Theory of Reinvention," *Public Administration Review* 60 (March/April 2000): 89–92. See also: Michael Spicer, "Public Administration, the History of Ideas, and the Reinventing Government Movement," *Public Administration Review* 64 (May/June

2004): 357–59; Larry D. Terry, "From Greek Mythology to the Real World of the New Public Management and Democratic Governance (Terry Responds)," *Public Administration Review* 59 (May/June 1999): 274–76.

41. James H. Svara and James R. Brunet, "Filling in the Skeletal Pillar: Addressing Social Equity in Introductory Courses in Public Administration," *Journal of Public Affairs Education* 10 (April 2004): 99–110.

42. John P. Burke, "Administrative Ethics and Democratic Theory," in *Handbook of Administrative Ethics*, 2nd ed., ed. Terry L. Cooper (New York: Marcel Dekker, 2001), 604–5; H. George Frederickson, "Public Administration and Social Equity," *Public Administration Review* 50 (March/April 1990): 228–37; H. George Frederickson and David K. Hart, "The Public Service and the Patriotism of Benevolence," *Public Administration Review* 45 (September/October 1985): 547–53.

43. John Rawls, *A Theory of Justice* (Cambridge, MA: Belknap Press, 1971), 136–38, 182–83.

44. H. George Frederickson, *New Public Administration* (Tuscaloosa: University of Alabama Press, 1980); David K. Hart, "Social Equity, Justice, and the Equitable Administrator," *Public Administration Review* 34 (January 1974): 3–11; Frank Marini, "The Minnowbrook Perspective and the Future of Public Administration," in *Toward a New Public Administration: The Minnowbrook Perspective, ed. Frank Marini* (New York, NY: Chandler, 1971), 346–67.

45. O. C. McSwite, *Legitimacy in Public Administration: A Discourse Analysis* (Thousands Oaks, CA: Sage Publications, 1997); Douglas F. Morgan, "The Public Interest," in *Handbook of Administrative Ethics*, 2nd ed., ed. Terry L. Cooper (New York: Marcel Dekker, 2001), 168–70.

46. Bozeman, *Public Values and Public Interest*, 83–99; Morgan, "The Public Interest," 154–57.

47. Bozeman, *Public Values and Public Interest*, 84.

48. Bozeman, *Public Values and Public Interest*, 83–84; Richardson, *Democracy, Bureaucracy, & Character*, 97–102.

49. Martinez and Richardson, *Administrative Ethics in the Twenty-first Century*, 15–18.

CHAPTER 2

1. Curtis Ventriss, "The Relevance of Public Ethics to Administration and Policy," in *Handbook of Administrative Ethics*, 2nd ed., ed. Terry L. Cooper (New York: Marcel Dekker, 2001), 263–89; James D. Wallace, *Virtues and Vices* (Ithaca, NY: Cornell University Press, 1978), 10–12.

2. A discussion about the history of philosophy and the various schools of thought would require multiple volumes. For a short introduction to the use of

philosophy in public administration, see, for example, Frank Fischer, "Ethical Discourse in Public Administration," *Administration & Society* 15 (May 1983): 5–42; Charles J. Fox, "The Use of Philosophy in Administrative Ethics," in *Handbook of Administrative Ethics*, 2nd ed., ed. Terry L. Cooper (New York: Marcel Dekker, 2001), 105–30; David K. Hart, "The Honorable Bureaucrat Among the Philistines," *Administration & Society* 15 (May 1983): 43–48.

3. Jeremy Bentham, *An Introduction to the Principles of Morals and Legislation* (New York: Hafner, 1948), 1; David E. Cooper, *World Philosophies: An Historical Introduction* (Cambridge, MA: Blackwell, 1996), 348–49.

4. John Stuart Mill, *On Liberty* (Arlington Heights, IL: AHM Publishing, 1947), 9.

5. Mortimer J. Adler and Seymour Cain, *Ethics: The Study of Moral Values* (Chicago: Encyclopedia Britannica, Inc., 1962), 262–63.

6. Thomas L. Friedman, *Hot, Flat, and Crowded: Why We Need a Green Revolution—And How It Can Renew America* (New York: Farrar, Straus and Giroux, 2008).

7. John Rawls, *A Theory of Justice* (Cambridge, MA: Belknap Press, 1971), 182–83.

8. G. E. Moore, *Principia Ethica* (Mineola, NY: Courier Dover Publications, 2004); Michael Smith, "Neutral and Relative Value after Moore," *Ethics* 113 (April 2003): 576–98.

9. Cooper, *World Philosophies*, 348–50.

10. Robert S. Hill, "David Hume," 518. See also David Hume, *An Enquiry Concerning Human Understanding* (Indianapolis: Hackett Publishing, 1977), 111–12.

11. Hill, "David Hume," in *History of Political Philosophy*, 2nd ed., eds. Leo Strauss and Joseph Cropsey (Chicago: Rand McNally & Company, 1972), 509–31.

12. Hill, "David Hume," 516–18.

13. Immanuel Kant, *Fundamental Principles of the Metaphysics of Morals*, trans. T. Abbott (New York: Prometheus, 1987), 49.

14. Pierre Hassner, "Immanuel Kant," in *History of Political Philosophy*, 2nd ed., ed. Leo Strauss and Joseph Cropsey (Chicago: Rand McNally & Company, 1972), 554–93.

15. Sir William David Ross, *The Right and the Good* (Oxford: Clarendon Press, 2002).

16. Henry Campbell Black, *Black's Law Dictionary*, 5th ed. (St. Paul, MN: West Publishing Company, 1979), 1347–48.

17. Edward S. Corwin, "The 'Higher Law' Background of American Constitutional Law," in *American Government: Readings and Cases*, 3rd ed., ed. Peter Woll (Boston: Little Brown & Company, 1969), 37–54; Paschal Larkin, *Property in the Eighteenth Century: With Special Reference to England and Locke*

(London: Cork University Press, 1930); Will Morrisey, "The Moral Foundations of the American Republic: An Introduction," in *The Moral Foundations of the American Republic*, 3rd ed., ed. Robert H. Horwitz (Charlottesville: The University Press of Virginia, 1986), 1–23; William D. Richardson, *Democracy, Bureaucracy, & Character: Founding Thought* (Lawrence: University Press of Kansas, 1997), 86–90; Gordon Wood, "The Political Ideology of the Founders," in *Toward a More Perfect Union: Six Essays on the Constitution*, ed. Neil L. York (Provo, UT: Brigham Young University, 1988), 7–27.

18. See, for example, Ming Hsu, Cedric Anen, and Steven R. Quartz, "The Right and the Good: Distributive Justice and Neural Encoding of Equity and Efficiency," *Science* 320 (23 May 2008): 1092–95; John T. Scholz and B. Dan Wood, "Efficiency, Equity, and Politics: Democratic Controls Over the Tax Collector," *American Journal of Political Science* 43 (October 1999): 1166–88.

19. See, for example, Ann Coulter, *Treason: Liberal Treachery from the Cold War to the War on Terrorism* (New York: Crown Forum, 2003); Lewis L. Gould, *Grand Old Party: A History of the Republicans* (New York: Random House, 2003), 483–94.

20. See, for example, Jules Witcover, *Party of the People: A History of the Democrats* (New York: Random House, 2003), 725–32.

21. Laurence Berns, "Thomas Hobbes," in *History of Political Philosophy*, 2nd ed., ed. Leo Strauss and Joseph Cropsey (Chicago: Rand McNally & Company, 1972), 370–94; Nicholas Dungey, "Thomas Hobbes's Materialism, Language, and the Possibility of Politics," *Review of Politics* 70 (Spring 2008): 190–220; David Gauthier, "Thomas Hobbes: Moral Theorist," *The Journal of Philosophy* 76 (October 1979): 547; Jimmy Casas Klausen, "Room Enough: America, Natural Liberty, and Consent in Locke's *Second Treatise*," *The Journal of Politics* 69 (August 1007): 760–69.

22. Merrill Jensen, *The Articles of Confederation: An Interpretation of the Social-Constitutional History of the American Revolution, 1774–1781* (Madison: The University of Wisconsin Press, 1963), 244; Andrew C. McLaughlin, "The Articles of Confederation," in *Essays on the Making of the Constitution*, ed. Leonard W. Levy (New York: Oxford University Press, 1969), 53.

23. Andrew Heywood, *Political Ideas and Concepts: An Introduction* (New York: St. Martin's Press, 1994), 44–46, 311; Kenneth R. Hoover, *Ideology and Political Life*, 2nd ed. (Belmont, CA: Wadsworth, 1994), 160–61, 191.

24. Heywood, *Political Ideas and Concepts*, 9–10, 256–83; Sidney Webb, "What Socialism Means: A Call to the Unconverted," in *The Quest for Justice: Readings in Political Ethics*, 3rd ed., ed. Leslie G. Rubin and Charles T. Rubin (Needham Heights, MA: Ginn Press, 1992), 219–24.

25. James David Barber, *The Book of Democracy* (Englewood Cliffs, NJ: Prentice Hall, 1995), 354–96.

26. Heywood, *Political Ideas and Concepts*, 113–16; Hoover, *Ideology and Political Life*, 40–41; Irving Kristol, "'When Virtue Loses All Her Loveliness'—Some Reflections on Capitalism and 'The Free Society,'" in *The Quest for Justice: Readings in Political Ethics*, 3rd ed., ed. Leslie G. Rubin and Charles T. Rubin (Needham Heights, MA: Ginn Press, 1992), 189–96; Robert Nozick, *Anarchy, State, and Utopia* (New York: Basic Books, 1974), 96–101.

27. R. Kenneth Godwin and John C. Wahlke, *Introduction to Political Science: Reason, Reflection, and Analysis* (Ft. Worth, TX: Harcourt Brace, 1997), 26–30, 59–60; Hoover, *Ideology and Political Life*, 84–88; Scholz and Wood, "Efficiency, Equity, and Politics," 1166–88.

28. Godwin and Wahlke, *Introduction to Political Science: Reason, Reflection, and Analysis*, 51–52; Heywood, *Political Ideas and Concepts*, 274–77; Hoover, *Ideology and Political Life*, 36–39; Adam Smith, "Selections from an Inquiry into the Nature and Causes of the Wealth of Nations," in *The Quest for Justice: Readings in Political Ethics*, 3rd ed., ed. Leslie G. Rubin and Charles T. Rubin (Needham Heights, MA: Ginn Press, 1992), 115–38.

29. Nick Crossley, "(Net)working Out: Social Capital in a Private Health Club," *British Journal of Sociology* 59 (September 2008): 475–500; Anthony Downs, *An Economic Theory of Democracy* (Old Tappan, NJ: Addison Wesley, 1997); Heywood, *Political Ideas and Concepts*, 190–91; Elinor Ostrom and T. K. Ahns, eds., *Foundations of Social Capital* (Cheltenham, UK: Edward Elgar, 2003); Robert Putnam, *Bowling Alone: The Collapse and Revival of American Community* (New York: Simon and Schuster, 2000).

30. Manuela Mosca, "On the Origins of the Concept of Natural Monopoly: Economies of Scale and Competition," *European Journal of the History of Economic Thought* 15 (June 2008): 317–53; Niko P. Paech, "Contestability Reconsidered: The Meaning of Market Exit Costs," *Journal of Economic Behavior & Organization* 34 (1 March 2008): 435–43; David L. Weimer and Aidan R. Vining, *Policy Analysis: Concepts and Practice*, 2nd ed. (Englewood Cliffs, NJ: 1992).

31. Robert Haveman, *Economics of the Public Sector* (Santa Barbara, CA: John Wiley & Sons, 1976).

32. Dan Campbell, "When the Lights Came On; USDA Program Brought Electricity and a Better Way of Life to Rural America," *Rural Cooperatives* 67 (July/August 2000): 6–9; Sherle R. Schwenninger, "Democratizing Capital," *Nation* 286 (7 April 2008): 27–28.

33. Ronald H. Coase, "The Institutional Structure of Production," *The American Economic Review* 82 (September 1992): 713–19; Alfred Endres and Bianca Rundshagen, "A Note on Coasean Dynamics," *Environmental Economics & Policy Studies* 9 (2008): 57–66; Joseph Farrell, "Information and the Coase Theorem," *The Journal of Economic Perspectives* 1 (Autumn 1987): 113–29;

Lawrence W. C. Lai and Connie W. Y. Hung, "The Inner Logic of the Coase Theorem and a Coasian Planning Research Agenda," *Environment & Planning B: Planning & Design* 35 (March 2008): 207–26; Fred S. McChesney, "Coase, Demsetz, and the Unending Externality Debate," *CATO Journal* 26 (Winter 2006): 179–200; Andrew L. Schlafly, "The Coase Theorem: The Greatest Economic Insight of the 20th Century," *Journal of American Physicians & Surgeons* 12 (Summer 2007): 45–47.

34. Anna Bergek, Staffan Jacobsson, and Bjorn A. Sanden, "'Legitimation' and 'Development' of Positive Externalities: Two Key Processes in the Formation Phase of Technological Innovation Systems," *Technology Analysis & Strategic Management* 20 (September 2008): 575–92; Jacob Dijkstra, Marcel A. L. M. Van Assen, and Frans N. Stokman, "Outcomes of Collective Decisions with Externalities Predicted," *Journal of Theoretical Politics* 20 (October 2008): 415–41.

35. James Andreoni, "Warm-Glow versus Cold-Pickle: The Effects of Positive and Negative Framing on Cooperation in Experiments," *The Quarterly Journal of Economics* 110 (February 1995): 1–21; A. H. Barnett, "The Pigouvian Tax Rule Under Monopoly," *The American Economic Review* 70 (December 1980): 1037–41.

36. Deborah Stone, *Policy Paradox: The Art of Political Decision Making*, rev. ed. (New York: W. W. Norton, 2002), 376–83.

37. Michael T. Heaney, "Issue Networks, Information, and Interest Group Alliances: The Case of Wisconsin Welfare Policies, 1993-99," *State Politics & Policy* 4 (Fall 2004): 237–70; Hugh Heclo, "Issue Networks and the Executive Establishment," in *The New American Political System*, ed. Anthony King (Washington, DC: American Enterprise Institute, 1978), 87–124; Mark Zschoch, "Why Policy Issue Networks Matter: The Advanced Technology Program and the Manufacturing Extension Partnership," *Canadian Journal of Political Science* 39 (June 2006): 443–45.

38. Stone, *Policy Paradox*, 38–83.

39. David S. Churchill, "Spectres of Anti-communism: Richard Rorty and Leftist Thought in Twentieth-Century America," *Canadian Review of American Studies* 38 (2008): 275–91; Alasdair MacIntyre, "Richard Rorty (1931–2007)," *Common Knowledge* 14 (Spring 2008): 183–92; Richard Rorty, *Contingency, Irony, Solidarity* (Cambridge, UK: Cambridge University Press, 1989); Keith F. Snider, "Expertise or Experimenting?," *Administration & Society* 32 (July 2000): 329–54; Ian Ward, "Bricolage and Low Cunning: Rorty on Pragmatism, Politics and Poetic Justice," *Legal Studies* 28 (June 2008): 281–305.

40. John P. Murphy, *Pragmatism from Peirce to Davidson* (Boulder, CO: Westview Press, 1990); Snider, "Expertise or Experimenting?," 330–33; Andrew C. Wicks and R. Edward Freeman, "Organization Studies and the New

Pragmatism: Positivism, Anti-Positivism, and the Search for Ethics," *Organization Science* 9 (February 1998): 123–40.

41. Murphy, *Pragmatism from Peirce to Davidson*, 1–6.

42. Jari I. Niemi, "Jurgen Habermas's Theory of Communicative Rationality: The Foundational Distinction Between Communicative and Strategic Action," *Social Theory and Practice* 31 (October 2005): 513–32.

43. Janet E. Day, "Emma Goldman and Ayn Rand: Ethical Egoism and Constraint," *Conference Papers—Midwestern Political Science Association* (2005): 1–28; Smith, "Neutral and Relative Value after Moore," 576–98.

44. Laurence Thomas, "The Reality of the Moral Self," *Monist* 76 (January 1993): 3–21.

45. Brian T. Trainor, "Politics as the Quest for Unity: Perspectivism, Incommensurable Values and Agonistic Politics," *Philosophy & Social Criticism* 34 (November 2008): 889–908; Kwasi Wiredu, "Democracy by Consensus: Some Conceptual Considerations," *Socialism and Democracy* 21 (November 2007): 155–70.

46. Heywood, *Political Ideas and Concepts*, 138–47; Ronald Dworkin, *Taking Rights Seriously* (Cambridge, MA: Harvard University Press, 1978), 90–94; Will Sarvis, "Americans and Their Land: The Deep Roots of Property and Liberty," *Contemporary Review* 290 (Spring 2008): 40–46.

47. Richardson, *Democracy, Bureaucracy, & Character*, 43–45, 84–86, 106; Herbert J. Storing, "American Statesmanship: Old and New," in *Bureaucrats, Policy Analysts, Statesmen: Who Leads?*, ed. Robert A. Goldwin (Washington, DC: American Enterprise Institute, 1980), 88–113.

48. Berns, "Thomas Hobbes," 370–94; Richardson, *Democracy, Bureaucracy, & Character*, 29, 85.

49. Dworkin, *Taking Rights Seriously*, 90–94; Heywood, *Political Ideas and Concepts*, 144.

50. H. L. A. Hart, "Positivism and the Separation of Law and Morals," *Harvard Law Review* 71 (February 1958): 593–629; Natalya Varlamova, "Legal Positivism and Human Rights," *Social Sciences* 39 (2008): 129–41.

51. Roger Guesnerie, "Pareto Optimality in Non-Convex Economies," *Econometrica* 43 (January 1975): 1–30; Yew-Kwang Ng, "The Economic Theory of Clubs: Pareto Optimality Conditions," *Economica* 40 (August 1973): 219–98; John Rawls, "Justice as Fairness: Political Not Metaphysical," *Philosophy and Public Affairs* 14 (Summer 1985): 223–51.

52. Nozick, *Anarchy, State, and Utopia*, 96–101.

53. Dworkin, *Taking Rights Seriously*, 90–94; Godwin and Wahlke, *Introduction to Political Science*, 22–23; Heywood, *Political Ideas and Concepts*, 144.

54. David Held, *Democracy and the Global Order: From the Modern States to Cosmopolitan Governance* (Palo Alto, CA: Stanford University Press), 125.

55. Robert C. Bartlett, "Political Philosophy and Sophistry: An Introduction to Plato's *Protagoras,*" *American Journal of Political Science* 47 (October 2003): 612–24; W. T. Jones, *The Classical Mind: A History of Western Philosophy,* 2nd ed. (New York: Harcourt Brace Jovanovich, 1970), 108, 215.

56. See, for example, Peter Berger, "Moral Certainty, Theological Doubt," *American Interest* 3 (May/June 2008): 74–81; James Blachowicz, "The Beginning and End of Negative Morality: An Evolutionary Perspective," *Philosophical Forum* 39 (Spring 2008): 21–51; Berit Brogaard, "Moral Contextualism and Moral Relativism," *Philosophical Quarterly* 58 (July 2008): 385–409; Richard Garner, "Abolishing Morality," *Ethical Theory & Moral Practice* 10 (November 2007): 499–513; John Greco, "What's Wrong with Contextualism?" *Philosophical Quarterly* 58 (July 2008): 416–36; Ian Jarvie, "Boudon's European Diagnosis of and Prophylactic against Relativism," *Philosophy of the Social Sciences* 38 (June 2008): 279–92.

57. Dworkin, *Taking Rights Seriously,* 171–73; Dennis F. Thompson, "Moral Responsibility of Public Officials: The Problem of Many Hands," *The American Political Science Review* 74 (December 1980): 905–16.

58. See, for example, Zygmunt Bauman, *Postmodern Ethics* (Oxford, UK: Blackwell, 1993), 16–36; John R. Taylor, *Linguistic Categorization: Prototypes in Linguistic Theory,* 3rd ed. (New York: Oxford University Press, 2003); Ventriss, "The Relevance of Public Ethics to Administration and Policy," 278–80.

59. James Kreines, "Between the Bounds of Experience and Divine Intuition: Kant's Epistemic Limits and Hegel's Ambitions," *Inquiry* 50 (June 2007): 306–34; Kenneth R. Westphal, "Contemporary Epistemology: Kant, Hegel, McDowell," *European Journal of Philosophy* 14 (August 2006): 274–301; James Schmidt, "What Enlightenment Was, What It Still Might Be, and Why Kant May Have Been Right After All," *American Behavioral Science* 49 (January 2006): 647–63.

60. Jean-Francois Lyotard, *The Postmodern Condition: A Report on Knowledge* (Minneapolis: The University of Minnesota Press, 1984); Michael Roberts, "Rethinking the Postmodern Perspective: Excavating the Kantian System to Rebuild Social Theory," *Sociological Theory* 41 (September 2000): 681–98.

61. Friedrich Nietzsche, *Beyond Good and Evil,* trans. Walter Kaufmann (New York: Vintage Books, 1966), 3, 19.

62. Lyotard, *The Postmodern Condition.* For other books on postmodernism, see also: Roland Barthes, *Mythologies* (New York: Hill and Wang, 1957); Jacques Derrida, *Of Grammatology,* trans. G. Spivak (Baltimore: Johns Hopkins University Press, 1976); Jacques Derrida, *Writing and Difference,* trans. A. Bass (Chicago: University of Chicago Press, 1978); Jacques Derrida, *Margins of Philosophy,* trans. A. Bass (Chicago: University of Chicago Press, 1982); Michel Foucault, *The Archaeology of Knowledge,* trans. A. Sheridan (New York: Pantheon

Books, 1972); Michel Foucault, *The Order of Things: An Archaeology of the Human Sciences* (London: Tavistock, 1980).

63. Jacques Martain, *An Introduction to Philosophy* (London and New York: Continuum International Publishing Group, 2005), 56–60.

64. O. C. McSwite, "Postmodernism, Public Administration, and the Public Interest," in *Refounding Public Administration: Modern Paradoxes, Postmodern Challenges*, eds. Gary L. Wamsley and James F. Wolf (Thousand Oaks, CA: Sage Publications, 1996), 198–224; Gary M. Woller and Kelly D. Patterson, "Public Administration Ethics," *American Behavioral Science* 41 (September 1997): 103–18.

65. John P. Burke, *Bureaucratic Responsibility* (Baltimore: Johns Hopkins University Press, 1986), 20–22; Henry Kariel, *The Decline of American Pluralism* (Palo Alto, CA: Stanford University Press, 1961), 51.

CHAPTER 3

1. Richard L. Daft, *Organization Theory and Design*, 8th ed. (Mason, OH: Thomson South-Western, 2004), 373–79; Richard P. Nielsen and Ron Dufresne, "Can Ethical Organizational Character Be Stimulated and Enabled? 'Upbuilding' Dialog as Crisis Management Method," *Journal of Business Ethics* 57 (April 2005): 311–26; Derek S. Pugh, David J. Hickson, and C. Ransom Hinings, "An Empirical Taxonomy of Work Organizations," *Administrative Science Quarterly* 14 (March 1969): 115–26; Montgomery Van Wart and Kathryn G. Denhardt, "Organizational Structure: A Reflection of Society's Values and a Context for Individual Ethics," in *Handbook of Administrative Ethics*, 2nd ed., ed. Terry L. Cooper (New York: Marcel Dekker, 2001), 230–36; Wallace S. Sayre, "Premises of Public Administration: Past and Emerging," *Public Administration Review* 18 (Spring 1958): 104–5; Curtis Ventriss, "The Relevance of Public Ethics to Administration and Policy," in *Handbook of Administrative Ethics*, 2nd ed., ed. Terry L. Cooper (New York: Marcel Dekker, 2001), 281–84; Bart Victor and John B. Cullen, "The Organizational Bases of Ethical Work Climates," *Administrative Science Quarterly* 33 (March 1988): 101–25.

2. Harold F. Gortner, Julianne Mahler, and Jeanne Bell Nicholson, *Organization Theory: A Public Perspective* (Pacific Grove, CA: Brooks/Cole Publishing Company, 1989), 2–5; Peter M. Blau and W. Richard Scott, "The Concept of Formal Organization," in *Classics of Organization Theory*, 2nd ed., ed. Jay M. Shafritz and J. Steven Ott (Pacific Grove, CA: Brooks/Cole Publishing Company, 1987), 187–92; Marianne M. Jennings, "Preventing Organizational Ethical Collapse," *The Journal of Government Financial Management* 53 (Spring 2004): 12–19.

3. Dwight Waldo, *The Enterprise of Public Administration* (Novato, CA: Chandler and Sharp, 1980), 164. See also: Gortner, Mahler, and Nicholson, *Organization Theory: A Public Perspective*, 3–5; James L. Perry and Hal G. Rainey, "The Public-Private Distinction in Organization Theory: A Critique and Research Strategy," *Academy of Management Review* 13 (April 1988): 182–201; Hal G. Rainey and Barry Bozeman, "Comparing Public and Private Organizations: Empirical Research and the Power of the *A Priori*," *Journal of Public Administration Research and Theory* 10 (April 2000): 447–70.

4. Robert T. Golembiewski, *Ironies in Organizational Development*, 2nd ed. (New York: Marcel Dekker, 2003), 197–204; Gortner, Mahler, and Nicholson, *Organization Theory: A Public Perspective*, 395–401; Jennings, "Preventing Organizational Ethical Collapse," 13–18; J. Michael Martinez and William D. Richardson, *Administrative Ethics in the Twenty-first Century* (New York: Peter Lang USA, 2008), 119–27.

5. Kathryn G. Denhardt, *The Ethics of Public Service: Resolving Moral Dilemmas in Public Organizations* (Westport, CT: Greenwood Press, 1988), 33–36; Harold F. Gortner, "Values and Ethics," in *Handbook of Administrative Ethics*, 2nd ed., ed. Terry L. Cooper (New York: Marcel Dekker, 2001), 511–15; April Hejka-Ekins, "Ethics in In-Service Training," in *Handbook of Administrative Ethics*, 2nd ed., ed. Terry L. Cooper (New York: Marcel Dekker, 2001), 86–87; Paul K. J. Sheeran, *Ethics in Public Administration: A Philosophical Approach* (Westport, CT: Praeger, 1993), 83–87.

6. Leigh E. Grosenick and Pamela A. Gibson, "Governmental Ethics and Organizational Culture," in *Handbook of Administrative Ethics*, 2nd ed., ed. Terry L. Cooper (New York: Marcel Dekker, 2001), 243–61; Jennings, "Preventing Organizational Ethical Collapse," 12–13; David M. Levitan, "The Neutrality of the Public Service," *Public Administration Review* 2 (Autumn 1942): 317–23; Van Wart and Denhardt, "Organizational Structure: A Reflection of Society's Values and a Context for Individual Ethics," 233–36; Ventriss, "The Relevance of Public Ethics to Administration and Policy," 281–82.

7. See, for example, Philip R. P. Coelho, James E. McClure, and John A. Spry, "The Social Responsibility of Corporate Management: A Classical Critique," *Mid-American Journal of Business* 18 (Spring 2003): 15–24; Robert Jackall, *Moral Mazes: The World of Corporate Managers* (New York: Oxford University Press, 1988); Brenda E. Joyner and Dinah Payne, "Evolution and Implementation: A Study of Values, Business Ethics and Corporate Social Responsibility," *Journal of Business Ethics* 41 (December 2002): 297–311; Cecily A. Railborn and Dinah Payne, "Corporate Codes of Conduct: A Collective Conscience and Continuum," *Journal of Business Ethics* 9 (November 1990): 879–89.

8. Denhardt, *The Ethics of Public Service*, 24–26; Gortner, Mahler, and Nicholson, *Organization Theory: A Public Perspective*, 342–81; J. Michael

Martinez, "Law versus Ethics: Reconciling Two Concepts of Public Service Ethics," *Administration & Society* 29 (January 1998): 698–99.

9. Chris Argyris, "Organization Man: Rational and Self-Actualizing," *Public Administration Review* 33 (July/August 1973): 354–57; John P. Burke, "Administrative Ethics and Democratic Theory," in *Handbook of Administrative Ethics*, 2nd ed., ed. Terry L. Cooper (New York: Marcel Dekker, 2001), 603–6; Denhardt, *The Ethics of Public Service*, 100–107; T. W. Fletcher, "The Nature of Administrative Loyalty," *Public Administration Review* 18 (Winter 1958): 37–42.

10. Denhardt, *The Ethics of Public Service*, 2–6; Gortner, Mahler, and Nicholson, *Organization Theory: A Public Perspective*, 3–4; Martinez and Richardson, *Administrative Ethics in the Twenty-first Century*, 112–16; Richard J. Stillman II, *Preface to Public Administration: A Search for Themes and Direction*, 2nd ed. (Burke, VA: Chatelaine Press, 1999), 111–12.

11. Martinez and Richardson, *Administrative Ethics in the Twenty-first Century*, 112–13, 164; David H. Rosenbloom, *Public Administration: Understanding Management, Politics, and Law in the Public Sector*, 2nd ed. (New York: Random House, 1989), 204–10; Stillman, *Preface to Public Administration*, 96–97.

12. Gortner, Mahler, and Nicholson, *Organization Theory: A Public Perspective*, 58–64; Andrew Heywood, *Political Ideas and Concepts: An Introduction* (New York: St. Martin's Press, 1994), 89–93; Vincent Ostrom, *The Intellectual Crisis in American Public Administration*, 2nd ed. (Tuscaloosa: The University of Alabama Press, 1989), 25–29; Max Weber, "Bureaucracy," in *Classics of Organization Theory*, 2nd ed., ed. Jay M. Shafritz and J. Steven Ott (Pacific Grove, CA: Brooks/Cole Publishing Company, 1987), 81–87; James Q. Wilson, *Bureaucracy: What Government Agencies Do and Why They Do It* (New York: Basic Books, 1989), 334–35.

13. Brian R. Fry and Lloyd G. Nigro, "Max Weber and U.S. Public Administration: The Administrator as Neutral Servant," *Journal of Management History* 2 (1996): 37–46; Gortner, Mahler, and Nicholson, *Organization Theory: A Public Perspective*, 58, 63; Ostrom, *The Intellectual Crisis in American Public Administration*, 30–31; Wilson, *Bureaucracy*, 131–34.

14. Frederick Winslow Taylor, "The Principles of Scientific Management," in *Classics of Organization Theory*, 2nd ed., ed. Jay M. Shafritz and J. Steven Ott (Pacific Grove, CA: Brooks/Cole Publishing Company, 1987), 74. See also Frederick Taylor, *The Principles of Scientific Management* (New York: Harper & Brothers, 1917).

15. Martinez and Richardson, *Administrative Ethics in the Twenty-first Century*, 113–14; Marshall W. Meyer, "Expertness and Span of Control," *American Sociological Review* 33 (December 1968): 944–51; Ben Nefzger, "The Ideal Type: Some Conceptions and Misconceptions," *Sociological Quarterly* 6 (Spring 1965): 166–74; Wilson, *Bureaucracy*, 334–45.

16. Gortner, Mahler, and Nicholson, *Organization Theory: A Public Perspective*, 64–69; Martinez and Richardson, *Administrative Ethics in the Twenty-first Century*, 117–18; Ostrom, *The Intellectual Crisis in American Public Administration*, 36–41; Herbert A. Simon, "The Proverbs of Administration," in *Classics of Organization Theory*, 2nd ed., ed. Jay M. Shafritz and J. Steven Ott (Pacific Grove, CA: Brooks/Cole Publishing Company, 1987), 102–18; Dwight Waldo, *The Administrative State*, 2nd ed. (New York: Holmes & Meier, 1984), 49–63.

17. Pamela S. Tolbert and Lynne G. Zucker, "Institutional Sources of Change in the Formal Structure of Organizations: The Diffusion of Civil Service Reform, 1880–1935," *Administrative Science Quarterly* 28 (March 1983): 23.

18. Donald F. Kettl, *The Transformation of Governance: Public Administration for Twenty-First Century America* (Baltimore: Johns Hopkins University Press, 2002), 39–43; Ostrom, *The Intellectual Crisis in American Public Administration*, 23–25; David H. Rosenbloom, *Federal Service and the Constitution* (Ithaca, NY: Cornell University Press, 1971), 70–71; Richard Stillman II, *American Bureaucracy: The Core of Modern Government*, 3rd ed. (Belmont, CA: Wadsworth/Thomson, 2004), 158–59.

19. Michael Nelson, "A Short, Ironic History of American National Bureaucracy," *Journal of Politics* 44 (August 1982): 747–78; Patrick Overeem, "The Value of the Dichotomy: Politics, Administration, and the Political Neutrality of Administrators," *Administrative Theory & Praxis* 27 (June 2005): 311–29; Stillman, *American Bureaucracy: The Core of Modern Government*, 49–54; Tolbert and Zucker, "Institutional Sources of Change in the Formal Structure of Organizations," 22–39.

20. Frank Goodnow, *Politics and Administration* (New York: MacMillan, 1900); Frank Goodnow, *The Principles of the Administrative Law of the United States* (New York: G. P. Putnam's Sons, 1905). See also John P. Burke, *Bureaucratic Responsibility* (Baltimore and London: Johns Hopkins University Press, 1986), 10; Carl J. Friedrich, "Public Policy and the Nature of Administrative Responsibility," in *Combating Corruption/Encouraging Ethics: A Sourcebook for Public Service Ethics*, ed. William L. Richter, Frances Burke, and Jameson W. Doig (Washington, DC: American Society for Public Administration, 1990), 43–44; Stillman, *Preface to Public Administration*, 69–70.

21. Martinez and Richardson, *Administrative Ethics in the Twenty-first Century*, 114–15; Stillman, *Preface to Public Administration*, 118–20; Leonard D. White, *Introduction to the Study of Public Administration* (New York: MacMillan, 1926).

22. Herbert J. Storing, "Leonard D. White and the Study of Public Administration," *Public Administration Review* 25 (March 1965): 38.

23. Luther Gulick, "Notes on the Theory of Organization," in *Classics of Organization Theory*, 2nd ed., ed. Jay M. Shafritz and J. Steven Ott (Pacific Grove,

CA: Brooks/Cole Publishing Company, 1987), 96. See also: Luther Gulick and Lyndall Urwick, ed., *Papers on the Science of Administration* (New York: Augustus M. Kelley, 1937); Ostrom, *The Intellectual Crisis in American Public Administration*, 31–36; Stillman, *Preface to Public Administration*, 120–22.

24. Martinez and Richardson, *Administrative Ethics in the Twenty-first Century*, 114–16; Ostrom, *The Intellectual Crisis in American Public Administration*, 113–15; Waldo, *The Administrative State*, 55–59.

25. Charles Goodsell, *The Case for Bureaucracy: A Public Administration Polemic*, 3rd ed. (Chatham, NJ: Chatham House Publishers, 1994), 151–60; Stillman, *Preface to Public Administration*, 111–12. See also Jeffrey L. Pressman and Aaron Wildavsky, *Implementation* (Berkeley: University of California Press, 1973).

26. Steven Ferrey, *Environmental Law: Examples and Explanations* (New York: Aspen Law & Business, 1997), 178–81; Sonya Lunder, Tracey J. Woodruff, and Daniel A. Axelrad, "An Analysis of Candidates for Addition to the Clean Air Act List of Hazardous Air Pollutants," *Journal of the Air & Waste Management Association* 54 (February 2004): 157–71; Thomas O. McGarity, "Hazardous Air Pollutants, Migrating Hot Spots, and the Prospect of Data-Driven Regulation of Complex Industrial Complexes," *Texas Law Review* 86 (June 2008): 1445–92; Elizabeth H. Mikols and Amarjit S. Gill, "The Regulation of Hazardous Air Pollutants Under the Clean Air Act Amendments of 1990," *IEEE Transactions on Industry Applications* 32 (July/August 1996): 760–65; Christopher Moore and Don Courter, "Reducing HAP Emissions to Avoid NESHAP Applicability," *Pollution Engineering* 30 (November 1998): 21–23; Olga L. Moya and Andrew L. Fono, *Federal Environmental Law: The User's Guide* (St. Paul, MN: West Publishing Company, 1997), 271–75.

27. Roger H. Davidson and Walter J. Oleszek, *Congress and Its Members*, 3rd ed. (Washington, DC: Congressional Quarterly Press, 1990), 269–74; Kettl, *The Transformation of Governance*, 149; Martinez and Richardson, *Administrative Ethics in the Twenty-first Century*, 144–45.

28. Goodsell, *The Case For Bureaucracy*, 151–60; Kettl, *The Transformation of Governance*, 100–103; Stillman, *Preface to Public Administration*, 132–33.

29. Kettl, *The Transformation of Governance*, 10–11; Stillman, *Preface to Public Administration*, 111–32; Tolbert and Zucker, "Institutional Sources of Change in the Formal Structure of Organizations," 22–39.

30. Terry L. Cooper, "Big Questions in Administrative Ethics: A Need for Focused, Collaborative Effort," *Public Administration Review* 64 (July/August 2004): 395–407; Denhardt, *The Ethics of Public Service*, 131–58; Sheeran, *Ethics in Public Administration*, 147–53.

31. Waldo, *The Administrative State*, xxxiii–xxxiv.

32. Kettl, *The Transformation of Governance*, 84–85; Stillman, *Preface to Public Administration*, 126–28.

33. Vincent Ostrom, *The Political Theory of a Compound Republic: Designing the American Experiment*, 2nd ed. (Lincoln: University of Nebraska Press, 1987), 31–59; William D. Richardson, *Democracy, Bureaucracy, & Character: Founding Thought* (Lawrence: University Press of Kansas, 1997), 20–26; John A. Rohr, *Ethics for Bureaucrats: An Essay on Law and Values*, 2nd ed. (New York: Marcel Dekker, 1989), 67–68.

34. Cooper, "Big Questions in Administrative Ethics," 395–96; Ostrom, *The Intellectual Crisis in American Public Administration*, 12–19; Stillman, *Preface to Public Administration*, 140–43.

35. Ronald Dworkin, *Taking Rights Seriously* (Cambridge, MA: Harvard University Press, 1978), 81; H. L. A. Hart, *The Concept of Law* (Oxford: Oxford University Press, 1961), 92.

36. Cooper, "Big Questions in Administrative Ethics," 396–97; Richardson, *Democracy, Bureaucracy, & Character*, 20–26; Rohr, *Ethics for Bureaucrats*, 68.

37. Barry Bozeman, *Public Values and Public Interest: Counterbalancing Economic Individualism* (Washington, DC: Georgetown University Press, 2007), 76–80; Kettl, *The Transformation of Governance*, 69–73; Laurence J. O'Toole, Jr., "Different Public Managements? Implications of Structural Context in Hierarchies and Networks," in *Advancing Public Management: New Developments in Theory, Methods, and Practice*, ed. Jeffrey L. Brudney, Laurence J. O'Toole, Jr., and Hal G. Rainey (Washington, DC: Georgetown University Press, 2000), 19–21.

38. Daft, *Organization Theory and Design*, 17–24; Gortner, Mahler, and Nicholson, *Organization Theory: A Public Perspective*, 58–59; Michael E. Milakovich and George J. Gordon, *Public Administration in America* (Belmont, CA: Wadsworth/Thomson, 2004), 154–56; Weber, "Bureaucracy," 81–86.

39. Chris Argyris, "Empowerment: The Emperor's New Clothes," in *Organization Development and Transformation: Managing Effective Change*, 5th ed., ed. Wendell L. French, Cecil H. Bell, Jr., and Robert A. Zawacki (Boston: Irwin, McGraw-Hill, 2000), 452–59; Robert T. Golembiewski, *Men, Management, and Morality: Toward a New Organizational Ethic* (New York: McGraw-Hill, 1965), 65; Van Wart and Denhardt, "Organizational Structure," 235–39.

40. Van Wart and Denhardt, "Organizational Structure," 235–36. See also: Michael Beer and Anna Elise Walton, "Organization Change and Development," *Annual Review of Psychology* 38 (January 1987): 339–67; Carolyn J. Hill and Laurence E. Lynn, Jr., "Is Hierarchical Governance in Decline? Evidence from Empirical Research," *Journal of Public Administration Research and Theory* 15 (April 2005): 187.

41. David W. Cravens, Nigel F. Piercy, and Shannon H. Shipp, "New Organizational Forms for Competing in Highly Dynamic Environments: The

Network Paradigm," *British Journal of Management* 7 (September 1996): 203–18; Louis P. White and Melanie J. Rhodeback, "Ethical Dilemmas in Organization Development: A Cross-Cultural Analysis," *Journal of Business Ethics* 11 (September 1992): 663–70.

42. Linda de Leon and Robert B. Denhardt, "The Political Theory of Reinvention," *Public Administration Review* 60 (March/April 2000): 89–92; Ostrom, *The Intellectual Crisis in American Public Administration*, 97–100; Michael Spicer, "Public Administration, the History of Ideas, and the Reinventing Government Movement," *Public Administration Review* 64 (May/June 2004): 357–59; Larry D. Terry, "From Greek Mythology to the Real World of the New Public Management and Democratic Governance (Terry Responds)," *Public Administration Review* 59 (May/June 1999): 274–76.

43. Daft, *Organization Theory and Design*, 376–86; Van Wart and Denhardt, "Organizational Structure," 230–36; Victor and Cullen, "The Organizational Bases of Ethical Work Climates," 101–25.

44. Donald F. Kettl, *The Global Public Management Revolution*, 2nd ed. (Washington, DC: Brookings Institution Press, 2005), 36–37; Milakovich and Gordon, *Public Administration in America*, 38–41; Stephen Page, "What's New About the New Public Management? Administrative Change in the Human Services," *Public Administration Review* 65 (November 2005): 713–14; James R. Thompson, "Reinvention as Reform: Assessing the National Performance Review," *Public Administration Review* 60 (November/December 2000): 517–18.

45. Linda L. M. Bennett and Stephen Earl Bennett, *Living with Leviathan: Americans Coming to Terms with Big Government* (Lawrence: The University Press of Kansas, 1990), 80–81; Goodsell, *The Case For Bureaucracy*, 9–11; Gortner, Mahler, and Nicholson, *Organization Theory: A Public Perspective*, 112–31.

46. Gerald E. Caiden and Naomi J. Caiden, "Understanding Fraud, Waste, Abuse and Corruption," in *Combating Corruption/Encouraging Ethics: A Sourcebook for Public Service Ethics*, ed. William L. Richter, Francis Burke, and Jameson W. Doig (Washington, DC: The American Society for Public Administration, 1990), 61–69; Terry L. Cooper, *The Responsible Administrator: An Approach to Ethics for the Administrative Role*. 3rd ed. (San Francisco: Jossey-Bass, 1990), 155–86; Gortner, Mahler, and Nicholson, *Organization Theory: A Public Perspective*, 390–92.

47. Daft, *Organization Theory and Design*, 376; Martinez, "Law versus Ethics," 698–701; Richardson, *Democracy, Bureaucracy, & Character*, 11–16.

48. Daft, *Organization Theory and Design*, 376–77; Joshua Halberstam, *Everyday Ethics: Inspired Solutions to Real-Life Dilemmas* (New York: Penguin, 1993), xv–xix.

49. Daft, *Organization Theory and Design*, 377–78; Edgar H. Schein, "Defining Organizational Culture," in *Classics of Organization Theory*, 2nd ed.,

ed. Jay M. Shafritz and J. Steven Ott (Pacific Grove, CA: Brooks/Cole Publishing Company, 1987), 381–95; Alan L. Wilkins and William G. Ouchi, "Efficient Cultures: Exploring the Relationship Between Culture and Organizational Performance," *Administrative Science Quarterly* 28 (September 1983): 468–81; Wilson, *Bureaucracy*, 91–93.

50. Daft, *Organization Theory and Design*, 378; Gortner, Mahler, and Nicholson, *Organization Theory: A Public Perspective*, 100–47; Arthur H. Walker and Jay W. Lorsch, "Organizational Choice: Product versus Function," in *Classics of Organization Theory*, 2nd ed., ed. Jay M. Shafritz and J. Steven Ott (Pacific Grove, CA: Brooks/Cole Publishing Company, 1987), 192–204.

51. Daft, *Organization Theory and Design*, 378–79; Stillman, *Preface to Public Administration*, 67–68; Shann Turnbull, "Stakeholder Democracy: Redesigning the Governance of Firms and Bureaucracies," *Journal of Socio-Economics* 23 (Fall 1994): 321–60.

52. Ralph Clark Chandler, "Deontological Dimensions of Administrative Ethics, Revisited," *Public Personnel Management* 28 (Winter 1999): 512–13; Daft, *Organization Theory and Design*, 379–81; John Rehfuss, *The Job of the Public Manager* (Chicago: The Dorsey Press, 1989), 50–54; Gary Yukl, *Leadership in Organizations*, 5th ed. (Upper Saddle River, NJ: Prentice Hall, 2002), 401–10.

53. Daft, *Organization Theory and Design*, 379–81; Kenneth Kernaghan, "Integrating Values into Public Service: The Values Statement as Centerpiece," *Public Administration Review* 63 (November/December 2003): 711–19; Lorna Storr, "Leading with Integrity: A Qualitative Research Study," *Journal of Health Organization and Management* 18 (2004): 415–34; Neil R. Vance and Brett V. Trani, "The Ethical Grounding to 21st Century Public Leadership," *International Journal of Organization Theory and Behavior* 11 (Fall 2008): 372–80; Yukl, *Leadership in Organizations*, 409–10.

54. O. C. Ferrell and Steven J. Skinner, "Ethical Behavior and Bureaucratic Structure in Marketing Research," *Journal of Marketing Research* 25 (February 1988): 103–9; Laurence E. Lynn, Jr., *Public Management as Art, Science, and Profession* (Chatham, NJ: Chatham House Publishers, 1996), 56–59.

CHAPTER 4

1. Kathryn G. Denhardt, *The Ethics of Public Service: Resolving Moral Dilemmas in Public Organizations* (Westport, CT: Greenwood Press, 1988), 10. See also: John P. Burke, "Administrative Ethics and Democratic Theory," in *Handbook of Administrative Ethics*, 2nd ed., ed. Terry L. Cooper (New York: Marcel Dekker, 2001), 612.

2. J. D. Thompson, *Organizations in Action* (New York: McGraw-Hill, 1967), 28.

3. Quoted in Sally Babidge, Shelley Greer, Rosita Henry, and Christine Pam, "Management Speak: Indigenous Knowledge and Bureaucratic Engagement," *Social Analysis* 51(Winter 2007): 148–64; See also Susan Michie, Marie Johnston, Jill Francis, Wendy Hardeman, and Martin Eccles, "From Theory to Intervention: Mapping Theoretically Derived Behavioural Determinants to Behaviour Change Techniques," *Applied Psychology: An International Review* 57 (October 2008): 660–80.

4. R. Kenneth Godwin and John C. Wahlke, *Introduction to Political Science: Reason, Reflection, and Analysis* (Fort Worth, TX: Harcourt Brace, 1997), 140–46; Richard G. Niemi and Herbert F. Weisberg, "What Determines the Vote?," in *Controversies in Voting Behavior*, 3rd ed., ed. Richard G. Niemi and Herbert F. Weisberg (Washington, DC: Congressional Quarterly Press, 1993), 137–51.

5. Thomas J. Barth, "Administering the Public Interest: The Facilitative Role for Public Administrators," in *Refounding Public Administration: Modern Paradoxes, Postmodern Challenges*, ed. Gary L. Wamsley and James F. Wolf (Thousand Oaks, CA: Sage Publications, 1996), 172–73; Donald F. Kettl, *The Global Public Management Revolution*, 2nd ed. (Washington, DC: Brookings Institution Press, 2005), 52–54; Richard J. Stillman II, *Preface to Public Administration: A Search for Themes and Direction*, 2nd ed. (Burke, VA: Chatelaine Press, 1999), 100.

6. Charles Goodsell, *The Case For Bureaucracy: A Public Administration Polemic*, 3rd ed. (Chatham, NJ: Chatham House Publishers, 1994), 151–60; Stillman, *Preface to Public Administration*, 40–41; Lisa Weinberg, "Understanding Social Process: The Key to Democratic Government," in *Refounding Public Administration: Modern Paradoxes, Postmodern Challenges*, ed. Gary L. Wamsley and James F. Wolf (Thousand Oaks, CA: Sage Publications, 1996), 290–92.

7. Carolyn Bourdeaux, "Politics versus Professionalism: The Effect of Institutional Structure on Democratic Decision-making in a Contested Policy Area," *Journal of Public Administration Research and Theory* 18 (July 2008): 349–73; Kettl, *The Global Public Management Revolution*, 52–54; Constance A. Nathanson, "Social Movements as Catalysts for Policy Change: The Case of Smoking and Guns," *Journal of Health Politics, Policy and Law* 24 (1999): 421–88.

8. D. D. Riley, *Controlling the Federal Bureaucracy* (Philadelphia: Temple University Press, 1987), 60–63. See also: Goodsell, *The Case For Bureaucracy*, 15–17.

9. Denhardt, *The Ethics of Public Service*, 100.

10. Terry L. Cooper, *The Responsible Administrator: An Approach to Ethics for the Administrative Role*, 3rd ed. (San Francisco: Jossey-Bass, 1990), 35–44;

Goodsell, *The Case For Bureaucracy*, 159–60; Stillman, *Preface to Public Administration*, 189–91.

11. J. Michael Martinez, "Law versus Ethics: Reconciling Two Concepts of Public Service Ethics," *Administration & Society* 29 (January 1998): 696–704; Gerald J. Postema, "Moral Responsibility in Professional Ethics," *New York University Law Review* 55 (1980): 63–89.

12. Dwight Waldo, *The Administrative State*, 2nd ed. (New York: Holmes & Meier, 1984), 103–6. See also: Barth, "Administering the Public Interest," 172–86; Cooper, *The Responsible Administrator*, 58–76.

13. Cooper, *The Responsible Administrator*, 166–67; Kenneth J. Meier and Laurence J. O'Toole, Jr., "Political Control versus Bureaucratic Values: Reframing the Debate," *Public Administration Review* 66 (March/April 2006): 177–92; Patrick Overeem, "The Value of the Dichotomy: Politics, Administration, and the Political Neutrality of Administrators," *Administrative Theory & Praxis* 27 (June 2005): 311–29.

14. Richard M. Cyert and James G. March, *A Behavioral Theory of the Firm* (Englewood Cliffs, NJ: Prentice-Hall, 1963); James G. March, ed., *Handbook of Organizations* (Chicago: Rand McNally, 1965); Robert K. Merton, *On Theoretical Sociology* (New York: The Free Press, 1967), 39.

15. Richard C. Feiock and Jered B. Carr, "Incentives, Entrepreneurs, and Boundary Change," *Urban Affairs Review* 36 (January 2001): 382–405; W. R. Mack, Deanna Green, and Arnold Vedlitz, "Innovation and Implementation in the Public Sector: An Examination of Public Entrepreneurship," *Review of Policy Research* 25 (May 2008): 233–52.

16. Court Carney, "The Contested Image of Nathan Bedford Forrest," *Journal of Southern History* 67 (August 2001), 601–29; Jack Hurst, "Tennessee Turning Point: Nathan Bedford Forrest Took Matters into His Own Hands at Fort Donelson—And a Legend Was Born," *America's Civil War* 21 (January 2009): 28–37; Charles G. Jones, "Forrest: A Mixture of Genius and Guile," *Washington Times*, June 3, 1995, B3; J. Michael Martinez, *Carpetbaggers, Cavalry, and the Ku Klux Klan: Exposing the Invisible Empire During Reconstruction* (Lanham, MD: Rowman & Littlefield, 2007), 18–23; Andrew Lytle, *Bedford Forrest and His Critter Company* (New York: McDowell, Obolensky, 1960), 382–83.

17. Drew Gilpin Faust, *This Republic of Suffering: Death and the American Civil War* (New York: Alfred A. Knopf, 2008), 43–55; William A. Gladstone, *United States Colored Troops* (Gettysburg, PA: Thomas Publications, 1990), 104; James M. McPherson, *Battle Cry of Freedom: The Civil War Era* (New York: Oxford University Press, 1988), 788–96; Edgar A. Toppin, "African Americans and the Confederacy," in *Macmillan Information Now Encyclopedia: The Confederacy*, ed. Richard N. Current (New York: Simon & Schuster Macmillan Reference USA, 1993), 1–5.

18. Brian Steel Wills, *A Battle from the Start: The Life of Nathan Bedford Forrest* (New York: HarperCollins, 1992), 182.

19. John Cimprich and Robert C. Mainfort, Jr., "Fort Pillow Revisited: New Evidence About an Old Controversy," *Civil War History* 28 (Winter 1982): 293–306; Faust, *This Republic of Suffering*, 44–45, 53–54; Shelby Foote, *The Civil War, A Narrative: Red River to Appomattox* (New York: Vintage, 1986), 110; Jack Hurst, *Nathan Bedford Forrest: A Biography* (New York: Knopf, 1993), 174; Wills, *A Battle from the Start*, 182.

20. Carol Becker, "Pilgrimage to My Lai: Social Memory and the Making of Art," *Art Journal* 62 (Winter 2003): 50–65; Kendrick Oliver, "Atrocity, Authenticity and American Exceptionalism: (Ir)rationalising the Massacre at My Lai," *Journal of American Studies* 37 (August 2003): 247–68; Lt. Gen. W. R. Peers, USA, *The My Lai Inquiry* (New York: W. W. Norton, 1979), 3–11.

21. Truda Gray and Brian Martin, "My Lai: The Struggle Over Outrage," *Peace & Change* 33 (January 2008): 90–113; Peers, *The My Lai Inquiry*, 221–56.

22. Becker, "Pilgrimage to My Lai," 51–53; Oliver, "Atrocity, Authenticity and American Exceptionalism," 247–68; Peers, *The My Lai Inquiry*, 221–56.

23. David Cesarani, *Becoming Eichmann: Rethinking the Life, Crimes, and Trial of a "Desk Murderer"* (New York: Da Capo Books, 2004), 349–50; Carsten Bagge Laustsen and Rasmus Ugilt, "Eichmann's Kant," *Journal of Speculative Philosophy* 21 (2007): 166–80; Amit Pinchevski and Roy Brand, "Holocaust Perversions: The Stalags Pulp Fiction and the Eichmann Trial," *Critical Studies in Media Communication* 24 (December 2007): 387–407.

24. Quoted in Cesarani, *Becoming Eichmann*, 281. See also: Laustsen and Ugilt, "Eichmann's Kant," 166–68.

25. Paul Formosa, "Is Radical Evil Banal? Is Banal Evil Radical?," *Philosophy and Social Criticism* 33 (September 2007): 717–35; Peter Schotten, "Hannah Arendt's Eichmann Reconsidered," *Modern Age* 49 (Spring 2007): 139–47.

26. Elizabeth Mehren, "She's on Activist Duty Now: Mary Ann Wright Quit a 30-Year Army and Diplomatic Career in Protest of the Iraq War; She's Now a Soldier for the Antiwar Movement," *Los Angeles Times*, January 20, 2006, A1.

27. Mary Ann Wright, "Resigning as Resistance," in *America and the World: The Double Bind*, ed. Majid Tehranian and Kevin P. Clements (East Brunswick, NJ: Transaction Publishers, 2005), 91–94.

28. Wright, "Resigning as Resistance," 91. See also: Shane Harris, "Diplomat Resigns to Protest War," Government Executive.com (21 March 2003), http://www.govexec.com/dailyfed/0303/032103wright.htm (accessed January 20, 2009).

29. Wright, "Resigning as Resistance," 93. See also: J. C. Reindl, "Iraq War Critic Who Was U.S. Colonel to Speak at UT," *The [Toledo] Blade*, March 10, 2008, B2.

30. Mehren, "She's on Activist Duty Now," A1; Wright, "Resigning as Resistance," 93–94.

31. Quoted in Harris, "Diplomat Resigns to Protest War." See also: Mehren, "She's on Activist Duty Now," A1.

32. Harris, "Diplomat Resigns to Protest War"; Mehren, "She's on Activist Duty Now," A1; Reindl, "Iraq War Critic Who Was U.S. Colonel to Speak at UT," B2; Robin Wright, "Rice Declines to Give Senators Timeline for Iraq Withdrawal," *The Washington Post*, October 20, 2005, A22.

33. Wright, "Resigning as Resistance," 96.

34. Steve Barnes, "Southwest Texas: 12 Arrested in Protest Near Bush Ranch," *The New York Times*, November 24, 2005, A30; Reindl, "Iraq War Critic Who Was U.S. Colonel to Speak at UT," B2; Wright, "Rice Declines to Give Senators Timeline for Iraq Withdrawal," A22.

35. Barnes, "Southwest Texas," A30; Kari Browne, "A Diplomat's Battle," *Ms.* 13 (Winter 2003): 22; Mehren, "She's on Activist Duty Now," A1; Reindl, "Iraq War Critic Who Was U.S. Colonel to Speak at UT," B2; Wright, "Rice Declines to Give Senators Timeline for Iraq Withdrawal," A22.

36. Cooper, *The Responsible Administrator*, 58–76; Denhardt, *The Ethics of Public Service*, 99–130; Ciaran O'Kelly and Melvin J. Dubnick, "Taking Tough Choices Seriously: Public Administration and Individual Moral Agency," *Journal of Public Administration Research and Theory* 16 (July 2006): 393–415.

37. Ronald Dworkin, *Taking Rights Seriously* (Cambridge, MA: Harvard University Press, 1978), 14–22; H. L. A. Hart, *The Concept of Law* (Oxford: Oxford University Press, 1961), 89–96; Martinez, "Law versus Ethics," 691–94.

38. O'Kelly and Dubnick, "Taking Tough Choices Seriously," 394–96; Debra Stewart, "Ethics and the Profession of Public Administration: The Moral Responsibility of Individuals in Public Sector Organizations," *Public Administration Quarterly* 45 (Winter 1985): 487–95; Susan Wakefield, "Ethics and the Public Service: A Case for Individual Responsibility," *Public Administration Review* (November/December 1976): 661–66.

39. James S. Bowman, "Whistle Blowing in the Public Sector: An Overview of the Issues," in *Combating Corruption/Encouraging Ethics: A Sourcebook for Public Service Ethics*, ed. William L. Richter, Francis Burke, and Jameson W. Doig (Washington, DC: The American Society for Public Administration, 1990), 195–202; Terry L. Cooper, "Hierarchy, Virtue, and the Practice of Public Administration: A Perspective for Normative Ethics," *Public Administration Review* 47 (July/August 1987): 320–28; Gregory D. Foster, "Law, Morality, and the Public Servant," *Public Administration Review* (January/February 1981): 29–34; Mary P. Rowe, "Organizational Response to Assessed Risk: Complaint Channels," in *Combating Corruption/Encouraging Ethics: A Sourcebook for Public Service Ethics*, ed. William L. Richter, Francis Burke, and Jameson W. Doig (Washington, DC: The American Society for Public Administration, 1990), 194–95.

40. Stephen K. Bailey, "Ethics and the Public Service," *Public Administration Review* 24 (December 1964): 234–43; John A. Rohr, *Ethics for Bureaucrats: An Essay on Law and Values*, 2nd ed. (New York: Marcel Dekker, 1989), 54–56; Wakefield, "Ethics and the Public Service," 661–66.

CHAPTER 5

1. Charles J. Fox, "The Use of Philosophy in Administrative Ethics," in *Handbook of Administrative Ethics*, 2nd ed., ed. Terry L. Cooper (New York: Marcel Dekker, 2001), 116. See also F. Neil Brady, "'Publics' Administration and the Ethics of Particularity," *Public Administration Review* 63 (September/October 2003): 525–26; Michael E. Milakovich and George J. Gordon, *Public Administration in America* (Belmont, CA: Wadsworth/Thomson, 2004); David H. Rosenbloom, *Public Administration: Understanding Management, Politics, and Law in the Public Sector*, 2nd ed. (New York: Random House, 1989); Keith F. Snider, "Expertise or Experimenting?," *Administration & Society* 32 (July 2000): 329–30.

2. Martin Diamond, "Democracy and *The Federalist*: A Reconsideration of the Framers' Intent," *American Political Science Review* 53 (March 1959): 52–68; Gottfried Dietze, *The Federalist: A Classic on Federalism and Free Government* (Westport, CT: Greenwood Press, 1960), 316; David F. Epstein, *The Political Theory of the Federalist* (Chicago: The University of Chicago Press, 1984), 4–5, 66; Maynard Smith, "Reason, Passion, and Political Freedom in *The Federalist*," *Journal of Politics* 22 (August 1960): 525–44; Morton White, *Philosophy, The Federalist, and the Constitution* (New York: Oxford University Press, 1987), 57, 73; Garry Wills, *Explaining America: The Federalist* (Garden City, NY: Doubleday & Company, Inc., 1981), 270.

3. Terry L. Cooper, "Big Questions in Administrative Ethics: A Need for Focused, Collaborative Effort," *Public Administration Review* 64 (July/August 2004): 395–407; Terry L. Cooper, "Hierarchy, Virtue, and the Practice of Public Administration: A Perspective for Normative Ethics," *Public Administration Review* 47 (July/August 1987): 320–28; H. George Frederickson, "Ethics and the New Managerialism," *Public Administration & Management: An Interactive Journal* 4 (1999): 299–324; John A. Rohr, "On Cooper's 'Big Questions,'" *Public Administration Review* 64 (July/August 2004): 408–9.

4. Brady, "'Publics' Administration and the Ethics of Particularity," 525–34; Fox, "The Use of Philosophy in Administrative Ethics," 115–17; George A. Graham, "Ethical Guidelines for Public Administrators: Observations on Rules of the Game," *Public Administration Review* 34 (January/February 1974): 90–92.

5. Sarah R. Adkins, "Democracy's Quiet Virtues," in *Ethics and Character: The Pursuit of Democratic Virtues*, ed. William D. Richardson, J. Michael

Martinez, and Kerry R. Stewart (Durham, NC: Carolina Academic Press, 1998), 210–18; Kathryn G. Denhardt, "Character Ethics and the Transformation of Governance," *International Journal of Public Administration* 17 (October 1994): 2165–93; Richard T. Green, "Character Ethics and Administration," *International Journal of Public Administration* 17 (October 1994): 2137–64; William D. Richardson and J. Michael Martinez, "Introduction," in *Ethics and Character: The Pursuit of Democratic Virtues*, ed. William D. Richardson, J. Michael Martinez, and Kerry R. Stewart (Durham, NC: Carolina Academic Press, 1998), 5–17; James Q. Wilson, "The Rediscovery of Character: Private Virtue and Public Policy," *The Public Interest* 81 (Fall 1985): 3–16.

6. American Society for Public Administration, "ASPA Workbook: Responsibility and Accountability," in *Combating Corruption/Encouraging Ethics: A Sourcebook for Public Service Ethics*, ed. William L. Richter, Francis Burke, and Jameson W. Doig (Washington, DC: The American Society for Public Administration, 1990), 54–55; Terry L. Cooper, *The Responsible Administrator: An Approach to Ethics for the Administrative Role*, 3rd ed. (San Francisco: Jossey-Bass, 1990), 58–82; Melvin J. Dubnick, "Accountability and Ethics: Reconsidering the Relationships," *International Journal of Organization Theory and Behavior* 6 (Fall 2003): 405–41.

7. Kathryn G. Denhardt, *The Ethics of Public Service: Resolving Moral Dilemmas in Public Organizations* (Westport, CT: Greenwood Press, 1988), 140–43; J. Michael Martinez and William D. Richardson, *Administrative Ethics in the Twenty-first Century* (New York: Peter Lang USA, 2008), 96–101; Patrick J. Sheeran, *Ethics in Public Administration: A Philosophical Approach* (Westport, CT: Praeger, 1993), 83–86.

8. Terry L. Cooper, "The Emergence of Administrative Ethics as a Field of Study in the United States," in *Handbook of Administrative Ethics*, 2nd ed., ed. Terry L. Cooper (New York: Marcel Dekker, 2001), 24–28; Lloyd G. Nigro and William D. Richardson, "Between Citizen and Administrator: Administrative Ethics and *PAR*," *Public Administration Review* 50 (November-December 1990): 623–35; Montgomery Van Wart, "The Sources of Ethical Decision-making for Individuals in the Public Sector," *Public Administration Review* 56 (November/December 1996): 525–33.

9. William D. Richardson, *Democracy, Bureaucracy, & Character: Founding Thought* (Lawrence: University Press of Kansas, 1997), 67.

10. William L. Richter, Frances Burke, and Jameson W. Doig, "Combating Unethical Behavior: What to Do When the Angels Are Missing," in *Combating Corruption/Encouraging Ethics: A Sourcebook for Public Service Ethics*, ed. William L. Richter, Francis Burke, and Jameson W. Doig (Washington, DC: The American Society for Public Administration, 1990), 150; Diane E. Yoder and Kathryn G. Denhardt, "Ethics Education in Public Affairs: Preparing Graduates

for Workplace Moral Dilemmas," in *Handbook of Administrative Ethics*, 2nd ed., ed. Terry L. Cooper (New York: Marcel Dekker, 2001), 61.

11. David John Farmer, "Against Myopia: Public Administration and Ethics," *Journal of Public Affairs Education* 4 (January 1998): 34; John R. Walton, James M. Stearns, and Charles T. Crespy, "Integrating Ethics into the Public Administration Curriculum: A Three-Step Process," *Journal of Policy Analysis and Management* 16 (Summer 1997): 470–83.

12. Ernest A. Engelbert, "University Education for Public Policy Analysis," *Public Administration Review* 37 (May/June 1977): 228–36; Donald C. Menzel, "To Act Ethically: The What, Why, and How of Ethics Pedagogy," *Journal of Public Affairs Education* 4 (January 1998): 11–18; Sharon Daloz Parks, "Is It Too Late? Young Adults and the Formation of Professional Ethics," in *Can Ethics Be Taught? Perspectives, Challenges, and Approaches at Harvard Business School*, ed. Thomas R. Piper, Mary C. Gentile, and Sharon Daloz Parks (Boston, MA: Harvard Business School Press), 13–72; Diane E. Yoder and Kathryn G. Denhardt, "Ethics Education in Public Affairs: Preparing Graduates for Workplace Moral Dilemmas," in *Handbook of Administrative Ethics*, 2nd ed., ed. Terry L. Cooper (New York: Marcel Dekker, 2001), 65–67.

13. Donald C. Menzel, "Teaching Ethics and Values in Public Administration: Are We Making a Difference?," *Public Administration Review* 57 (May/June 1997): 229–30. See also: Bayard Catron, "Teaching Ethics, Teaching Ethically," in *Combating Corruption/Encouraging Ethics: A Sourcebook for Public Service Ethics*, ed. William L. Richter, Francis Burke, and Jameson W. Doig (Washington, DC: The American Society for Public Administration, 1990), 283–89; April Hejka-Ekins, "Teaching Ethics in Public Administration," *Public Administration Review* 48 (September-October 1988): 885–91; John A. Perkins, "Higher Education and Training for Administrative Careers," *Public Administration Review* 18 (January/February 1958): 14–20.

14. N. Lee Cooper, "President's Message—The Harlan Standard: Former Associate Justice Can Teach Us the Value of Reasoned Dissent," *ABA Journal* 83 (June 1997): 8.

15. Richard L. Chapman and Frederic N. Cleaveland, "The Changing Character of the Public Service and the Administrator of the 1980s," *Public Administration Review* 33 (July/August 1973): 364–65; Cooper, "The Emergence of Administrative Ethics as a Field of Study in the United States," 4–5; William L. Richter, Frances Burke, and Jameson W. Doig, "The Timely, Ambiguous, and Fragile Nature of Ethical Concerns" in *Combating Corruption/Encouraging Ethics: A Sourcebook for Public Service Ethics*, ed. William L. Richter, Francis Burke, and Jameson W. Doig (Washington, DC: The American Society for Public Administration, 1990), 1–6.

16. Talcott Parsons, "Suggestions for a Sociological Approach to the Theory of Organizations," in *Classics of Organization Theory*, 2nd ed., ed. Jay M. Shafritz and J. Steven Ott (Pacific Grove, CA: Brooks/Cole Publishing Company, 1987), 134. See also: Edgar H. Schein, "Organizational Culture," in *Organization Development and Transformation: Managing Effective Change*, 5th ed., ed. Wendell L. French, Cecil H. Bell, Jr., and Robert A. Zawacki (Boston: Irwin, McGraw-Hill, 2000), 127–41; John Van Maanen, "People Processing: Strategies of Organizational Socialization," *Organizational Dynamics* 7 (Summer 1978): 18–36.

17. Leigh E. Grosenick and Pamela A. Gibson, "Governmental Ethics and Organizational Culture," in *Handbook of Administrative Ethics*, 2nd ed., ed. Terry L. Cooper (New York: Marcel Dekker, 2001), 248–49; Richard A. Loverd, "Styles and Strategies of Managing Openness," in *Combating Corruption/ Encouraging Ethics: A Sourcebook for Public Service Ethics*, ed. William L. Richter, Francis Burke, and Jameson W. Doig (Washington, DC: The American Society for Public Administration, 1990), 222; Vincent Ostrom, *The Intellectual Crisis in American Public Administration*, 2nd ed. (Tuscaloosa: The University of Alabama Press, 1989), 38–39.

18. Peter M. Blau and W. Richard Scott, "The Concept of Formal Organization," in *Classics of Organization Theory*, 2nd ed., ed. Jay M. Shafritz and J. Steven Ott (Pacific Grove, CA: Brooks/Cole Publishing Company, 1987), 187–92; Cooper, *The Responsible Administrator*, 40–44; Harold F. Gortner, Julianne Mahler, and Jeanne Bell Nicholson, *Organization Theory: A Public Perspective* (Pacific Grove, CA: Brooks/Cole Publishing Company, 1989), 69–76.

19. Denhardt, *The Ethics of Public Service*, 103. See also: Susan Michie, Marie Johnston, Jill Francis, Wendy Hardeman, and Martin Eccles, "From Theory to Intervention: Mapping Theoretically Derived Behavioural Determinants to Behaviour Change Techniques," *Applied Psychology: An International Review* 57 (October 2008): 660–80; J. D. Thompson, *Organizations in Action* (New York: McGraw-Hill, 1967), 28.

20. American Society for Public Administration, "ASPA Code of Ethics and Guidelines," in *Combating Corruption/Encouraging Ethics: A Sourcebook for Public Service Ethics*, ed. William L. Richter, Francis Burke, and Jameson W. Doig (Washington, DC: The American Society for Public Administration, 1990), 265–69; James S. Bowman, "From Codes of Conduct to Codes of Ethics: The ASPA Case," in *Handbook of Administrative Ethics*, 2nd ed., ed. Terry L. Cooper (New York: Marcel Dekker, 2001), 341–44; Cooper, *The Responsible Administrator*, 139–40; Denhardt, *The Ethics of Public Service*, 127–28; J. Michael Martinez, "Law versus Ethics: Reconciling Two Concepts of Public Service Ethics," *Administration & Society* 29 (January 1998): 705–17.

21. Richard Blake, Jill A. Grob, and Donald H. Potenski, "The Nature and Scope of State Government Codes of Ethics," *Public Productivity & Management Review* 21 (June 1998): 453–59; Ralph Clark Chandler, "The Problem of Moral Reasoning in American Public Administration: The Case for a Code of Ethics," *Public Administration Review* 43 (January/February 1983): 32–39; Peter J. Dean, "Making Codes of Ethics 'Real,'" *Journal of Business Ethics* 11 (April 1992): 285–90; Jeremy F. Plant, "Codes of Ethics," in *Handbook of Administrative Ethics*, 2nd ed., ed. Terry L. Cooper (New York: Marcel Dekker, 2001), 309–33; Dennis Thompson, "The Possibility of Administrative Ethics," *Public Administration Review*, 45 (September/October 1985): 555–61; Dennis Thompson, "Moral Responsibility of Public Officials: The Problem of Many Hands," *American Political Science Review* 74 (December 1980): 905–16; Greg Wood and Malcolm Rimmer, "Codes of Ethics: What Are They Really and What Should They Be?," *International Journal of Value-Based Management* 16 (May 2003): 181–95.

22. Benjamin Freedman, "A Meta-Ethics for Professional Morality," *Ethics* 89 (October 1978): 1–19; Alan Gewirth, "Professional Ethics: The Separatist Thesis," *Ethics* 96 (January 1986): 282–300; Philip H. Jos and Mark E. Tompkins, "Administrative Practice and the Waning Promise of Professionalism for Public Administration," *American Review of Public Administration* 25 (September 1995): 207–29.

23. Guy B. Adams, "Ethics and the Chimera of Professionalism: The Historical Context of an Oxymoronic Relationship," *American Review of Public Administration* 23 (June 1993): 117–39; John Ladd, "The Quest for a Code of Professional Ethics: An Intellectual and Moral Confusion," in *Combating Corruption/Encouraging Ethics: A Sourcebook for Public Service Ethics*, ed. William L. Richter, Francis Burke, and Jameson W. Doig (Washington, DC: The American Society for Public Administration, 1990), 271–74; Darrell L. Pugh, "Professionalism in Public Administration: Problems, Perspectives, and the Role of the ASPA," *Public Administration Review* 49 (January/February 1989): 1–8; Dean L. Yarwood, "The Ethical World of Organizational Professionals and Scientists," *Public Administration Quarterly* 8 (Winter 1985): 461–86.

24. David M. Levitan, "The Neutrality of the Public Service," *Public Administration Review* 2 (Autumn 1942): 317–23; Francis E. Rourke, "Responsiveness and Neutral Competence in American Bureaucracy," *Public Administration Review* 52 (November/December 1992): 539–46; Debra Stewart, "Ethics and the Profession of Public Administration: The Moral Responsibility of Individuals in Public Sector Organizations," *Public Administration Quarterly* 45 (Winter 1985): 487–95.

25. Brady, "'Publics' Administration and the Ethics of Particularity," 525–26; Cooper, *The Responsible Administrator*, 85–90; Martinez, "Law versus Ethics,"

704–12; Gary M. Woller and Kelly D. Patterson, "Public Administration Ethics," *American Behavioral Science* 41 (September 1997): 103–18; Neil R. Vance and Brett V. Trani, "The Ethical Grounding to 21st Century Public Leadership," *International Journal of Organization Theory and Behavior* 11 (Fall 2008): 372–80.

26. Denhardt, *The Ethics of Public Service*, 85–98; Montgomery Van Wart, "The Sources of Ethical Decision-making for Individuals in the Public Sector," *Public Administration Review* 56 (November/ December 1996): 526–27; Dennis P. Wittmer, "Ethical Decision-Making," in *Handbook of Administrative Ethics*, 2nd ed., ed. Terry L. Cooper (New York: Marcel Dekker, 2001), 491–92.

27. Harold F. Gortner, *Ethics for Public Managers* (Westport, CT: Praeger, 1991), 59–79; Martinez, "Law versus Ethics," 698–718; John A. Rohr, *Ethics for Bureaucrats: An Essay on Law and Values*, 2nd ed. (New York: Marcel Dekker, 1989), 73–84; Van Wart, "The Sources of Ethical Decision-making for Individuals in the Public Sector," 528–29; Natalya Varlamova, "Legal Positivism and Human Rights," *Social Sciences* 39 (2008): 129–41.

28. Gortner, *Ethics for Public Managers*, 37–52; John Rehfuss, *The Job of the Public Manager* (Chicago: The Dorsey Press, 1989), 263–77; James Q. Wilson, *Bureaucracy: What Government Agencies Do and Why They Do It* (New York: Basic Books, 1989), 128–29.

29. John P. Burke, "Administrative Ethics and Democratic Theory," in *Handbook of Administrative Ethics*, 2nd ed., ed. Terry L. Cooper (New York: Marcel Dekker, 2001), 617–18.

30. Aristotle, *The Nicomachean Ethics*, trans. David Ross (New York and Oxford: Oxford University Press, 1980), 142–43.

SELECTED REFERENCES

Adams, Guy B. 1993. "Ethics and the Chimera of Professionalism: The Historical Context of an Oxymoronic Relationship." *American Review of Public
Administration* 23 (June): 117–39.

Adkins, Sarah R. 1998. "Democracy's Quiet Virtues." Pp. 203–23 in *Ethics and
Character: The Pursuit of Democratic Virtues*, ed. William D. Richardson,
J. Michael Martinez, and Kerry R. Stewart. Durham, N.C.: Carolina Aca-
demic Press.

Adler, Mortimer J., and Seymour Cain. 1962. *Ethics: The Study of Moral Values*.
Chicago: Encyclopedia Britannica, Inc.

American Society for Public Administration. 1990. "ASPA Code of Ethics and
Guidelines." Pp. 265–69 in *Combating Corruption/Encouraging Ethics: A
Sourcebook for Public Service Ethics*, ed. William L. Richter, Francis Burke,
and Jameson W. Doig. Washington, D.C.: The American Society for Public Administration.

———. "ASPA Workbook: Responsibility and Accountability." 1990. Pp. 54–55
in *Combating Corruption/Encouraging Ethics: A Sourcebook for Public
Service Ethics*, ed. William L. Richter, Francis Burke, and Jameson W.
Doig. Washington, D.C.: The American Society for Public Administration.

Andreoni, James. 1995 "Warm-Glow versus Cold-Pickle: The Effects of Positive
and Negative Framing on Cooperation in Experiments." *The Quarterly
Journal of Economics* 110 (February): 1–21.

Appleby, Paul H. 1952. *Morality and Administration in Democratic Government*. Baton Rouge: Louisiana State University Press.

Argyris, Chris. 2000. "Empowerment: The Emperor's New Clothes." Pp. 452–59 in *Organization Development and Transformation: Managing Effective Change*, 5th Ed., ed. Wendell L. French, Cecil H. Bell, Jr., and Robert A. Zawacki. Boston: Irwin, McGraw-Hill.

———. 1973. "Organization Man: Rational and Self-Actualizing." *Public Administration Review* 33 (July/August): 354–57.

Aristotle. 1980. *The Nicomachean Ethics*. Translated by David Ross. New York and Oxford: Oxford University Press.

Babidge, Sally; Shelley Greer; Rosita Henry; and Christine Pam. 2007. "Management Speak: Indigenous Knowledge and Bureaucratic Engagement." *Social Analysis* 51 (Winter): 148–64.

Bailey, Stephen K. 1964. "Ethics and the Public Service." *Public Administration Review* 24 (December): 234–43.

Barber, James David. 1995. *The Book of Democracy*. Englewood Cliffs, N.J.: Prentice Hall.

Barnes, Steve. 2005. "Southwest Texas: 12 Arrested in Protest Near Bush Ranch." P. A30 in *The New York Times*.

Barnett, A. H. 1980 "The Pigouvian Tax Rule Under Monopoly." *The American Economic Review* 70 (December): 1037–41.

Barth, Thomas J. 1996. "Administering the Public Interest: The Facilitative Role for Public Administrators." Pp. 168–97 in *Refounding Public Administration: Modern Paradoxes, Postmodern Challenges*, ed. Gary L. Wamsley and James F. Wolf. Thousand Oaks, Ca.: Sage Publications.

Barthes, Roland. 1957. *Mythologies*. New York: Hill and Wang.

Bartlett, Robert C. "Political Philosophy and Sophistry: An Introduction to Plato's *Protagoras*." *American Journal of Political Science* 47 (October): 612–24.

Bass, Jack, and Walter DeVries. 2003. *The Transformation of Southern Politics: Social Change and Political Consequence Since 1945*. Athens: University Press of Georgia.

Baum, Lawrence. 1989. *The Supreme Court*. 3d. Ed. Washington, D.C.: Congressional Quarterly Press.

Bauman, Zygmunt. 1993. *Postmodern Ethics*. Oxford, U.K: Blackwell.

Becker, Carol. 2003. "Pilgrimage to My Lai: Social Memory and the Making of Art." *Art Journal* (Winter 2003) 62: 50–65.

Beer, Michael, and Anna Elise Walton. 1987. "Organization Change and Development." *Annual Review of Psychology* 38 (January): 339–67.

Bennett, Linda L. M., and Stephen Earl Bennett. 1990. *Living with Leviathan: Americans Coming to Terms with Big Government*. Lawrence: The University Press of Kansas.

Bentham, Jeremy. 1948. *An Introduction to the Principles of Morals and Legislation*. New York: Hafner.

Bergek, Anna; Staffan Jacobsson; and Bjorn A. Sanden. 2008. "'Legitimation' and 'Development' of Positive Externalities': Two Key Processes in the

Formation Phase of Technological Innovation Systems." *Technology Analysis & Strategic Management* 20 (September): 575–92.

Berger, Peter. 2008. "Moral Certainty, Theological Doubt." *American Interest* 3 (May/June): 74–81.

Berns, Laurence. 1972. "Thomas Hobbes." Pp. 370–94 in *History of Political Philosophy*, 2d. Ed. ed. Leo Strauss and Joseph Cropsey. Chicago: Rand McNally & Company.

Blachowicz, James. 2008. "The Beginning and End of Negative Morality: An Evolutionary Perspective." *Philosophical Forum* 39 (Spring): 21–51.

Black, Henry Campbell. 1979. *Black's Law Dictionary*, 5th ed. St. Paul, Minn.: West Publishing Company.

Blake, Richard; Jill A. Grob; and Donald H. Potenski. 1998. "The Nature and Scope of State Government Codes of Ethics." *Public Productivity & Management Review* 21 (June): 453–59.

Blau, Peter M., and W. Richard Scott. 1987. "The Concept of Formal Organization." Pp. 187–92 in *Classics of Organization Theory*, 2d. Ed. ed. Jay M. Shafritz and J. Steven Ott. Pacific Grove, Ca.: Brooks/Cole Publishing Company.

Bourdeaux, Carolyn. 2008. "Politics Versus Professionalism: The Effect of Institutional Structure on Democratic Decision-making in a Contested Policy Area." *Journal of Public Administration Research and Theory* 18 (July): 349–73.

Bowman, James S. 2001. "From Codes of Conduct to Codes of Ethics: The ASPA Case." Pp. 335–53 in *Handbook of Administrative Ethics,*. 2d Ed., ed. by Terry L. Cooper. New York: Marcel Dekker.

———. 1990. "Whistle Blowing in the Public Sector: An Overview of the Issues." Pp. 195–202 in *Combating Corruption/Encouraging Ethics: A Sourcebook for Public Service Ethics*, ed. William L. Richter, Francis Burke, and Jameson W. Doig. Washington, D.C.: The American Society for Public Administration.

Box, Richard C., and Deborah A. Sagen. 1998. "Working With Citizens: Breaking Down Barriers to Citizen Self-Governance." Pp. 158–74 in *Government Is Us: Public Administration in an Anti-Government Era*, ed. Cheryl Simrell King and Camilla Stivers. Thousand Oaks, Ca.: Sage Publications.

Bozeman, Barry. 2007. *Public Values and Public Interest: Counterbalancing Economic Individualism*. Washington, D.C.: Georgetown University Press.

Brady, F. Neil. 2003. "'Publics' Administration and the Ethics of Particularity." *Public Administration Review* 63 (September/October): 525–34.

Brady, F. Neil and David W. Hart. 2006. "An Aesthetic Theory of Conflict in Administrative Ethics." *Administration & Society* 38 (March): 113–34.

Brogaard, Berit. 2008. "Moral Contextualism and Moral Relativism." *Philosophical Quarterly* 58 (July): 385–409.

Brown v. Board of Education of Topeka. 1954. 347 U.S. 483.

Browne, Kari. 2003. "A Diplomat's Battle." *Ms.* 13 (Winter): 22.

Burke, John P. 2001. "Administrative Ethics and Democratic Theory." Pp. 603–22 in *Handbook of Administrative Ethics*, 2d Ed. ed. Terry L. Cooper. New York: Marcel Dekker.

———. *Bureaucratic Responsibility*. 1986. Baltimore: Johns Hopkins University Press.

Caiden, Gerald E., and Naomi J. Caiden. 1990. "Understanding Fraud, Waste, Abuse and Corruption." Pp. 61–69 in *Combating Corruption/Encouraging Ethics: A Sourcebook for Public Service Ethics*, ed William L. Richter, Francis Burke, and Jameson W. Doig. Washington, D.C.: The American Society for Public Administration.

Cameron, III, George D. 2000. "Ethics and Equity: Enforcing Ethical Standards in Commercial Relationships." *Journal of Business Ethics* 23 (January): 161–72.

Campbell, Dan. 2000. "When the Lights Came On; USDA Program Brought Electricity and a Better Way of Life to Rural America." *Rural Cooperatives* 67 (July/August): 6–9.

Carney, Court. 2001. "The Contested Image of Nathan Bedford Forrest." *Journal of Southern History* 67 (August): 601–29.

Catron, Bayard. 1990. "Teaching Ethics, Teaching Ethically." Pp. 283–89 in *Combating Corruption/Encouraging Ethics: A Sourcebook for Public Service Ethics*, ed. William L. Richter, Francis Burke, and Jameson W. Doig. Washington, D.C.: The American Society for Public Administration.

Cesarani, David. 2004. *Becoming Eichmann: Rethinking the Life, Crimes, and Trial of a "Desk Murderer."* New York: Da Capo Books.

Chandler, Ralph Clark. 1983. "The Civil Servant as Trustee: A Reorganization of the Professionalism Discussion." *Dialogue* 5 (Summer): 5–21.

———. 2001. "Deontological Dimensions of Administrative Ethics Revisited." Pp. 179–93 in *Handbook of Administrative Ethics*, 2d Ed., ed. Terry L. Cooper. New York: Marcel Dekker. Also: 1999. "Deontological Dimensions of Administrative Ethics, Revisited." *Public Personnel Management* 28 (Winter): 505–14.

———. 1983. "The Problem of Moral Reasoning in American Public Administration: The Case for a Code of Ethics." *Public Administration Review* 43 (January/February): 32–39.

Chapman, Richard L., and Frederic N. Cleaveland. 1973. "The Changing Character of the Public Service and the Administrator of the 1980s." *Public Administration Review* 33 (July/August): 358–65.

Churchill, David S. 2008. "Spectres of Anti-communism: Richard Rorty and Leftist Thought in Twentieth-Century America." *Canadian Review of American Studies* 38: 275–91.

Cimprich John, and Robert C. Mainfort, Jr. 1982. "Fort Pillow Revisited: New Evidence About An Old Controversy." *Civil War History* 28 (Winter): 293–306.

Coase, Ronald H. 1992. "The Institutional Structure of Production." *The American Economic Review* 82 (September): 713–19.

Coelho, Philip R. P.; James E. McClure; and John A. Spry. 2003. "The Social Responsibility of Corporate Management: A Classical Critique." *Mid-American Journal of Business* 18 (Spring): 15–24.

Cooper, David E. 1996. *World Philosophies: An Historical Introduction.* Cambridge, Mass.: Blackwell.

Cooper, N. Lee. 1997. "President's Message—The Harlan Standard: Former Associate Justice Can Teach Us the Value of Reasoned Dissent." *ABA Journal* 83 (June): 8.

Cooper, Terry L. 2004. "Big Questions in Administrative Ethics: A Need for Focused, Collaborative Effort." *Public Administration Review* 64 (July/August): 395–407.

———. 2001. "The Emergence of Administrative Ethics as a Field of Study in the United States." Pp. 1–36 in *Handbook of Administrative Ethics*, 2d Ed., ed. Terry L. Cooper. New York: Marcel Dekker, 2001.

———. 1991. *An Ethic of Citizenship for Public Administration.* Englewood Cliffs, N.J.: Prentice Hall.

———. 1987. "Hierarchy, Virtue, and the Practice of Public Administration: A Perspective for Normative Ethics." *Public Administration Review* 47 (July/August): 320–28.

———. 1990. *The Responsible Administrator: An Approach to Ethics for the Administrative Role*, 3d Ed. San Francisco: Jossey-Bass.

Corwin, Edward S. 1969. "The 'Higher Law' Background of American Constitutional Law." Pp. 37–54 in *American Government: Readings and Cases*, 3d. Ed., ed. Peter Woll. Boston: Little Brown & Company.

Coulter, Ann. 2003. *Treason: Liberal Treachery from the Cold War to the War on Terrorism.* New York: Crown Forum.

Cravens, David W., Nigel F. Piercy, and Shannon H. Shipp. 1996. "New Organizational Forms for Competing in Highly Dynamic Environments: The Network Paradigm." *British Journal of Management* 7 (September): 203–18.

Crossley, Nick. 2008. "(Net)working Out: Social Capital in a Private Health Club." *British Journal of Sociology* 59 (September): 475–500.

Cyert, Richard M., and James G. March. 1963. *A Behavioral Theory of the Firm.* Englewood Cliffs, N.J.: Prentice-Hall.

Daft, Richard L. 2004. *Organization Theory and Design*, 8th Ed. Mason, Ohio: Thomson South-Western.

Dahl, Robert A. 1956. *A Preface to Democratic Theory.* Chicago: The University of Chicago Press.

Davidson, Roger H., and Walter J. Oleszek. 1990. *Congress and Its Members*, 3d Ed. Washington, D.C.: Congressional Quarterly Press.

Day, Janet E. 2005. "Emma Goldman and Ayn Rand: Ethical Egoism and Constraint." *Conference Papers—Midwestern Political Science Association*: 1–28.

Dean, Peter J. 1992. "Making Codes of Ethics 'Real.'" *Journal of Business Ethics* 11 (April): 285–90.

De Leon, Linda, and Robert B. Denhardt. 2000. "The Political Theory of Reinvention." *Public Administration Review* 60 (March/April): 89–97.

Denhardt, Kathryn G. 1994. "Character Ethics and the Transformation of Governance." *International Journal of Public Administration* 17 (October): 2165–93.

———. 1988. *The Ethics of Public Service: Resolving Moral Dilemmas in Public Organizations.* Westport, Conn.: Greenwood Press.

Derrida, Jacques. 1982. *Margins of Philosophy.* Trans. A. Bass. Chicago: University of Chicago Press.

———. 1976. *Of Grammatology.* Trans. G. Spivak. Baltimore: Johns Hopkins University Press.

———. 1978. *Writing and Difference.* Trans. A. Bass. Chicago: University of Chicago Press.

Diamond, Martin. 1959. "Democracy and *The Federalist*: A Reconsideration of the Framers' Intent." *American Political Science Review* 53 (March): 52–68.

———. 1986. "Ethics and Politics: The American Way." Pp. 75–108 in *The Moral Foundations of the American Republic,* 3d Ed., ed. Robert H. Horwitz. Charlottesville: The University Press of Virginia.

Dietze, Gottfried. 1960. *The Federalist: A Classic on Federalism and Free Government.* Westport, Conn.: Greenwood Press.

Diggins, John Patrick. 1988. "Recovering 'First Principles': Critical Perspectives on the Constitution and the Fate of Classical Republicanism." Pp. 119–43 in *Toward a More Perfect Union: Six Essays on the Constitution,* ed. Neil L. York. Provo, Ut.: Brigham University.

Dijkstra, Jacob, Marcel A. L. M. Van Assen, and Frans N. Stokman. 2008. "Outcomes of Collective Decisions with Externalities Predicted." *Journal of Theoretical Politics* 20 (October): 415–41.

Dobel, J. Patrick. 1990. "Integrity in the Public Service." *Public Administration Review* 50 (May/June): 356–66.

Downs, Anthony. 1997. *An Economic Theory of Democracy.* Old Tappan, N.J.: Addison Wesley.

Dubnick, Melvin J. 2003. "Accountability and Ethics: Reconsidering the Relationships." *International Journal of Organization Theory and Behavior* 6 (Fall): 405–41.

Dungey, Nicholas. 2008. "Thomas Hobbes's Materialism, Language, and the Possibility of Politics." *Review of Politics* 70 (Spring): 190–220.

Dworkin, Ronald. 1978. *Taking Rights Seriously.* Cambridge, Mass.: Harvard University Press.

Endres, Alfred, and Bianca Rundshagen. 2008. "A Note on Coasean Dynamics." *Environmental Economics & Policy Studies* 9: 57–66.

Engelbert, Ernest A. 1977. "University Education for Public Policy Analysis." *Public Administration Review* 37 (May/June): 228–36.

Epstein, David F. 1984. *The Political Theory of the Federalist.* Chicago: The University of Chicago Press.

Farmer, David John. "Against Myopia: Public Administration and Ethics." *Journal of Public Affairs Education* 4 (January 1998): 33–38.

Farrell, Joseph. 1987. "Information and the Coase Theorem." *The Journal of Economic Perspectives* 1: 113–29.

Faust, Drew Gilpin. 2008. *This Republic of Suffering: Death and the American Civil War*. New York: Alfred A. Knopf.

Feiock, Richard C., and Jered B. Carr. 2001. "Incentives, Entrepreneurs, and Boundary Change." *Urban Affairs Review* 36 (January): 382–405.

Ferrell, O. C., and Steven J. Skinner. 1988. "Ethical Behavior and Bureaucratic Structure in Marketing Research." *Journal of Marketing Research* 25 (February): 103–9.

Ferrey, Steven. 1997. *Environmental Law: Examples and Explanations*. New York: Aspen Law & Business.

Finer, Herman. 1990. "Administrative Responsibility in Democratic Government." P. 44 in *Combating Corruption/Encouraging Ethics: A Sourcebook for Public Service Ethics*, ed. William L. Richter, Francis Burke, and Jameson W. Doig. Washington, D.C.: The American Society for Public Administration.

Fischer, Frank. 1983. "Ethical Discourse in Public Administration." *Administration & Society* 15 (May): 5–42.

Fletcher, T. W. 1958. "The Nature of Administrative Loyalty." *Public Administration Review* 18 (Winter): 37–42.

Foley, Dolores. 1998. "We Want Your Input: Dilemmas of Citizen Participation." Pp. 140–57 in *Government Is Us: Public Administration in an Anti-Government Era*, ed. Cheryl Simrell King and Camilla Stivers. Thousand Oaks, Ca.: Sage Publications.

Foote, Shelby. 1986. *The Civil War, A Narrative: Red River to Appomattox*. New York: Vintage.

Formosa, Paul. 2007. "Is Radical Evil Banal? Is Banal Evil Radical?" *Philosophy and Social Criticism* 33 (September): 717–35.

Foster, Gregory D. 1981. "Law, Morality, and the Public Servant." *Public Administration Review* 41 (January/February): 29–34.

Foucault, Michel. 1972. *The Archaeology of Knowledge*, trans. A. Sheridan. New York: Pantheon Books.

———. 1980. *The Order of Things: An Archaeology of the Human Sciences*. London: Tavistock.

Fox, Charles J. 2001. "The Use of Philosophy in Administrative Ethics." Pp. 105–30 in *Handbook of Administrative Ethics*, 2d Ed., ed. Terry L. Cooper. New York: Marcel Dekker.

Frederickson, H. George. 1999. "Ethics and the New Managerialism." *Public Administration & Management: An Interactive Journal* 4: 299–324.

———. 1980. *New Public Administration*. University, Ala.: University of Alabama Press.

———. 1990. "Public Administration and Social Equity." *Public Administration Review* 50 (March/April): 228–37.

Frederickson, H. George, and David K. Hart. 1985. "The Public Service and the Patriotism of Benevolence." *Public Administration Review* 45 (September/ October): 547–53.

Freedman, Benjamin. 1978. "A Meta-Ethics for Professional Morality." *Ethics* 89 (October): 1–19.

Friedman, Thomas L. 2008. *Hot, Flat, and Crowded: Why We Need a Green Revolution—And How It Can Renew America*. New York: Farrar, Straus and Giroux.

Friedrich, Carl J. 1990. "Public Policy and the Nature of Administrative Responsibility." Pp. 43–44 in *Combating Corruption/Encouraging Ethics: A Sourcebook for Public Service Ethics*, ed. William L. Richter, Francis Burke, and Jameson W. Doig. Washington, D.C.: The American Society for Public Administration.

Fry, Brian R., and Lloyd G. Nigro. 1996. "Max Weber and U.S. Public Administration: The Administrator as Neutral Servant." *Journal of Management History* 2: 37–46.

Garner, Richard. 2007. "Abolishing Morality." *Ethical Theory & Moral Practice* 10 (November): 499–513.

Gauthier, David. 1979. "Thomas Hobbes: Moral Theorist." *The Journal of Philosophy* 76 (October): 547–59.

Gawthrop, Louis C. 1984. "Civis, Civitas, and Civilitas: A New Focus for the Year 2000." *Public Administration Review* 44 (March): 101–7.

Gewirth, Alan. 1986. "Professional Ethics: The Separatist Thesis." *Ethics* 96 (January): 282–300.

Gladstone, William A. 1990. *United States Colored Troops*. Gettysburg, Pa.: Thomas Publications.

Godwin, R. Kenneth, and John C. Wahlke. 1997. *Introduction to Political Science: Reason, Reflection, and Analysis*. Ft. Worth, TX: Harcourt Brace.

Golembiewski, Robert T. 2003. *Ironies in Organizational Development*, 2d. Ed. New York: Marcel Dekker.

———. 1965. *Men, Management and Morality: Toward a New Organizational Ethic*. New York: McGraw-Hill.

Goodsell, Charles T. 1994. *The Case For Bureaucracy: A Public Administration Polemic*, 3d. Ed. Chatham, N.J.: Chatham House Publishers.

———. 2006. "Conflating Forms of Separation in Administrative Ethics." *Administration & Society* 38 (March): 135–41.

Gortner, Harold F. 1991. *Ethics for Public Managers*. Westport, Conn.: Praeger.

———. 2001. "Values and Ethics." Pp. 509–28 in *Handbook of Administrative Ethics*, 2d Ed., ed. Terry L. Cooper. New York: Marcel Dekker.

Gortner, Harold F., Julianne Mahler, and Jeanne Bell Nicholson. 1989. *Organization Theory: A Public Perspective*. Pacific Grove, Ca: Brooks/Cole Publishing Company.

Gould, Lewis L. 2003. *Grand Old Party: A History of the Republicans*. New York: Random House.

Graham, George A. 1974. "Ethical Guidelines for Public Administrators: Observations on Rules of the Game." *Public Administration Review* 34 (January/February): 90–92.

Gray, Truda, and Brian Martin. 2008. "My Lai: The Struggle Over Outrage." *Peace & Change* 33 (January): 90–113.

Greco, John. 2008. "What's Wrong with Contextualism?" *Philosophical Quarterly* 58 (July): 416–36.

Green, Richard T. 1994. "Character Ethics and Administration." *International Journal of Public Administration* 17 (October): 2137–64.

Grosenick, Leigh E., and Pamela A. Gibson. 2001. "Governmental Ethics and Organizational Culture." Pp. 243–61 in *Handbook of Administrative Ethics*, 2d Ed., ed. Terry L. Cooper. New York: Marcel Dekker.

Guesnerie, Roger. 1975. "Pareto Optimality in Non-Convex Economies." *Econometrica* 43 (January): 1–30.

Gulick, Luther. 1987. "Notes on the Theory of Organization." Pp. 87–97 in *Classics of Organization Theory*, 2d. Ed., ed. Jay M. Shafritz and J. Steven Ott. Pacific Grove, Ca.: Brooks/Cole Publishing Company.

Gulick, Luther and Lyndall Urwick, eds. 1937. *Papers on the Science of Administration*. New York: Augustus M. Kelley.

Halberstam, Joshua. 1993. *Everyday Ethics: Inspired Solutions to Real-Life Dilemmas*. New York: Penguin.

Hamilton, Alexander, James Madison, and John Jay. 1961. *The Federalist Papers*, ed. Clinton Rossiter. New York: The American Library.

Hardin, Garret. 1968. "The Tragedy of the Commons." *Science* 162 (December): 1243–48.

Harris, Cheryl I. 2005. "Symposium: Race Jurisprudence and the Supreme Court: Where Do We Go From Here? In The Shadow of *Plessy*." *University of Pennsylvania Journal of Constitutional Law* 7 (February): 889–901.

Harris, Shane. 2003. "Diplomat Resigns to Protest War." *Government Executive.com* (21 March) www.govexec.com/dailyfed/0303/ 032103wright.htm (accessed 20 January 2009).

Hart, David K. 2001. "A Dream of What We Could Be: The Founding Values, the Oath, and *Homo Virtutis Americanus*." Pp. 207–26 in *Handbook of Administrative Ethics*, 2d Ed., ed. L. Cooper. New York: Marcel Dekker.

———. 1983. "The Honorable Bureaucrat Among the Philistines." *Administration & Society* 15 (May): 43–48.

———. 1989. "A Partnership in Virtue Among All Citizens: The Public Service and Civic Humanism." *Public Administration Review* 49 (March-April): 101–5.

———. 1974. "Social Equity, Justice, and the Equitable Administrator." *Public Administration Review* 34 (January): 3–11.

Hart, David K., and P. Artell Smith. 1988. "Fame, Fame-Worthiness, and the Public Service." *Administration & Society* 20 (August): 131–51.

Hart, H. L. A. 1961. *The Concept of Law*. Oxford: Oxford University Press.

———. 1958. "Positivism and the Separation of Law and Morals." *Harvard Law Review* 71 (February): 593–629.

Hassner, Pierre. 1972. "Immanuel Kant." Pp. 554–94 in *History of Political Philosophy*, 2d. Ed., ed. Leo Strauss and Joseph Cropsey. Chicago: Rand McNally & Company, 1972.

Haveman, Robert. 1976. *Economics of the Public Sector.* Santa Barbara, Ca.: John Wiley & Sons.

Heaney, Michael T. 2004. "Issue Networks, Information, and Interest Group Alliances: The Case of Wisconsin Welfare Policies, 1993–99." *State Politics & Policy* 4 (Fall): 237–70.

Heclo, Hugh. 1978. "Issue Networks and the Executive Establishment." Pp. 87–124 in *The New American Political System*, ed. Anthony King. Washington, DC: American Enterprise Institute.

Hejka-Ekins, April. 2001. "Ethics in In-Service Training." Pp. 79–103 in *Handbook of Administrative Ethics*, 2d Ed., ed. Terry L. Cooper. New York: Marcel Dekker.

———. 1988. "Teaching Ethics in Public Administration." *Public Administration Review* 48 (September-October): 885–91.

Held, David. 1995. *Democracy and the Global Order.* Stanford, Ca.: Stanford University Press.

Heywood, Andrew. 1994. *Political Ideas and Concepts: An Introduction.* New York: St. Martin's Press.

Hill, Carolyn J., and Laurence E. Lynn, Jr. 2005. "Is Hierarchical Governance in Decline? Evidence from Empirical Research." *Journal of Public Administration Research and Theory* 15 (April): 173–95.

Hill, Robert S. 1972. "David Hume." Pp. 509–31 in *History of Political Philosophy*, 2d. Ed., ed. Leo Strauss and Joseph Cropsey. Chicago: Rand McNally & Company.

Hoover, Kenneth R. 1994. *Ideology and Political Life*, 2d. Ed., Belmont, Ca.: Wadsworth.

Hsu, Ming; Cedric Anen; and Steven R. Quartz. 2008. "The Right and the Good: Distributive Justice and Neural Encoding of Equity and Efficiency." *Science* 320 (23 May): 1092–95.

Hume, David. 1977. *An Enquiry Concerning Human Understanding.* Indianapolis: Hackett Publishing.

Hurst, Jack. 1993. *Nathan Bedford Forrest: A Biography.* New York: Knopf.

———. 2009. "Tennessee Turning Point: Nathan Bedford Forrest Took Matters Into His Own Hands at Fort Donelson—And a Legend Was Born," *America's Civil War* 21 (January): 28–37.

Jackall, Robert. 1988. *Moral Mazes: The World of Corporate Managers.* New York: Oxford University Press.

Jarvie, Ian. 2008. "Boudon's European Diagnosis of and Prophylactic against Relativism." *Philosophy of the Social Sciences* 38 (June): 279–92.

Jennings, Marianne M. 2004. "Preventing Organizational Ethical Collapse." *The Journal of Government Financial Management* 53 (Spring): 12–19.

Jensen, Merrill. 1963. *The Articles of Confederation: An Interpretation of the Social-Constitutional History of the American Revolution, 1774–1781.* Madison: The University of Wisconsin Press.

Jones, Charles G. 1995. "Forrest: A Mixture of Genius and Guile." *Washington Times*, June 3, p. B3.

Jones, W. T. 1970. *The Classical Mind: A History of Western Philosophy*, 2d. Ed. New York: Harcourt Brace Jovanovich.

Jos, Philip H., and Mark E. Tompkins. 1995. "Administrative Practice and the Waning Promise of Professionalism for Public Administration." *American Review of Public Administration* 25 (September): 207–29.

Joyner, Brenda E., and Dinah Payne. 2002. "Evolution and Implementation: A Study of Values, Business Ethics and Corporate Social Responsibility." *Journal of Business Ethics* 41 (December): 297–311.

Kalu, Kalu N. 2003. "Of Citizenship, Virtue, and the Administrative Imperative: Deconstructing Aristotelian Civic Republicanism." *Public Administration Review* 63 (July/August): 418–27.

Kant, Immanuel. 1990. "The Categorical Imperative." P. 27 in *Combating Corruption/Encouraging Ethics: A Sourcebook for Public Service Ethics*, ed. William L. Richter, Francis Burke, and Jameson W. Doig. Washington, D.C.: The American Society for Public Administration

———. 1987. *Fundamental Principles of the Metaphysics of Morals.* Trans. T. Abbott. New York: Prometheus.

Kariel, Henry. 1961. *The Decline of American Pluralism.* Palo Alto, Ca.: Stanford University Press.

Kernaghan, Kenneth. 2003. "Integrating Values into Public Service: The Values Statement as Centerpiece." *Public Administration Review* 63 (November/December): 711–19.

Kettl, Donald F. 2005. *The Global Public Management Revolution*, 2d. Ed. Washington, D.C.: Brookings Institution Press.

———. 2002. *The Transformation of Governance: Public Administration for Twenty-First Century America.* Baltimore: The Johns Hopkins University Press.

Klausen, Jimmy Casas. 2007. "Room Enough: America, Natural Liberty, and Consent in Locke's *Second Treatise*." *The Journal of Politics* 69 (August): 760–69.

Kreines, James. 2007. "Between the Bounds of Experience and Divine Intuition: Kant's Epistemic Limits and Hegel's Ambitions." *Inquiry* 50 (June): 306–34.

Kristol, Irving. 1992. "'When Virtue Loses All Her Loveliness'—Some Reflections on Capitalism and 'The Free Society.'" Pp. 189–96 in *The Quest for Justice: Readings in Political Ethics*, 3d. Ed., ed. Leslie G. Rubin and Charles T. Rubin. Needham Heights, Mass.: Ginn Press.

Ladd, John. 1990. "The Quest for a Code of Professional Ethics: An Intellectual and Moral Confusion." Pp. 271–74 in *Combating Corruption/Encouraging Ethics: A Sourcebook for Public Service Ethics*, ed. William L. Richter, Francis Burke, and Jameson W. Doig. Washington, D.C.: The American Society for Public Administration.

Lai, Lawrence W. C., and Connie W. Y. Hung. 2008. "The Inner Logic of the Coase Theorem and a Coasian Planning Research Agenda." *Environment & Planning B: Planning & Design* 35 (March): 207–26.

Larkin, Paschal. 1930. *Property in the Eighteenth Century: With Special Reference to England and Locke*. London: Cork University Press.

Laustsen, Carsten Bagge, and Rasmus Ugilt. 2007. "Eichmann's Kant." *Journal of Speculative Philosophy* 21: 166–80.

Le Grand, Julian. 1984. "Equity as an Economic Objective." *Journal of Applied Philosophy* 1 (March): 39–51.

Levitan, David M. 1942. "The Neutrality of the Public Service." *Public Administration Review* 2 (Autumn): 317–23.

Lilla, Mark T. 1981. "Ethos, 'Ethics,' and Public Service." *The Public Interest* 63 (Spring): 3–17.

Loverd, Richard A. 1990. "Styles and Strategies of Managing Openness." Pp. 217–23 in *Combating Corruption/Encouraging Ethics: A Sourcebook for Public Service Ethics*, ed. William L. Richter, Francis Burke, and Jameson W. Doig. Washington, D.C.: The American Society for Public Administration.

Luke, Jeffrey S., and David W. Hart. 2001. "Character and Conduct in the Public Service: A Review of Historical Perspectives." Pp. 529–54 in *Handbook of Administrative Ethics*, 2d Ed., ed. Terry L. Cooper. New York: Marcel Dekker.

Lunder, Sonya, Tracey J. Woodruff, and Daniel A. Axelrad. 2004. "An Analysis of Candidates for Addition to the Clean Air Act List of Hazardous Air Pollutants." *Journal of the Air & Waste Management Association* 54 (February): 157–71.

Lynn, Jr., Laurence E. 1996. *Public Management as Art, Science, and Profession*. Chatham, N.J.: Chatham House Publishers.

Lyotard, Jean-Francois. 1984. *The Postmodern Condition: A Report on Knowledge*. Minneapolis: The University of Minnesota Press.

Lytle, Andrew. 1960. *Bedford Forrest and His Critter Company*. New York: McDowell, Obolensky.

MacIntyre, Alasdair. 2008. "Richard Rorty (1931–2007)." *Common Knowledge* 14 (Spring): 183–92.

Mack, W. R., Deanna Green, and Arnold Vedlitz. 2008. "Innovation and Implementation in the Public Sector: An Examination of Public Entrepreneurship." *Review of Policy Research* 25 (May): 233–52.

March, James G., ed. 1965. *Handbook of Organizations*. Chicago: Rand McNally.

Marini, Frank. 1971. "The Minnowbrook Perspective and the Future of Public Administration." Pp. 346–67 in *Toward a New Public Administration: The Minnowbrook Perspective*, ed. Frank Marini. New York, N.Y.: Chandler.

Martain, Jacques. 2005. *An Introduction to Philosophy*. London and New York: Continuum International Publishing Group.

Martin, D. W. 1988. "The Fading Legacy of Woodrow Wilson." *Public Administration Review* 48 (March/April): 631–36

Martinez, J. Michael. 2007. *Carpetbaggers, Cavalry, and the Ku Klux Klan: Exposing the Invisible Empire During Reconstruction*. Lanham, Md.: Rowman & Littlefield.

———. 1998. "Law Versus Ethics: Reconciling Two Concepts of Public Service Ethics." *Administration & Society* 29 (January): 690–722.

Martinez, J. Michael, and William D. Richardson. 2008. *Administrative Ethics in the Twenty-first Century*. New York: Peter Lang USA.

———. 2000. "*The Federalist Papers* and Legal Interpretation." *South Dakota Law Review* 45 (Summer): 307–33.

Marx, Fritz Morstein. 1949. "Administrative Ethics and the Rule of Law." *The American Political Science Review* 43 (December): 1119–44.

McChesney, Fred S. 2006. "Coase, Demsetz, and the Unending Externality Debate." *CATO Journal* 26 (Winter): 179–200.

McGregor, Eugene B. 1974. "Social Equity and the Public Service." *Public Administration Review* 34 (January/February): 18–29.

McGarity, Thomas O. 2008. "Hazardous Air Pollutants, Migrating Hot Spots, and the Prospect of Data-Driven Regulation of Complex Industrial Complexes." *Texas Law Review* 86 (June): 1445–92.

McLaughlin, Andrew C. 1969. "The Articles of Confederation." Pp. 44–60 in *Essays on the Making of the Constitution*, ed. Leonard W. Levy. New York: Oxford University Press.

McPherson, James M. 1988. *Battle Cry of Freedom: The Civil War Era*. New York: Oxford University Press.

McSwite, O. C. 1997. *Legitimacy in Public Administration: A Discourse Analysis*. Thousands Oaks, Ca.: Sage Publications.

———. 1996. "Postmodernism, Public Administration, and the Public Interest." Pp. 198–224 in *Refounding Public Administration: Modern Paradoxes, Postmodern Challenges*, ed. Gary L. Wamsley and James F. Wolf. Thousand Oaks, Ca.: Sage Publications.

Mehren, Elizabeth. 2006. "She's on Activist Duty Now: Mary Ann Wright Quit a 30-Year Army and Diplomatic Career in Protest of the Iraq War; She's Now a Soldier for the Antiwar–Movement." *Los Angeles Times*, 20 January, p. A1.

Meier, Kenneth J., and Laurence J. O'Toole, Jr. 2006. "Political Control versus Bureaucratic Values: Reframing the Debate." *Public Administration Review* 66 (March/April): 177–92.

Menzel, Donald C. 1997. "Teaching Ethics and Values in Public Administration: Are We Making a Difference?" *Public Administration Review* 57 (May/June): 224–30.

———. 1998. "To Act Ethically: The What, Why, and How of Ethics Pedagogy." *Journal of Public Affairs Education* 4 (January): 11–18.

Merton, Robert K. 1967. *On Theoretical Sociology*. New York: The Free Press.

Meyer, Marshall W. 1968. "Expertness and Span of Control." *American Sociological Review* 33 (December): 944–51.

Meyerson, Michael I. 2008. *Liberty's Blueprint: How Madison and Hamilton Wrote The Federalist Papers, Defined the Constitution, and Made Democracy Safe for the World*. New York: Basic Books.

Michie, Susan; Marie Johnston; Jill Francis; Wendy Hardeman; and Martin Eccles. 2008. "From Theory to Intervention: Mapping Theoretically Derived Behavioural Determinants to Behaviour Change Techniques." *Applied Psychology: An International Review* 57 (October): 660–80.

Mikols, Elizabeth H., and Amarjit S. Gill. 1996. "The Regulation of Hazardous Air Pollutants Under the Clean Air Act Amendments of 1990." *IEEE Transactions on Industry Applications* 32 (July/August): 760–65.

Milakovich, Michael E., and George J. Gordon. 2004. *Public Administration in America*. Belmont, Ca: Wadsworth/Thomson.

Mill, John Stuart. 1947. *On Liberty*. Arlington Heights, IL: AHM Publishing.

Moe, Ronald C., and Robert S. Gilmour. 1995. "Rediscovering Principles of Public Administration: The Neglected Foundation of Public Law." *Public Administration Review* 55 (March/April): 135–46.

Moore, Christopher, and Don Courter. 1998. "Reducing HAP Emissions to Avoid NESHAP Applicability." *Pollution Engineering* 30 (November): 21–23.

Moore, G. E. 2004. *Principia Ethica*. Mineola, N.Y.: Courier Dover Publications.

Morgan, Douglas F. 2001. "The Public Interest." Pp. 151–78 in *Handbook of Administrative Ethics*, 2d Ed., ed. Terry L. Cooper. New York: Marcel Dekker.

Morrisey, Will. 1986. "The Moral Foundations of the American Republic: An Introduction." Pp. 1–23 in *The Moral Foundations of the American Republic*, 3d. Ed., ed. Robert H. Horwitz. Charlottesville, Va.: The University Press of Virginia.

Mosca, Manuela. 2008. "On the Origins of the Concept of Natural Monopoly: Economies of Scale and Competition." *European Journal of the History of Economic Thought* 15 (June): 317–53.

Moya, Olga L., and Andrew L. Fono. 1997. *Federal Environmental Law: The User's Guide*. St. Paul, Minn.: West Publishing Company.

Murphy, John P. 1990. *Pragmatism from Peirce to Davidson*. Boulder, Co.: Westview Press.

Nathanson, Constance A. 1999. "Social Movements as Catalysts for Policy Change: The Case of Smoking and Guns." *Journal of Health Politics, Policy and Law* 24: 421–88.

Nefzger, Ben. 1965. "The Ideal Type: Some Conceptions and Misconceptions." *Sociological Quarterly* 6 (Spring): 166–74.

Nelson, Michael. 1982. "A Short, Ironic History of American National Bureaucracy." *Journal of Politics* 44 (August): 747–78.

Ng, Yew-Kwang. 1973. "The Economic Theory of Clubs: Pareto Optimality Conditions." *Economica* 40 (August): 219–98.

Nielsen, Richard P., and Ron Dufresne. 2005. "Can Ethical Organizational Character Be Stimulated and Enabled? 'Upbuilding' Dialog as Crisis Management Method." *Journal of Business Ethics* 57 (April): 311–26.

Niemi, Jari, I. 2005. "Jurgen Habermas's Theory of Communicative Rationality: The Foundational Distinction Between Communicative and Strategic Action." *Social Theory and Practice* 31 (October): 513–32.

Niemi, Richard G., and Herbert F. Weisberg. 1993. "What Determines the Vote?" Pp. 137–51 in *Controversies in Voting Behavior*, 3d. Ed., ed. Richard G. Niemi and Herbert F. Weisberg. Washington, D.C.: Congressional Quarterly Press.

Nietzsche, Friedrich. 1966. *Beyond Good and Evil.* Trans. Walter Kaufmann. New York: Vintage Books.

Nigro, Lloyd G., and William D. Richardson. 1990. "Between Citizen and Administrator: Administrative Ethics and *PAR.*" *Public Administration Review* 50 (November December): 623–35.

Nozick, Robert. 1974. *Anarchy, State, and Utopia,* New York: Basic Books

O Brien, David M. 1986. *Storm Center: The Supreme Court in American Politics.* New York: W. W. Norton.

O'Kelly, Ciaran, and Melvin J. Dubnick. 2006. "Taking Tough Choices Seriously: Public Administration and Individual Moral Agency." *Journal of Public Administration Research and Theory* 16 (July): 393–415.

Oliver, Kendrick. 2003. "Atrocity, Authenticity and American Exceptional: (Ir)rationalising the Massacre at My Lai." *Journal of American Studies* 37 (August): 247–68.

Ostrom Elinor, and T. K. Ahns, eds. 2003. *Foundations of Social Capital.* Cheltenham, U.K.: Edward Elgar.

Ostrom, Vincent. 1989. *The Intellectual Crisis in American Public Administration*, 2d. Ed., Tuscaloosa: The University of Alabama Press.

———. 1987. *The Political Theory of a Compound Republic: Designing the American Experiment*, 2d. Ed. Lincoln: University of Nebraska Press.

O'Toole, Laurence J., Jr. 2000. "Different Public Managements? Implications of Structural Context in Hierarchies and Networks." Pp. 19–32 in *Advancing Public Management: New Developments in Theory, Methods, and Practice*, ed. Jeffrey L. Brudney, Laurence J. O'Toole, Jr., and Hal G. Rainey. Washington, D.C.: Georgetown University Press.

———. 1987. "Doctrines and Developments: Separation of Powers, the Politics-Administration Dichotomy, and the Rise of the Administrative State." *Public Administration Review* 47 (January/February): 17–25.

Overeem, Patrick. 2005. "The Value of the Dichotomy: Politics, Administration, and the Political Neutrality of Administrators." *Administrative Theory & Praxis* 27 (June): 311–29.

Paech, Niko P. 2008. "Contestability Reconsidered: The Meaning of Market Exit Costs." *Journal of Economic Behavior & Organization* 34 (1 March): 435–43.

Page, Stephen. 2005. "What's New About the New Public Management? Administrative Change in the Human Services." *Public Administration Review* 65 (November): 713–27.

Parks, Sharon Daloz. 1993. "Is It Too Late? Young Adults and the Formation of Professional Ethics." Pp. 13–72 in *Can Ethics Be Taught? Perspectives, Challenges, and Approaches at Harvard Business School*, ed. Thomas R. Piper, Mary C. Gentile, and Sharon Daloz Parks. Boston, Mass.: Harvard Business School Press.

Parsons, Talcott. 1987. "Suggestions for a Sociological Approach to the Theory of Organizations." Pp. 132–46 in *Classics of Organization Theory*, 2d. Ed., ed. Jay M. Shafritz and J. Steven Ott. Pacific Grove, Ca.: Brooks/Cole Publishing Company.

Perkins, John A. 1958. "Higher Education and Training for Administrative Careers." *Public Administration Review* 18 (January/February): 14–20.

Pinchevski, Amit, and Roy Brand. 2007. "Holocaust Perversions: The Stalags Pulp Fiction and the Eichmann Trial." *Critical Studies in Media Communication* 24 (December): 387–407.

Plant, Jeremy F. 2001. "Codes of Ethics." Pp. 309–33 in *Handbook of Administrative Ethics*, 2d Ed., ed. Terry L. Cooper. New York: Marcel Dekker.

Plessy v. Ferguson. 1896. 163 U.S. 163 U.S. 537.

Pops, Gerald M. 2001. "A Teleological Approach to Administrative Ethics." Pp. 195–206 in *Handbook of Administrative Ethics*, 2d Ed., ed. Terry L. Cooper. New York: Marcel Dekker.

Postema, Gerald J. 1980. "Moral Responsibility in Professional Ethics." *New York University Law Review* 55: 63–89.

Pressman, Jeffrey L., and Aaron Wildavsky. 1973. *Implementation*. Berkeley: University of California Press.

Pugh, Darrell L. 1989. "Professionalism in Public Administration: Problems, Perspectives, and the Role of the ASPA." *Public Administration Review* 49 (January/February): 1–8.

Pugh, Derek S.; David J. Hickson; and C. Ransom Hinings. 1969. "An Empirical Taxonomy of Work Organizations." *Administrative Science Quarterly* 14 (March): 115–26.

Putnam, Robert. 2000. *Bowling Alone: The Collapse and Revival of American Community*. New York: Simon and Schuster.

Railborn, Cecily A., and Dinah Payne. 1990. "Corporate Codes of Conduct: A Collective Conscience and Continuum." *Journal of Business Ethics* 9 (November): 879–89.

Rainey, Hal G., and Barry Bozeman. 2000. "Comparing Public and Private Organizations: Empirical Research and the Power of the *A Priori.*" *Journal of Public Administration Research and Theory* 10 (April): 447–70.

Rawls, John. 1985. "Justice as Fairness: Political Not Metaphysical." *Philosophy and Public Affairs* 14 (Summer): 223–51.

———. 1971. *A Theory of Justice.* Cambridge, Mass.: Belknap Press.

Rehfuss, John. 1989. *The Job of the Public Manager.* Chicago: The Dorsey Press.

Reindl, J. C. 2008. "Iraq War Critic Who Was U.S. Colonel to Speak at UT." *The [Toledo] Blade,* 10 March, p. B2.

Richardson, William D. 1997. *Democracy, Bureaucracy, & Character: Founding Thought.* Lawrence: University Press of Kansas.

Richardson, William D., and J. Michael Martinez. 1998. "Introduction." Pp. 5–17 in *Ethics and Character: The Pursuit of Democratic Virtues,* ed. William D. Richardson, J. Michael Martinez, and Kerry R. Stewart. Durham, N.C.: Carolina Academic Press.

———. 1987. "Administrative Ethics and Founding Thought: Constitutional Correctives, Honor, and Education." *Public Administration Review* 47 (September/October): 367–76.

———. 1987. "Self-Interest Properly Understood: The American Character and Public Administration." *Administration & Society* 19 (August): 157–77.

Richter, William L., Frances Burke, and Jameson W. Doig. 1990. "Combating Unethical Behavior: What to Do When the Angels are Missing." Pp. 147–51 in *Combating Corruption/Encouraging Ethics: A Sourcebook for Public Service Ethics,* ed. William L. Richter, Francis Burke, and Jameson W. Doig. Washington, D.C.: The American Society for Public Administration.

———. 1990. "The Timely, Ambiguous, and Fragile Nature of Ethical Concerns." Pp. 1–6 in *Combating Corruption/Encouraging Ethics: A Sourcebook for Public Service Ethics,* ed. William L. Richter, Francis Burke, and Jameson W. Doig. Washington, D.C.: The American Society for Public Administration.

Riley, D. D. 1987. *Controlling the Federal Bureaucracy.* Philadelphia: Temple University Press.

Roberts, Michael. 2000. "Rethinking the Postmodern Perspective: Excavating the Kantian System to Rebuild Social Theory," *Sociological Theory* 41 (September): 681–98.

Rodgers, Frederic. 2004. "'Our Constitution is Color Blind': Justice John Marshall Harlan and the *Plessy v. Ferguson* Dissent." *American Bar Association Judges' Journal* 43 (Spring): 15.

Rohr, John A. 1989. *Ethics for Bureaucrats: An Essay on Law and Values,* 2d. Ed. New York: Marcel Dekker.

———. 2004. "On Cooper's 'Big Questions.'" *Public Administration Review* 64 (July/August): 408–9.

Rorty, Richard. 1989. *Contingency, Irony, Solidarity.* Cambridge, U.K.: Cambridge University Press.

Rosenbloom, David H. 1971. *Federal Service and the Constitution*. Ithaca, NY: Cornell University Press.

———. 1989. *Public Administration: Understanding Management, Politics, and Law in the Public Sector*, 2d. Ed. New York: Random House.

———. 2000. "Retrofitting the Administrative State to the Constitution: Congress and the Judiciary's Twentieth-Century Progress." *Public Administration Review* 60 (January/February): 29–46.

Ross, Sir William David. 2002. *The Right and the Good*. Oxford: Clarendon Press.

Rourke, Francis E. 1992. "Responsiveness and Neutral Competence in American Bureaucracy." *Public Administration Review* 52 (November/December): 539–46.

Rowe, Mary P. 1990. "Organizational Response to Assessed Risk: Complaint Channels." Pp. 194–95 in *Combating Corruption/Encouraging Ethics: A Sourcebook for Public Service Ethics*, ed. William L. Richter, Francis Burke, and Jameson W. Doig. Washington, D.C.: The American Society for Public Administration.

Sarvis, Will. 2008. "Americans and Their Land: The Deep Roots of Property and Liberty." *Contemporary Review* 290 (Spring): 40–46.

Sayre, Wallace S. 1958. "Premises of Public Administration: Past and Emerging." *Public Administration Review* 18 (Spring): 102–5.

Schein, Edgar H. 1987. "Defining Organizational Culture." Pp. 381–95 in *Classics of Organization Theory*, 2d. Ed., ed. Jay M. Shafritz and J. Steven Ott. Pacific Grove, Ca.: Brooks/Cole Publishing Company.

———. 1987. "Organizational Culture." Pp. 127–41 in *Classics of Organization Theory*, 2d. Ed., ed. Jay M. Shafritz and J. Steven Ott. Pacific Grove, Ca.: Brooks/Cole Publishing Company.

Schlafly, Andrew L. 2007. "The Coase Theorem: The Greatest Economic Insight of the 20th Century." *Journal of American Physicians & Surgeons* 12 (Summer): 45–47.

Schmidt, James. 2006. "What Enlightenment Was, What It Still Might Be, and Why Kant May Have Been Right After All." *American Behavioral Science* 49 (January): 647–63.

Scholz, John T., and B. Dan Wood. 1999. "Efficiency, Equity, and Politics: Democratic Controls Over the Tax Collector." *American Journal of Political Science* 43 (October): 1166–88.

Schotten, Peter. 2007. "Hannah Arendt's Eichmann Reconsidered." *Modern Age* 49 (Spring): 139–47.

Schwenninger, Sherle R. 2008. "Democratizing Capital." *Nation* 286 (7 April): 27–28.

Sheeran, Patrick J. 1993. *Ethics in Public Administration: A Philosophical Approach*. Westport, Conn.: Praeger.

Simon, Herbert A. 1957. *Administrative Behavior*, 2d. Ed. New York: The Free Press.

———. 1987. The Proverbs of Administration." Pp. 102–18 in *Classics of Organization Theory*, 2d. Ed., ed. Jay M. Shafritz and J. Steven Ott. Pacific Grove, Ca.: Brooks/Cole Publishing Company.

Smith, Adam. 1992. "Selections from *An Inquiry into the Nature and Causes of the Wealth of Nations.*" Pp. 115–38 in *The Quest for Justice: Readings in Political Ethics*, 3d. Ed., ed. Leslie G. Rubin and Charles T. Rubin. Needham Heights, Mass.: Ginn Press.

Smith, Maynard. 1960. "Reason, Passion, and Political Freedom in *The Federalist.*" *Journal of Politics* 22 (August): 525–44.

Smith, Michael. 2003. "Neutral and Relative Value after Moore." *Ethics* 113 (April): 576–98.

Snider, Keith F. 2000. "Expertise or Experimenting?" *Administration & Society* 32 (July): 329–54.

Spicer, Michael. 2004. "Public Administration, the History of Ideas, and the Reinventing Government Movement," *Public Administration Review* 64 (May/June): 353–62.

Steed Robert P., and Laurence W. Moreland. 2000. "Southern Politics in Perspective." Pp. 67–86 in *Confederate Symbols in the Contemporary South*, ed. J. Michael Martinez, William D. Richardson, and Ron McNinch-Su. Gainesville, Fla.: Uinversity Press of Florida.

Stewart, Debra W. 1985. "Ethics and the Profession of Public Administration: The Moral Responsibility of Individuals in Public Sector Organizations." *Public Administration Quarterly* 45 (Winter): 487–95.

Stillman II, Richard J. 2004. *American Bureaucracy: The Core of Modern Government*, 3d. Ed. Belmont, Ca.: Wadsworth/Thompson

———. 1999. *Preface to Public Administration: A Search for Themes and Direction*, 2d. Ed. Burke, Va.: Chatelaine Press.

Stivers, Camilla. 2001. "Citizenship Ethics in Public Administration." Pp. 583–602 in *Handbook of Administrative Ethics*, 2d Ed., ed. Terry L. Cooper. New York: Marcel Dekker.

———. 1991. "Comments: Some Tensions in the Notion of 'The Public as Citizen': Rejoinder to Frederickson." *Administration & Society* 22 (February): 418–23.

———. 1990. "The Public Agency as Polis: Active Citizenship in the Administrative State." *Administration & Society* 22 (May): 86–105.

Stone, Deborah. 2002. *Policy Paradox: The Art of Political Decision Making*. Revised Edition. New York: W. W. Norton.

Storing, Herbert J. 1980. "American Statesmanship: Old and New." Pp. 88–113 in *Bureaucrats, Policy Analysts, Statesmen: Who Leads?*, ed. Robert A. Goldwin. Washington, D.C.: American Enterprise Institute.

———. 1965. "Leonard D. White and the Study of Public Administration." *Public Administration Review* 25 (March): 38–51.

Storr, Lorna. 2004. "Leading with Integrity: A Qualitative Research Study." *Journal of Health Organization and Management* 18: 415–34.

Strauss, Leo. 1972. "Niccolo Machiavelli, 1469–1527." Pp. 271–92 in *History of Political Philosophy*, 2d. Ed., ed. Leo Strauss and Joseph Cropsey. Chicago: The University of Chicago Press.

Streib, Gregory. 1992. "Ethics and Expertise in the Public Service: Maintaining Democracy in an Era of Professionalism." *Southeastern Political Review* 20 (Spring): 122–43.

Svara, James H., and James R. Brunet. 2004. "Filling in the Skeletal Pillar: Addressing Social Equity in Introductory Courses in Public Administration." *Journal of Public Affairs Education* 10 (April): 99–110.

Taylor, Frederick Winslow. 1917. *The Principles of Scientific Management.* New York: Harper & Brothers.

———. 1987. "The Principles of Scientific Management." Pp. 66–81 in *Classics of Organization Theory,* 2d Ed., ed. Jay M. Shafritz and J. Steven Ott. Pacific Grove, Ca.: Brooks/Cole Publishing Company.

Taylor, John R. 2003. *Linguistic Categorization: Prototypes in Linguistic Theory.* 3d Ed. New York: Oxford University Press.

Terry, Larry D. 1999. "From Greek Mythology to the Real World of the New Public Management and Democratic Governance (Terry Responds)." *Public Administration Review* 59 (May/June): 272–77.

Thomas, Laurence. 1993. "The Reality of the Moral Self." *Monist* 76 (January): 3–21.

Thompson, Dennis F. 1980. "Moral Responsibility of Public Officials: The Problem of Many Hands." *The American Political Science Review* 74 (December): 905–16.

———. 1985. "The Possibility of Administrative Ethics." *Public Administration Review* 45 (September/October): 555–61.

Thompson, J. D. 1967. *Organizations in Action.* New York: McGraw-Hill.

Thompson, James R. 2000. "Reinvention as Reform: Assessing the National Performance Review." *Public Administration Review* 60 (November/December): 508–21.

Timney, Mary M. 1998. "Overcoming Administrative Barriers to Citizen Participation: Citizens as Partners, Not Adversaries." Pp. 88–101 in *Government Is Us: Public Administration in an Anti-Government Era,* ed. Cheryl Simrell King and Camilla Stivers. Thousand Oaks, Ca.: Sage Publications.

Tolbert, Pamela S., and Lynne G. Zucker. 1983. "Institutional Sources of Change in the Formal Structure of Organizations: The Diffusion of Civil Service Reform, 1880–1935." *Administrative Science Quarterly* 28 (March): 22–39.

Toppin, Edgar A. 1993. "African Americans and the Confederacy." Pp. 1–5 in *Macmillan Information Now Encyclopedia: The Confederacy,* ed. Richard N. Current. New York: Simon & Schuster Macmillan Reference USA.

Trainor, Brian T. 2008. "Politics as the Quest for Unity: Perspectivism, Incommensurable Values and Agonistic Politics." *Philosophy & Social Criticism* 34 (November): 889–908.

Turnbull, Shann. 1994. "Stakeholder Democracy: Redesigning the Governance of Firms and Bureaucracies." *Journal of Socio-Economics* 23 (Fall): 321–60.

Van Maanen, John. 1978. "People Processing: Strategies of Organizational Socialization." *Organizational Dynamics* 7 (Summer): 18–36.

Van Wart, Montgomery. 1996. "The Sources of Ethical Decision-making for Individuals in the Public Sector." *Public Administration Review* 56 (November/December): 525–33.

Van Wart, Montgomery, and Kathryn G. Denhardt. 2001. "Organizational Structure: A Reflection of Society's Values and a Context for Individual Ethics." Pp. 227–41 in *Handbook of Administrative Ethics*, 2d Ed., ed. Terry L. Cooper. New York: Marcel Dekker.

Vance, Neil R., and Brett V. Trani. 2008. "The Ethical Grounding to 21st Century Public Leadership." *International Journal of Organization Theory and Behavior* 11 (Fall): 372–80.

Varlamova, Natalya. 2008. "Legal Positivism and Human Rights," *Social Sciences* 39: 129–41.

Ventriss, Curtis. 2001. "The Relevance of Public Ethics to Administration and Policy." Pp. 263–89 in *Handbook of Administrative Ethics*, 2d Ed., ed. Terry L. Cooper. New York: Marcel Dekker.

Victor, Bart, and John B. Cullen. 1988. "The Organizational Bases of Ethical Work Climates." *Administrative Science Quarterly* 33 (March): 101–25.

Wakefield, Susan. 1976. "Ethics and the Public Service: A Case for Individual Responsibility." *Public Administration Review* (November/December): 661–66.

Waldo, Dwight. 1984. *The Administrative State*. 2d Ed. New York: Holmes & Meier.

———. 1980. *The Enterprise of Public Administration*. Novato, Ca.: Chandler and Sharp.

———. 1974. "Reflections on Public Morality." *Administration & Society* 6 (November): 267–82.

Walker, Arthur H., and Jay W. Lorsch. 1987. "Organizational Choice: Product Versus Function." Pp. 192–204 in *Classics of Organization Theory*, 2d Ed., ed. Jay M. Shafritz and J. Steven Ott. Pacific Grove, Ca.: Brooks/Cole Publishing Company.

Wallace, James D. 1978. *Virtues & Vices*. Ithaca, N.Y.: Cornell University Press.

Walton, John R., James M. Stearns, and Charles T. Crespy. 1997. "Integrating Ethics into the Public Administration Curriculum: A Three-Step Process." *Journal of Policy Analysis and Management* 16 (Summer): 470–83.

Ward, Ian. 2008. "Bricolage and Low Cunning: Rorty on Pragmatism, Politics and Poetic Justice." *Legal Studies* 28 (June): 281–305.

Webb, Sidney. 1992. "What Socialism Means: A Call to the Unconverted." Pp. 219–24 in *The Quest for Justice: Readings in Political Ethics*, 3d Ed., ed. Leslie G. Rubin and Charles T. Rubin. Needham Heights, Mass.: Ginn Press.

Weber, Max. 1987. "Bureaucracy." Pp. 81–87 in *Classics of Organization Theory*, 2d Ed., ed. Jay M. Shafritz and J. Steven Ott. Pacific Grove, Ca.: Brooks/Cole Publishing Company.

Weimer, David L., and Aidan R. Vining. 1992. *Policy Analysis: Concepts and Practice.* 2d Ed. Englewood Cliffs, N.J.

Weinberg, Lisa. 1996. "Understanding Social Process: The Key to Democratic Government." Pp. 279–92 in *Refounding Public Administration: Modern Paradoxes, Postmodern Challenges,* ed. Gary L. Wamsley and James F. Wolf. Thousand Oaks, Ca.: Sage Publications.

Westphal, Kenneth R. 2006. "Contemporary Epistemology: Kant, Hegel, McDowell." *European Journal of Philosophy* 14 (August): 274–301.

White, Leonard D. 1926. *Introduction to the Study of Public Administration.* New York: MacMillan.

———. 1958. *The Republican Era, 1869–1901.* New York: MacMillan.

White, Louis P., and Melanie J. Rhodeback. 1992. "Ethical Dilemmas in Organization Development: A Cross-Cultural Analysis." *Journal of Business Ethics* 11 (September): 663–70.

White, Morton. 1987. *Philosophy, The Federalist, and the Constitution.* New York: Oxford University Press.

Wicks, Andrew C., and R. Edward Freeman. 1998. "Organization Studies and the New Pragmatism: Positivism, Anti-Positivism, and the Search for Ethics." *Organization Science* 9 (February): 123–40.

Wilkins, Alan L., and William G. Ouchi. 1983. "Efficient Cultures: Exploring the Relationship Between Culture and Organizational Performance." *Administrative Science Quarterly* 28 (September): 468–81.

Wills, Brian Steel. 1992. *A Battle from the Start: The Life of Nathan Bedford Forrest.* New York: HarperCollins.

Wills, Garry. 1981. *Explaining America: The Federalist.* Garden City, N.Y.: Doubleday & Company, Inc.

Wilson, James Q. 1989. *Bureaucracy: What Government Agencies Do and Why They Do It.* New York: Basic Books.

———. 1985. "The Rediscovery of Character: Private Virtue and Public Policy." *The Public Interest* 81 (Fall): 3–16.

Wiredu, Kwasi. 2007. "Democracy by Consensus: Some Conceptual Considerations." *Socialism and Democracy* 21 (November): 155–70.

Wise, Charles R. 2001. "The Supreme Court's Constitutional Federalism: Implications for Public Administration." *Public Administration Review* 61 (May/June): 343–58.

Witcover, Jules. 2003. *Party of the People: A History of the Democrats.* New York: Random House.

Wittmer, Dennis P. "Ethical Decision-Making." Pp. 481–507 in *Handbook of Administrative Ethics,* 2d Ed., ed. Terry L. Cooper. New York: Marcel Dekker.

Woller, Gary M., and Kelly D. Patterson. 1997. "Public Administration Ethics." *American Behavioral Science* 41 (September): 103–18.

Wood, Gordon. 1988. "The Political Ideology of the Founders." Pp. 7–27 in *Toward a More Perfect Union: Six Essays on the Constitution,* ed. Neil L. York. Provo, Ut.: Brigham University.

Wood, Greg, and Malcolm Rimmer. 2003. "Codes of Ethics: What Are They Really and What Should They Be?" *International Journal of Value-Based Management* 16 (May): 181–95.

Wright, Mary Ann. 2005. "Resigning as Resistance." Pp. 91–99 in *America and the World: The Double Bind*, ed. Majid Tehranian and Kevin P. Clements. East Brunswick, N. J.: Transaction Publishers.

Wright, Robin. 2005. "Rice Declines to Give Senators Timeline for Iraq Withdrawal." *The Washington Post*, 20 October, p. A22.

Yarwood, Dean L. 1985. "The Ethical World of Organizational Professionals and Scientists." *Public Administration Quarterly* 8 (Winter): 461–86.

Yoder, Diane E., and Kathryn G. Denhardt. 2001. "Ethics Education in Public Affairs: Preparing Graduates for Workplace Moral Dilemmas." Pp. 59–77 in *Handbook of Administrative Ethics*, 2d Ed., ed. Terry L. Cooper. New York: Marcel Dekker.

Yukl, Gary. 2002. *Leadership in Organizations*, 5th Ed. Upper Saddle River, N.J.: Prentice Hall.

Zschoch, Mark. 2006. "Why Policy Issue Networks Matter: The Advanced Technology Program and the Manufacturing Extension Partnership." *Canadian Journal of Political Science* 39 (June): 443–45.

INDEX

About the Author

J. Michael Martinez currently works as a corporate attorney in Monroe, GA, and teaches political science as a part-time faculty member at Kennesaw State University in Kennesaw, GA. He is the author of numerous articles and books on southern history, American government, and public administration.